the hamlyn vegetable book

the hamlyn vegetable book

Clare Connery

photography by Sandra Lane

Bounty
BOOKS

To my daughter, Clare – for health and happiness

Publishing Director: Laura Bamford

Project Manager: Jeni Wright
Editor: Katey Day

Creative Director: Keith Martin
Senior Designer: Geoff Fennell

Photographer: Sandra Lane
Home Economist: Oona van den Berg
Stylist: Mary Norden
Picture Researcher: Wendy Gay

Indexer: Hilary Bird

Senior Production Controller: Bonnie Ashby

First published in Great Britain in 1998 by
Hamlyn, a division of Octopus Publishing Group Ltd

This edition published in 2008 by Bounty Books,
a division of Octopus Publishing Group Ltd
2–4 Heron Quays, London E14 4JP
www.octopusbooks.co.uk

An Hachette Livre UK Company
www.hachettelivre.co.uk

Design, text & illustrations copyright © Octopus Publishing Group Ltd 1998

ISBN: 978-0-753717-78-3

A CIP catalogue record for this book is available from the British Library

Printed and bound in China

contents

introduction 6

directory 10

leafy greens & brassicas 12

stalks & stems 32

the onion family 44

roots & tubers 56

podded vegetables 70

fruiting vegetables 80

mushrooms 98

recipes 106

soups 108

starters 126

stews 144

stir-fries, pan-fries & grills 166

roasts & bakes 190

dips & salsas 208

sauces & dressings 226

accompaniments 236

index 252

acknowledgements & notes 256

Not for me a childhood in which the image of vegetables was blighted by the odour of overcooked greens in a steamy kitchen. I had a green-fingered grandmother who, widowed before I was born, had refined her household budgeting to a fine art, walked everywhere and revered her small kitchen garden. My happiest childhood times were spent in her company in her little wooden cottage close to the sea. Sitting at her tiny kitchen table, or on the kitchen steps surveying her vegetable patch, it was always a pleasure to eat up my greens. My adventurous granny introduced me to the avocado and the aubergine, to kohlrabi and celeriac, and it was with her that I went on my first mushroom hunt.

For my grandmother, food was the greatest pleasure, her homegrown vegetables were a special daily treat. For me food has been the focal point of my working life, the way in which I have earned my living, but I have never lost that initial fascination with growing things of all colours, shapes, sizes and flavours, implanted by Granny Smyth. I was extremely fortunate to have had such a wonderful educational 'supplement'.

Today we live in a highly automated, ready-prepared, pre-packed, just-heat-and-serve society. Basic knowledge about food, what it is, how it grows, what goodness it contains, how to prepare it efficiently and hygienically bypasses many children altogether. The standard of teaching of such things in schools is variable, to say the least. If all schools provided information about the nutritional benefits and sheer tasty delight of a different vegetable every week, then I believe we would have a healthier society. But, I must get down from my soapbox!

One never stops hearing about food. Hardly a week goes by than we read about the nutritional benefits of some vegetable or other, all those vitamins, minerals and trace elements, the newly discovered protection against some disease or other. The preparation for this book not only involved me in learning about these nutritional attributes but also in studying the history and geographical origins of each vegetable. In addition of course I immersed myself in the creation and testing of all the recipes. What an illuminating story can be told about vegetables, and how fascinating it is to follow their progress through history. I was transported to ancient origins in the Andean foothills and Asia Minor, visited the tables of the Aztecs and the Egyptians and learnt about the health-giving properties of vegetables known to the Greeks and Romans. So, with the aid of modern scientific and medical analysis, we are really learning about nutritional benefits already known many centuries ago.

Styles of cooking, like fashions, come and go but we are fortunate in the late 20th century that the variety of ingredients available to us now is unprecedented in history. Not only has horticulture progressed so that natural seasons can be extended, but easy transportation means that vegetables from all around the world reach our shops in tip-top condition throughout the year.

For me this book has been a true labour of love, with the seeds of inspiration planted all those years ago in that wooden cottage by the sea. How appropriate that I should be writing these words looking out of my window over the sea in County Down. The book is finished, but the memory of a late summer and early autumn writing in a summerhouse just above the little harbour, lingers.

introduction

The book presents portraits of over sixty different vegetables from all over the world, from the essential onion to decorative mizuna greens, grouped into sections. First there are Leafy Greens & Brassicas, which include those relative newcomers to our supermarket shelves, the several types of oriental greens, crisp and delicious. Next come Stalks & Stems (far more interesting than its name implies), including the aristocratic asparagus and the dramatic globe artichoke, which looks so imposing in the garden. The Onion Family, flavour enhancers and medicinal marvels through the centuries, come next, then Roots & Tubers, from king potato and his carbohydrate rivals from around the world (the taro and the yam), to the radishes essential in the diet of the workers who built the pyramids, and the Jerusalem artichoke, whose identity in soups always mystifies my dinner guests. Podded Vegetables – from the ancient pea and bean to the New World sweetcorn and the mucilaginous okra – follow, then the gloriously coloured Fruited Vegetables, including the family of peppers and chillies, the squashes, which bring brightness as the days draw in towards winter, and the aubergine. Finally, and strictly not vegetables at all, but so important for flavour and texture, come Mushrooms, cultivated and wild, mass produced and plentiful, or fickle and hidden in jealously guarded secret locations.

No one can entirely deny their origins, however widely travelled he or she may be. As a very personal selection, the recipes chosen to illustrate these vegetables reflect my own wanderings through life, linking the traditional with the very modern, the rustic with the sophisticated. There are some timeless recipes like Rustic Greek Salad, then there are those which owe much to the growing popularity of exotic cuisines such as Wilted Greens with Water Chestnuts & Black Bean Sauce. I am not a vegetarian and this book is deliberately not written solely for non-meat eaters. It is rather a celebration of the central role that vegetables should play in our everyday diet. Not only because of their nutritional value, but because of the variety of flavours they offer. There are dishes intended for all occasions, from rapid snacks and light lunches to informal suppers and stylish dinner parties. They also reflect our growing international tastes. I believe that this selection of recipes has something to offer all age groups, and certainly there is nothing here which my intrepid grandmother or my very modern daughter could not have sat at the same table and enjoyed.

For convenience the recipes are divided conventionally into soups, starters and main-course dishes. This main category has been further divided into cooking methods – Stews; Stir-fries, Pan-fries & Grills; and Roasts & Bakes. In addition I have included some essential Sauces & Dressings, and a selection of Dips & Salsas, so important for modern entertaining. Finally, there is Accompaniments, a selection of breads, scones, crisps and other savoury tit-bits to eat with vegetable dishes. Everything one could want in a vegetable book and all beautifully illustrated with evocative photographs.

I hope you will enjoy my selection and be inspired not only to try the recipes but also to experiment to create many others for yourself.

Clare Connery
Strangford, 1998

directory

leafy greens & brassicas

Swiss chard

Beta vulgaris

This leafy vegetable is high in vitamins A and C, and also contains some vitamin B and the minerals, sodium, potassium and iron.

Also called silver chard, seakale beet and silver beet, why this vegetable is commonly known as Swiss chard is a bit of a mystery. What is known is that it can be traced back to the ancient Greeks, and that the Romans introduced it to central and northern Europe and from there to Persia and China. In its wild form, it can be found all around the Mediterranean and British coasts.

Swiss chard is from the same family as beetroot, but it is grown for its leaves rather than its roots. It comes in two varieties, the technicolour red or ruby chard (also called rhubarb chard), and the more familiar white variety, which has broad white leaf stalks and midribs supporting glossy green fleshy leaves. Both the stalks and leaves can be eaten. The stalks are succulent and juicy, not unlike celery. The leaves are similar in taste to spinach and are often substituted for it, although chard leaves are larger, more fleshy and substantial. Chard has one particular advantage over spinach in that it contains less oxalic acid, which means that its iron content can be more readily absorbed by our bodies.

When buying chard, look for shiny, crisp, brightly coloured leaves and crisp spines. It is often sold in heads rather than leaves, and these should be firm and tightly packed. Because the stalks and leaves are different in texture and thickness, separate them before cooking by cutting round the central rib of the stalk which runs up into the leaf (scissors are good for this). Wash both the stalks and leaves well, then spin or shake the leaves dry. Either shred the leaves and cook them as you would spinach or cabbage, or leave them whole to be blanched and stuffed with rice, beans or other vegetables. Cut the stalks and central spine into 5–10 cm (2–4 inch) lengths about 1 cm (½ inch) wide, stripping off any stringy parts, then cook them until tender in boiling water with some lemon juice. Serve with melted butter, or with a cream, white or tomato sauce. Swiss chard is also very popular used in stir-fries.

Chinese mustard greens

Brassica juncea

These are a good source of vitamins C and D and the B group. They are high in calcium, iron and potassium.

These are thought to have originated in Central Asia and grow wild throughout the Mediterranean. For flavour, they are certainly the most interesting of the oriental greens and in no way bland – on the contrary, they are hot and spicy with a strong mustard flavour, as their name suggests. In Europe they are grown solely for their mustard seeds, in India and Asia for their seed oil, but in China they have been developed for their leaves as well. Look for them in the oriental vegetable sections of large supermarkets and in oriental shops, where they are called gai choy and sometimes described as mustard cabbage.

In appearance mustard greens are not unlike spring greens, slightly elongated in shape, with loose, almost puckered leaves in varying shades of green, from light lime to deep bottle green with a purple tinge. The leaves are coarse in texture and are best cooked like spring greens – shredded then boiled or steamed, with any coarse stalks removed. They can also be cooked quickly in a wok, which is the way I favour, either torn into pieces or shredded, and served with a light Chinese dressing or sauce.

If you grow your own, the seedlings or small young leaves can be eaten raw and are delicious in salads. I just love to pick and nibble every time I pass a plant.

Older leaves are more pungent than young leaves, but they lose some of their fire when cooked.

kale

Brassica oleracea
Acephala group

A good source of calcium, iron and vitamins A, E and C.

We in Ireland have a strong affinity with this hardy vegetable, mainly because of its partnership with potato in the preparation of colcannon, one of Ireland's national dishes. Of the two vegetables, the potato may be the better known, but kale has a much longer European pedigree. It is aptly described as a sort of primitive cabbage, thick stalked and loose leaved, no doubt closer in appearance to the brassicas known to the Greeks and Romans than to the hard-hearted and headed cabbages we know today. Wild or sea cabbage, its wild ancestor, is still found here and there along the coasts of western Europe, although it is not always certain whether these plants are truly wild or are simply escapes from cultivation which have reverted to their original form.

Curly kale Also known as cottage kale, curled kale, German kale, true kale and borecole (the anglicized version of the Dutch word *Boerenkool*, meaning peasant's cabbage), this is the most commonly available kale, although even then it is not always easy to find. Other names for it include Scotch kale, for this enormously robust and hardy vegetable which thrives on frost and snow, was once a staple in Scotland, where vegetable gardens in the Lowlands were formerly known as kale-yards or kailyards. Kail brose was peasant food in Scotland, a soup made by boiling an ox head or cow heel and then stirring cooked kale and a large handful of oatmeal into the cooking liquid. Green or pan kale was a meatless variation of this dish which was eaten during Lent. Kailkenny is a similar dish to colcannon and is found in northern Scotland.

Available all year, curly kale is probably the strongest tasting of all the brassicas. It has attractive frilled, curly leaves which grow from a coarse central stalk. In some varieties the leaves are crimped rather like parsley, or even serrated like small palm leaves. The colour is a dark, luscious green. Some curly kale plants can grow to over 1 metre (3 feet) high, giving the effect of being almost tree like. As a result, gardeners often use kale for foliage in borders. Indeed, some curly kale stems can become so thick and straight that they can be dried and made into walking sticks.

Collards or collard greens These are milder in taste with smooth leaves, thinner than those of true kale, and without the frilly or crimped edges. Although they were originally used in the 18th century as a winter feed for cattle, today collards have become a popular vegetable and are frequently used in the one-pot stews of the southern United States.

Purple or silver kale This is an ornamental variety, grown almost exclusively for display, and is especially popular with Japenese gardeners.

When buying kale, look for heads with crisp leaves, vibrant colour and stiff and firm stalks. As with all leafy vegetables, check for obvious signs of age, discoloration, bruising and limpness. Leaves should be crisp, their colour vibrant and the stalk stiff and firm. Kale is a robust leafy vegetable, so when bought fresh and in good condition, it should keep well for several days in a cool place or in a plastic bag in the refrigerator. Simplicity is the essence in both preparation and cooking. Remove any leaves you don't like the look or feel of, then break those remaining from the stalk, cutting out any thick stalky spines from the leaves. Wash the leaves (discard the stalks), drain well and either leave whole, tear into pieces or roll into a cigar shape and shred.

Boil in no more than 2.5 cm (1 inch) of water for 3–5 minutes, then drain, return to the pan, season with salt and pepper and finish with melted butter. Another method is to toss the kale in bacon fat after boiling and serve with fried bacon and mashed potatoes – an Irish speciality. Simply boiled and served slightly crisp, kale is excellent with fried fish. In contrast, when combined with mashed potatoes to make colcannon, it needs to be very well cooked so that it can be mashed with the potatoes to produce a speckled green mass. Because of its robust nature in both taste and texture, kale is ideally suited to combining with strong hot spices and using in stir-fries.

cauliflower

Brassica oleracea

Botrytis group

A rich source of vitamins A and C, folic acid, phosphorus, sulphur, calcium and sodium.

The cauliflower's early progress from its ancient Middle Eastern origins as a sort of spindly cabbage with a small flower head are a little obscure, but what we do know is that the resourceful Moors introduced it to Spain in the early Middle Ages, and that it has grown on the island of Cyprus with great success for many centuries. Cauliflower was certainly grown widely in Europe and Britain in the 17th century, and the description 'coleflower' or 'cabbage flower' dates from this time.

The cauliflower is a close cousin of broccoli, but it is distinctive enough to have its own name – *Botrytis*, from the Greek word for a bunch of grapes, because of the obvious similarity. In addition to the familiar large white and dwarf varieties, other cauliflowers vary in colour from snowy white through lime green to purple. Romanesco is one of several varieties seen in specialist grocers. It looks like a cross between broccoli and cauliflower and has very pretty, textured heads. The taste of Romanesco is similar to cauliflower and the colour can be white or pale green.

Believe your own eyes when choosing cauliflower, because freshness really does stand out. When in tip-top condition, the head should be tightly packed with a mass of creamy white curds swathed in crisp green leaves. Above all, it should look and smell fresh and beautiful.

Trim off any coarse bottom leaves and the woody base of the stalk. Very large cauliflowers are best cut into halves, quarters or broken into florets. The tender leaves can be left on or trimmed off and steamed or boiled as a separate vegetable. When I break cauliflower into florets I try to leave a little stalk attached to each one or group of curds. This I peel with a vegetable peeler to ensure that it cooks in the same time as the head.

I generally steam whole cauliflower or florets until just tender. When it is whole, test it after 10 minutes: it should feel tender but still have plenty of bite. If you prefer to boil cauliflower, use only a small amount of water and time in the same way. Whole cauliflower is good coated with a rich cheese sauce and browned under the grill, either as a main dish with crusty bread or as an accompaniment to roast beef or lamb.

Cauliflower is also good broken into bite-sized pieces and stir-fried in a little hot oil with chilli and cumin, either on its own or with other crisp vegetables. Before stir-frying it is best par-boiled for 1 minute, refreshed until cold, then drained and dried. Bite-sized florets can also be included in stews and stir-fries and any leftover raw florets can be used to make to make a creamy cauliflower soup. For this I use small florets and leave them whole rather than puréeing. More often than not, I snap the head into bite-sized pieces and eat them raw with creamy yogurt. You can also serve them as part of a crudité collection with dips, or include them in a cold salad.

Cabbage is a rich source of vitamins A, B, C, D and E, and a good source of iron, potassium and calcium.

One smell inextricably linked with my schooldays is that of cabbage and floor polish, somehow united and suspended above a damp and dismal dining hall – the result of the execution of the cabbage by drowning in gallons of boiling water. Fortunately, I made no connection between that colourless watery mass and the crisp green delicacy, topped with a knob of country butter, which was grown and presented with love and understanding by my mother and grandmother.

It would appear that the earliest type of cabbage was a wild loose-leaved plant, prevalent around the coasts of Europe. The modern-day equivalent still grows in coastal regions of France and Italy, a tall, thick-stemmed variety. Both the ancient Greeks and the Romans held it in high esteem, and it is believed that the Celts, originating themselves in central Europe, were the first to grow 'headed' cabbage – the word 'brassica' is derived from the Celtic word *bresic* meaning cabbage. By medieval times these round tight-headed cabbages were an important part of the diet of the poor, and by the 16th century the crinkled-leaf Savoy was becoming established in Europe.

cabbage
Brassica oleracea
Capitata group

Freshness is all when buying cabbage. A hearted cabbage should feel substantial and heavy. To prepare, remove the outer leaves where necessary. If the cabbage is loose-leaved, cut off as many leaves as required, removing the core. Store the rest in a bag in the refrigerator for future use. Rinse well under cold running water, shake dry, then place the leaves on top of each other in a pile. Roll up like a cigar and shred finely (opposite page). If the cabbage is tight-headed, cut it into quarters and cut out the tough stalk before shredding finely, then wash and drain. If the leaves are to be stuffed, leave them whole.

To cook shredded cabbage, put it into a large saucepan with a knob of butter and just enough water to prevent burning. Cover and cook over a high heat for a few minutes until just tender, shaking the pan and turning the cabbage occasionally. Drain and serve immediately, with lots of freshly ground black pepper and more butter. Take care not to overcook cabbage as this will cause it to lose much of its nutritional value. Shredded cabbage can also be steamed, and is excellent stir-fried, on its own or with other vegetables.

Only when blanching (part-cooking) whole leaves for stuffing should you use a large pan full of boiling water. Drop the leaves in for just long enough to make them pliable enough to be rolled.

Heavy-headed winter cabbage can be cooked, whole or quartered, in lots of boiling water, or along with boiled beef, bacon or ham (this is one of the traditional ways of cooking cabbage in Ireland). Winter cabbage can also be shredded, when it lends itself to long, slow cooking in stews and soups as well as braised dishes. It adds texture to stir-fried dishes, as does red cabbage, which is well suited to these cooking methods, as well as pickling.

Cabbages belong to the brassica clan of vegetables, and there are many varieties. However, all cabbages contain the sulphur compounds which are responsible for the famous smell given off by overcooked cabbage.

Red cabbage Wonderful to look at, this purple-headed cabbage is crisp and crunchy when raw or pickled, but needs long, slow cooking. It is ideal stewed or braised, particularly with apples, vine fruits, honey and red wine.

Savoy cabbage (opposite page) This handsome cabbage has deep green crinkly leaves that are tender and require little cooking. It is a great all-rounder, good boiled, steamed or braised. The head can be cooked whole, or the large leaves used for stuffing. As the leaves are crisp and delicate in flavour, they are excellent raw in salads.

Spring greens With their vibrant colours and delicate loose leaves, these are something to look forward to after the hard tight heads of winter. They often have slightly pointed heads and little or no heart because it is usual to eat them when they are still young.

White or Dutch cabbage With its hard round head, this cold weather cabbage is composed of silky, creamy white to pale green leaves packed tightly together. Its crisp texture makes it perfect for raw salads, particularly coleslaw. It can also be boiled, steamed and braised, but it lacks some of the depth of flavour of its leafy green relatives.

Brussels sprouts

Brassica oleracea

Gemmifera group

Brussels sprouts are an excellent source of vitamins C, A, and E, as well as potassium and iron.

As inventions go, the Brussels sprout is one of the most remarkable. Take a cabbage, cut off the head and develop the stem so that nine cabbages sprout like rosebuds along its length. Ingenious.

To the cook, there is only one variety, whose dark green tightly packed heads appear in the shops from late summer into winter (though purists say they are not worth eating until they have experienced the first frosts). Better known to gardener-cooks is a magnificent red variety, which not only tastes good but also makes an excellent ornamental border plant.

The maxim 'small is beautiful' certainly applies to sprouts. Here the German word *Rosenkohl* does the little wonders justice. If sprouts were treated more like delicate rosebuds, the end result would be more satisfying more often. When they are at their freshest, all compact greenness and with a minimum amount of cooking, their nutty flavour is a delight.

Choose small, tightly packed, bright green sprouts. Try to avoid really large sprouts – my rule is a maximum of 2.5 cm (1 inch): any larger and you run the risk of coarse texture and flavour. It is best to cook them within a couple of days of purchase.

All you need to do before cooking is to trim off the outer leaves along with a sliver from the stalky base, then give the sprouts a quick wash. If the leaves are loose and there is a risk of insects inside, soak the sprouts in cold salted water for about 15 minutes, then rinse well. Make a small cross in the stalk end and either cook them in a large saucepan of fast-boiling water to cover, for a maximum of 5 minutes until just tender, or steam for 3–5 minutes. Sprouts get soft and squashy, lose their colour and develop a rank smell if overcooked. After draining, toss them in butter and salt and freshly ground black pepper before serving. At Christmas it is traditional to toss them with chestnuts, on other occasions you can substitute slivers of toasted almonds or whole roasted hazelnuts for chestnuts. As an accompaniment to game, top them with crisp and golden butter-fried breadcrumbs.

Alternatively, stir-fry sprouts, either halved, quartered or sliced, or serve them raw as a crudité, left whole if small or cut in half. Raw sprouts are also good in salads, whole, halved, quartered, shredded, sliced or grated. This way there is little loss of vitamins, minerals, taste or texture.

High in vitamin A, with significant amounts of vitamin C, folic acid and iron, broccoli also has moderate levels of calcium.

Originating in ancient Asia Minor and the Eastern Mediterranean, broccoli in its sprouting form seems to have been popular with the Romans – the word broccoli comes from *brocco*, the Italian for sprout or shoot.

Sprouting broccoli has a mass of delicate flower heads loosely arranged at the top of long slender stalks. The colour ranges from white (not often found) through green to blue green and the original dusky purple, which turns green when cooked. Chinese sprouting broccoli, also called Chinese kale, looks like sprouting broccoli, but is more spindly, with looser yellow or white florets. Calabrese is an Italian creation of the late Middle Ages. It takes its name from Calabria, where it was developed. It is what most people today consider as broccoli, often sold wrapped in clingfilm. It has a large heavy head of blue-green flower buds on a chunky stalk.

Broccoli stalks should be firm and crisp and the leaves vigorous. Sprouting broccoli has a shorter shelf life than calabrese, so should be used within 1–2 days. Trim the ends of sprouting broccoli, cut off any tough or damaged stalks, then remove any bruised or wilted leaves. Rinse in cold running water then peel the stalk from below the

broccoli

Brassica oleracea
Italica group

flower head to the end. This allows the stalk and delicate head to cook in the same time. For calabrese, cut the head into even-sized florets, each with a section of stalk, which should be peeled.

Steam the stalks of sprouting broccoli for 3–5 minutes until just tender. Alternatively, lay them in a large deep frying pan, cover with boiling water and boil quickly until tender. Cook calabrese in boiling water for the same length of time. Broccoli and calabrese respond well to stir-frying. To prevent the florets burning before the stalks cook, remove the heads from the stalks and add these to the pan when the stalks are almost cooked. Broccoli requires little embellishment other than melted butter and freshly ground black pepper, but it is also delicious with lemon butter or grated Parmesan cheese, or with a cheese hollandaise, béarnaise or maltaise sauce. It can be used in gratins, stews, stir-fries or soups, and in crudités.

A good source of vitamins C and D and the B group, with a high content of calcium, iron and potassium.

There really isn't anything exotic about oriental vegetables, particularly brassicas like pak-choi and Chinese cabbage (page 27), supermarkets now stock a wide range. They are also in the gourmet gardener's repertoire, since they are fairly easy to grow, even in the smallest of spaces. Their attractive appearance, both before and after they bolt or

develop flowers, lends them to be grown along paths, in herbaceous borders, or in tubs and pots. Like the more familiar salad leaves and spring greens, they are also grown as 'cut and come again' vegetables. Pak-choi, also called bok-choi and bok-choy, comes in many varieties, the smallest being no more than 7–10 cm (3–4 inches) high. In some varieties its stalky base is reminiscent of celery, hence its alternative name of Chinese celery cabbage, but its leaves are smoother and more glossy, spoon-like in shape, and a deep rich green in colour. The creamy white mid rib and leaf stems are striking in contrast. Each plant is joined at the base of the thick stem by a small root, which holds the leaves together.

Pak-choi is a delicate plant and consequently does not keep long. When buying, look for plants with fresh green leaves. The stems should be crisp and bright. Pay attention to the smell: it should be fresh. Check the heads of pak-choi at home, remove any damaged or less than fresh leaves. Put the head in an open container, cover lightly with kitchen paper and place in the salad drawer of the refrigerator; it should keep fresh for several days.

When pak-choi is young, small and tender, it can be eaten raw as a salad leaf. It is slightly peppery in taste, with more flavour than Chinese cabbage.

Bigger plants can be prepared and cooked like Swiss chard. The thick stems, which are juicy and sweet, can be boiled or steamed and served with butter, an oil dressing or a sweet and sour sauce. The leaves can be torn or shredded and lightly boiled in the minimum of water, like spinach or other delicate leafy greens. Alternatively, both the leaves and stems can be sliced and braised together as in chow mein, or stir-fried in a fragrant oil and dressed with a flavoursome sauce or seasoning.

pak-choi
Brassica rapa Chinensis

mizuna
greens
Brassica rapa nipposinica

This Japanese brassica is a good source of vitamins C and D and the B group. It is also valued for its calcium, iron and potassium content. These are a particularly attractive variety of oriental greens, loved as much for their delicate spiky fronds as for their mild peppery flavour. Although originally from China, it is the Japanese who use them most frequently in their cooking. They are a handsome vegetable with finely divided and glossy deep green leaves on slender white stalks. They are especially decorative in the garden, either lining the edges of a path or creating an attractive display in a herbaceous border. They grow in loose bushy clumps, which can reach a height of about 23 cm (9 inches).

A relative of parsley and coriander, mizuna greens are only just finding their way into the shops, so it is best to sow your own for a guaranteed supply.

Before using, pick the greens over carefully and wash them under cold running water. Spin-dry like other salad leaves and store in a rigid container in the bottom of the refrigerator. Use as quickly as possible.

The leaves are perfect in salads when small and young. As they get older, they can be stir-fried with other leafy greens. Mizuna greens can also be used as a garnish for oriental dishes.

Chinese cabbage

Brassica rapa Pekinensis

Chinese cabbage contains moderate levels of vitamins A, B, C and D, with folic acid, potassium and calcium.

This is the best known of the oriental brassicas, also confusingly called Chinese leaves, pe-tsai, Peking cabbage, wong-bok, Shantung cabbage, celery cabbage and nappa cabbage. It is assumed that its history in China is ancient, although the first written record is from the 5th century AD – recent in terms of Chinese history.

It looks like a substantial chunky lettuce, a huge head of celery or a form of Cos lettuce, but it is much more leafy and substantial, weighing anything from 1–2 kg (2–4 lb). The leaves are slightly crinkly in texture, striped with long, wide, smooth white ribs fanning out towards frilled edges. It has a pleasant crunchy texture and the robust leaves are excellent in leafy salads. In taste they are reminiscent of celery and cabbage put together.

There are two other types of Chinese cabbage available. The round-hearted or barrel-shaped variety is more like conventional cabbage, with wrinkly leaves tightly wrapped around a dense heart. The loose-headed variety has more textured leaves, fluffy tops and a cream-coloured centre.

Chinese cabbage should look fresh and lively, be well filled out, and feel heavy and substantial. When bought in its prime, it will keep for several weeks in a plastic bag in the bottom of the refrigerator; if stored in a cool and dark, dry place, it will keep for several months. Don't wash it before it is needed.

To prepare, take off the coarse outer leaves, then use the rest. For a salad, I slice the whole head finely across the leaves. Or I cut away the spine and stalk and cut them into fine sticks for contrasting textures, then tear the large leaves into pieces and shred the heart. When used raw in salad, Chinese cabbage is best combined with other salad leaves, like rocket and endive which are more forceful in flavour, and tossed in a well-flavoured dressing.

To cook, cut the spines or stalks out of the leaves and cut them into pieces, then boil or steam. Serve with a light creamy sauce, or toss in butter or oil and season with salt and pepper. In oriental cooking, shredded leaves are most often stir-fried. A fast toss in a light sesame oil flavoured with garlic, chilli and ginger is delicious. A little sugar can be added, or a dash of rice wine or dry sherry, with a little chilli, oyster or black bean sauce.

chicory
Cichorium intybus

A good source of vitamins A and C, calcium, potassium and phosphorus, chicory is low in calories.

I first encountered witloof chicory as a student in London many years ago. I was fascinated by the tight, uniformly shaped heads wrapped in brilliant blue paper to preserve their pale colour and laid out in rows in shallow boxes.

A creamy yellow-leafed vegetable, chicory has been grown in Europe for hundreds of years, but the practice of roasting and grinding its root to add to coffee only goes back to the 18th century, and was indirectly responsible for the blanched vegetable we refer to as chicory today. It was discovered by chance when, in the middle of the last century, Monsieur Bezier of the Brussels Botanical Gardens, wanting a supply of chicory for his coffee in the winter, removed some roots from his salad bed, cut off most of the foliage and planted the roots in a darkened shed. The result: small compact shoots of tightly furled leaves without the harsh bitterness normally associated with chicory. Monsieur Bezier kept his discovery secret and it was only after his death that his wife passed on details of

the process. This blanched form of chicory became big business in Belgium, hence its name of Belgian chicory. Witloof, meaning 'white leaf', is its Flemish name.

There is also a red form of witloof chicory, the same as the white except for the pigmentation on the leaf tips. As a decorative addition to the salad bowl it is very pretty, but the colour runs as soon as it is subjected to heat so it is not good in cooking.

Radicchio is red, unforced chicory that grows green until exposed to cold weather. It is petite and round rather like a small cabbage, with wine-red leaves and cream ribs (opposite page). Its flavour is very distinctive like chicory, with a pleasant, slightly bitter edge.

The third variety of chicory, also unforced and perhaps less well known, is sugarloaf. It looks quite like a Cos lettuce, but with a noticeable 'back of the tongue' flavour to the crisp green leaves.

When in prime condition, all forms of chicory should have firm, tightly furled leaves. The chicons of witloof should taper to a neat point and not look as if they are about to burst into flower. Choose even-sized heads, preferably individually wrapped if you can find them.

If not, wrap them in brown paper as soon as you get them home and store them in the bottom of the refrigerator, where they should keep for 4–5 days.

To prepare chicory, remove any damaged leaves and trim the root end, cutting off any discoloured parts. Wash gently under cold running water and pat dry. If using the chicory raw in a salad, remove individual leaves and toss with a light fruit-flavoured vinaigrette, or combine with segments of citrus fruit or other sweet firm fruits such as apple or pear. The whole leaves are also good in crudités, and perfect for dipping in sauces or light pâtés. Alternatively, keep the chicory heads intact and cut into diagonal 5 mm (¼ inch) slices, then toss with other leaves or salad ingredients such as celery, walnuts, ham, cold chicken and strong cheese.

Cooking changes the nature of chicory, intensifying its flavour and bitterness, but never so much that it makes it unpleasant. Heat also changes its colour and texture, and it can look rather unattractive unless browned slightly in butter after boiling or steaming, or covered with a sauce, dressing or garnish.

When preparing chicory heads for cooking, it is received wisdom to whittle out a small cone from the core of the vegetable. This is said to reduce bitterness, but I am not altogether convinced, so experiment for yourself.

To boil chicory, drop the heads into a large saucepan of fast boiling water to which the juice of ½–1 lemon has been added. This helps to retain its colour. During cooking, push the chicory heads under the water with a spoon as they tend to rise and float. Boil for 4–5 minutes until just tender, then drain well and squeeze the heads carefully between your hands to remove the very last drop of unwanted liquid. Before serving, toss the heads in melted butter until browning slightly and season with a little sugar or orange juice. I often part-cook chicory by boiling, then braise it in the oven in cream, a sauce or stock. My favourite recipe is for Chicory & Smoked Bacon Gratin (page 202) which is baked in cream flavoured with Dijon mustard and cheese.

Radicchio is prepared in the same way as chicory, but it turns a murky rust-brown when cooked. One of the best methods of cooking it is to cut it in half lengthways, brush it with oil and sear the cut leaves on a hot ridged cast iron grill pan. Serve warm with a squeeze of lemon juice and plenty of salt and freshly ground pepper.

An excellent source of vitamins C, A and B, particularly when eaten very fresh and raw. Spinach is a good source of calcium, potassium and iron, although this is 'bound up' by oxalic acid and not easily available to our bodies.

Originating in ancient Persia, spinach appeared in China and then North Africa, and it was from there that it was brought by the Moors into medieval Spain. It was popular in monastic gardens throughout Europe, eventually finding its way across the channel. By the 16th century, its virtues of being quick, easy to grow and cook, were well known to the English.

Spinach is an annual plant which can be grown all year round, which means that if you are a gardener and plant it successionally you should never be without it. There are basically two varieties of true or real spinach, one with long-lobed leaves and the other a less hardy variety with round leaves. It is available as loose leaves with the stalks attached, or trimmed, washed and pre-packed ready for use. When selecting, make sure it is absolutely fresh as it deteriorates very quickly. The leaves should have a crisp

spinach
Spinacea oleracea

texture and be bright green in colour. Check the bags in particular, paying attention to the 'sell by' and 'use by' dates. Store in the refrigerator and use as soon as possible.

Spinach is best when the leaves are small, young and vibrant in colour, then they need very little preparation and are perfect for eating raw in a salad. Pick the spinach over and remove any damaged or discoloured leaves, trimming off any thick, coarse or long stalks. Fill the sink with cold water, add some salt, then the prepared leaves. Swirl the leaves in the water to wash away any sand, dirt or grit that might be clinging to them, then if they are very gritty, drain off the water and repeat the process. If serving raw, spin-dry in a salad spinner. For cooking, lift out a large handful at a time, shake off the excess water and pack into a very large saucepan with a knob of butter and only the water that is clinging to the leaves. Press the spinach well into the pan to get in as much as possible, cover closely with greaseproof paper and clamp on the lid. Cook over a moderate heat, shaking the pan occasionally to prevent the leaves from sticking, until the spinach has collapsed and is tender. This will take 5–8 minutes. Don't overcook or the leaves will become slimy. Now your full pan of spinach will be almost empty – it is surprising just how much a large volume of leaves breaks down on cooking. Remove the lid and paper and drain in a colander or conical sieve, pressing the leaves against the sides to squeeze out the liquid (this makes a refreshing and nutritious drink). The spinach is now ready to use. As an accompaniment, simply return it to the pan with a generous knob of butter and season well with salt and pepper and perhaps a pinch of freshly grated nutmeg. Shake over a high heat to warm through, then serve immediately.

The slightly astringent and very distinctive flavour of spinach goes well with cheese, butter, cream and eggs. It combines well with meat and fish. It is particularly good in the fruity stews popular in Middle Eastern cooking, as well as in the pastry tarts and pies of France, Italy and Greece. It is good in soups, soufflés and purées, superb with lentils, chickpeas, beans and potatoes, and is also popular stir-fried on its own or with other ingredients.

Not the real thing

There are two leafy greens that are not true spinach at all, but they bear the name spinach and are prepared and cooked in the same way.

New Zealand spinach (Tetragonia tetragonoides) is a useful substitute for true spinach because it can stand the hottest weather without running to seed. It has smaller and softer leaves, which are roughly triangular in shape with blunt tips. It tastes slightly milder than true spinach. Indeed, it was these greens that Captain Cook gave his sailors to prevent scurvy, and they were introduced to the Royal Botanical Gardens at Kew in 1771 by the botanist Joseph Banks after his voyage on board the *Endeavour*.

Leaf beet (Beta vulgaris cicula), also called perpetual spinach or spinach beet, is easier to grow than true spinach because it is not so sensitive to drought. It is also biennial and will not run to seed. The leaves are small and oval (below) with a coarser, less delicate flavour than true spinach. They are ideal for salads.

stalks & stems

Celery is high in potassium and raises alkaline levels in the blood, so it is good for gout and rheumatism. Low in calories, it helps reduce blood pressure and is also a diuretic.

Celery has been cultivated· for many centuries. The inspiration for those first gardeners (probably Greek) was the wild celery that still flourishes close to seashores in many parts of Europe and the British Isles. Smallage, a cultivated wild celery, has been grown in continental Europe since medieval times for its flavour and medicinal properties, and the tradition of adding it to soups, broths, stews and stocks is still very important in rural areas.

There are three types of celery: smallage, with its thin green stems and head of bushy green leaves, has a strong flavour and is used mainly for its heads, which are cut off rather than dug up. Then there is the green or yellow/green self-blanching variety, most often sold in plastic sleeves. The flavour of this mass-produced product is bland and may be the reason why celery's popularity has waned. The third variety is the British white celery, also known as trench celery because it was originally grown in deep trenches. Its stems are blanched by being progressively covered in earth or soot, which accounts for its other name of dirty celery. It has a crisp texture and nutty flavour, and reaches a peak of availability around Christmas.

All celery should be crisp, firm and pure in colour. The leaves should be fresh and lively. If the celery is to be used whole, wash under cold running water, separating the

celery
Apium graveolens
var. dulce

stalks slightly. Remove any strings from the stalks, trim a slice off the root end and pull away the tough outer leaves to expose the more delicate inner heart. Trim across the stalks, leaving a bulbous head about 15 cm (6 inches) long. Reserve the leaves and cut off stalks for salads, stocks, soups and stews. The whole head can be boiled or braised in stock, then served with a rich white sauce or the well-reduced braising liquor. Chopped, raw celery gives a spark of life and crunch to mixed salad leaves, and has a similar effect when combined with crunchy fruit like apples.

Celery adds a very distinctive flavour and texture to soups and stews. Cut it into appropriate lengths and boil, braise or stew until tender. Sticks or pieces of celery are also excellent fried on their own to be combined with other ingredients, or stir-fried with other mixed vegetables.

celeriac

Apium graveolens
var. rapaceum

A storehouse of energy, celeriac is high in carbohydrates, rich in iron with some quantities of vitamins C and B.

Celeriac was introduced into Britain from Egypt in the early 18th century by Stephen Switzer, a writer and seeds-man. Although strictly classed as a root vegetable, it is in fact a swollen stem that grows just above the ground. It is roughly spherical in shape with a knobbly surface, which accounts for its other names, turnip-rooted celery and knob celery. The spindly stalks and leafy foliage are similar to smallage or soup celery, and can be used in the same way. Celeriac has a distinctive nutty, slightly tangy taste similar to celery, but to my mind it is more powerful.

Its season is October to May (any later and it is inclined to be fibrous), when you should look out for smallish, firm bulbs, about the size of an orange rather than a grapefruit. Choose those with the smoothest skin you can find, because there will be less waste when peeling. Any leaves should be lively and a strong green colour. The root should also look fresh. Celeriac will keep well for up to a week in the vegetable compartment of the refrigerator. Before peeling, scrub thoroughly with a firm vegetable brush under cold running water to remove any dirt. Cut off the roots and any stems and leaves. Discard the roots, but reserve the stems and leaves to use as a flavouring for stocks, soups and stews. Both, if fresh and crisp, are also excellent chopped and added to salads. The skin should be peeled off using a firm sharp knife. If you are unsure of

the thickness of the skin or how much to take off, cut the celeriac in half first so you can judge how much to remove. Once peeled, celeriac turns brown quickly. To prevent this, place it immediately in cold water mixed with the juice of ½ lemon or 1–2 tablespoons of white vinegar. This is known as acidulated water. Prepare celeriac in cubes, chunks, sticks or crisps as the recipe requires.

The most usual way of cooking celeriac is by boiling it in acidulated water until tender. It is then drained, tossed in butter and served as an accompaniment or used in a gratin. Celeriac can also be mashed after boiling and served like mashed potato. It can be roasted in chunks, cut into chips or slices like potato crisps and deep-fried, or shredded or grated with raw potatoes, shaped into pancakes and fried. Cut into cubes, it is used in soups and stews. Celeriac is also used raw in salads, the best-known of which is the French *rémoulade du céléri-rave*, thin sticks of celeriac mixed with mayonnaise.

asparagus
Asparagus officinalis

Asparagus is low in calories, a rich source of vitamins A, B2 and C and a moderate source of E. It is also high in potassium, folic acid, calcium and iron.

The season for this delicate yet distinctively flavoured vegetable lasts only 6 weeks for British asparagus, from May into June. At other times of the year, asparagus is imported from America, Thailand, Hungary, Holland and Cyprus, but for me the best is British, and its short season makes it something not to tire of or take for granted.

Wild asparagus has grown along the river banks and seashores of southern Europe, Asia and north-west Africa for centuries, and thrived in the dry meadows, sand dunes, limestone cliffs and volcanic hills of northern Europe. It was favoured by the Greeks and cultivated by the Romans. It was elevated to the vegetable pantheon by aristocrats at the court of Louis XV in France, in particular by his mistress Madame de Pompadour who believed, as many people still do, that it had aphrodisiac powers. But that is not all asparagus is noted for. It has traditionally been used in folk medicine as a tonic and sedative and has been recommended for treating rheumatism, poor eyesight and toothache; it is also a diuretic.

Asparagus is a member of the lily family. It is available in three varieties: green, white and purple. Green-stemmed asparagus, mainly grown and certainly preferred in Britain, North America, Italy and France, is allowed to grow naturally into the light before being harvested when it is about 15 cm (6 inches) tall. It is graded into three sizes: 'special', very thick, juicy prime asparagus; 'medium', about 1 cm (½ inch) in diameter and good for most recipes; and 'sprue', the short spindly type that is very tender, cooks quickly and is particularly good for grilling and stir-frying. Green asparagus is also produced in France, Thailand, Holland and Cyprus. White asparagus, which has a creamy white stalk and ivory tips, is favoured by the Spanish, and also by the Dutch, Germans and Italians. It is grown under mounds of soil and cut just as the tips begin to show. Purple or violet asparagus is mostly grown in France. The spears are cut once the tips have grown about 4 cm (1½ inches) above the ground, consequently the stalks are white and the tops tinged with purple or green.

As with many delicate plants, asparagus is at its best when eaten as fresh as possible. Deterioration is rapid once it is picked. Harvesting asparagus from your own garden is the best way to enjoy it, but this is not always possible. When buying, look for firm, straight and sprightly spears, the tips tightly furled.

Unless the asparagus comes straight from the garden, cut off the bottom or 'butt' end of the stalk, removing 1–2.5 cm (½–1 inch) of any hard dried or woody parts. With freshly pulled asparagus this is not necessary, and sprue hardly needs trimming at all. Like this it is perfect eaten raw with rock salt and perhaps a squeeze of lemon juice, some balsamic vinegar and extra virgin olive oil.

To prepare asparagus for cooking, use a small serrated knife or vegetable peeler, start about 5 cm (2 inches) below the tip and peel down to the butt. This will expose the tender flesh of the stalk and enable it to cook in the same time as the delicate tip. If you are using baby asparagus, you will only need to trim the base of each stalk.

Asparagus can be prepared in advance to this point, wrapped in damp kitchen paper and stored in the bottom of the refrigerator for a few hours.

To cook asparagus, bring a large, shallow frying pan, sauté pan or oval casserole full of water to the boil. Add 1 tablespoon salt and lay the asparagus in a single layer over the bottom of the pan so that it is completely covered with water. Cover with a lid and quickly return to the boil. Remove the lid and boil for 5 minutes. Test to see if the asparagus is tender by spearing the stalk with the point of a sharp knife. If it is not tender, cook for another minute and test again, continuing to do this until the asparagus is ready. Lift quickly from the water using tongs and place on kitchen paper to drain, then serve immediately. For an entirely different taste and texture, fine asparagus spears or sprue can be grilled on a ridged cast iron grill pan, seasoned with salt and pepper and given a lift with dash of lemon juice.

Simplicity of serving is always the best for asparagus. Its flavour should be coaxed out and enhanced, not over-powered. All it needs is some melted butter, rock salt and freshly ground black pepper or, for a change, a dressing of balsamic vinegar, a little extra virgin oil and maybe a shaving or two of Parmesan cheese. It is also delicious with Hollandaise Sauce (page 233). One of my favourite dishes is Asparagus & White Wine Risotto (page 143), but asparagus also tastes good in soups, quiches, pancakes and gratins, with scrambled eggs, wrapped in Parma ham, stirred into omelettes, and served cold with mayonnaise.

Kohlrabi is rich in vitamin C, with traces of minerals, particularly potassium, and fibre.

Although it is also known as turnip-rooted cabbage, kohlrabi is not a root, but the swollen part of the lower stem. It is a most interesting looking vegetable, with its green or purple bulbous stem and bizarrely shaped leaf shoots sticking out from it – rather like a visitor from another planet. It is much more distinctive than the turnip or swede which it resembles in flavour. Kohlrabi has been cultivated in continental Europe since the 17th century, and is particularly popular in Germany and Switzerland. It is also widely available in India, China and other parts of Asia. There are two varieties, the pale green and the purple. In flavour they are akin to turnip and cabbage but more refined, with the additional hint of exotic flavours – water chestnut and celeriac. A word of warning: these subtleties can be lost if kohlrabi is overcooked.

The swollen kohlrabi stem can grow to the size of a grapefruit, but it is best eaten when much smaller, no bigger than a small orange or a large beef tomato – when too large it tends to be coarse, woody and fibrous. Its skin should look fresh, with a rich bloom. Kohlrabi will keep well for just over a week if stored in the bottom of the refrigerator or in a cool place.

To prepare kohlrabi for cooking, trim away the leaves and reserve them if you like, to be boiled like spinach or stir-fried like leafy greens. Peel off a thin layer of skin, then cut the kohlrabi into cubes, sticks or slices as the recipe

kohlrabi

Brassica oleracea
Gongylodes group

requires. It can be sliced into thicker sticks or chips and deep-fried, or cut into very thin slices and fried like potato crisps. It can be cut into wedges, blanched until almost tender, drained and refreshed, then served as part of a platter of crudités. Diced or cubed, kohlrabi can be added to soups and stews, boiled like turnips and served with butter and salt and pepper, or mashed like potatoes. It is also good topped with cheese and breadcrumbs and made into a gratin, or roasted with other root vegetables. The crispness and pure flavour of raw kohlrabi can be enjoyed like celeriac, cut into very thin sticks or grated, added to a salad or mixed with vinaigrette.

Botanically and nutritionally similar to the globe artichoke, the cardoon is also rich in potassium.

The cardoon is a giant edible thistle closely related to the globe artichoke, found wild in much of North Africa and the Mediterranean. It has bold, spiky silver green foliage and tall thistle-like purple flower heads, smaller and more compact than the globe artichoke, but equally stunning. Cultivated plants often grow to 2 metres (6 feet) in height and are valued not only as a vegetable but as an attractive garden plant. Unlike the globe artichoke, the cardoon is grown for its succulent leaf stalks rather than its flower head. The leaves look rather like very long celery and are blanched when they reach maturity, in order to retain their pale green colour.

The history of the cardoon is sketchy, but it is thought to have been held in high esteem by the Romans before the birth of Christ. Nowadays it is extremely popular in Spain, southern France, Italy and Morocco. In Britain cardoons have traditionally been used in much the same way as celery but only the inner ribs and hearts are used, the outer stalks and leaves being too tough and stringy. Their flavour is somewhere between celery, globe artichoke and asparagus.

To prepare, cut away the leaves, roots and prickly outer stems, leaving the inner stalks and firm succulent heart. Wash well under cold running water and remove any strings. Trim and cut into manageable lengths, then put them immediately into cold acidulated water to prevent discoloration. Very young stems may be tender enough to eat raw as part of a selection of crudités, in which case, cut them into 15 cm (6 inch) lengths. One of the most famous sauces served with cardoons is *bagna cauda*, a rich warm combination of anchovies, olive oil and butter from Piedmont in Italy. If you feel the stalks are not quite tender enough to eat raw, drop them into boiling salted and acidulated water for 4–5 minutes to tenderize them slightly. This will also remove any trace of bitterness. Drain, refresh under running water until cold, then dry before serving. To fully cook the stems, boil them for up to 30 minutes until tender. Drain well and serve with melted butter, olive oil or vinaigrette and salt and pepper. They also taste good with anchovies and shavings of Parmesan, or simply with butter, cream and cheese, and can be used in most recipes where celery or fennel features.

cardoon

Cynara cardunculus

globe artichoke

Cynara scolymus

Composed almost entirely of water but with a little carbohydrate, iodine and iron, globe artichokes are a slimmer's dream.

One of the great joys of my vegetable garden in County Down is the corner where globe artichokes grow beside the gooseberry bush. They make a spectacular show. The huge bluey-purple thistle heads and big jagged green leaves look so striking against the white of a lime-washed wall and the spectacular backdrop of the muted blues and purples of the Mourne Mountains. I enjoy their visual beauty as much as their taste, and make sure that I grow enough to satisfy both plate and vase.

The globe artichoke is an edible thistle, a close relative of the cotton thistle and the cardoon. Given its Arab name, *al-kharshuf*, it is thought to have grown originally in North Africa, from where it then found its way to southern Europe where it still grows wild. It has been prized by many for centuries, particularly by the Greeks and Romans, but it is believed to have been the Italians who were responsible for its popularity in the courts of Renaissance Europe. The globe artichoke reached England in the 16th century, and rapidly became a popular feature in kitchen gardens.

The artichoke flourishes in a light sandy soil and a mild climate. The flower buds are edible at various stages of the plant's maturity – but if you eat them, there will be no flowers. The plant grows to about 1.2–1.5 metres (4–5 feet) tall with a 90 cm (3 foot) spread of attractive leaves, which range in colour from brilliant bottle green to silvery/grey green and are topped with large thistle-like flowers. There are two main types – green and purple. Either colour can be round or egg-shaped and there is no marked difference in the flavour.

If you grow your own artichokes, harvest them when they are young and the flower buds small, then they can be eaten raw or lightly grilled while they are delicate and tender. If you prefer artichokes boiled or steamed, allow them to grow slightly larger. However you prefer to eat artichokes, harvest them only just before use. Whether picked straight from the garden or selected from the supermarket shelf, globe artichokes should be bright in colour, whether green or purple. The leaves on the flower heads should be firm and fleshy, forming a tightly shaped globe. They should have a healthy bloom, feel heavy and be of an even size.

To prepare artichokes, soak them, stem-side up, for about 15 minutes in a large bowl or bucket of cold water to which the juice of a lemon or a few tablespoons of white wine vinegar have been added, then wash in cold running water. Drain and continue the preparation.

Small artichokes If very small, remove the leaves from the base, trim the stem to about 2.5 cm (1 inch) and peel it. The stem is very tender and can be eaten. The hairy choke has not yet formed, so the inner yellow leaves can be gouged out with a knife. Keep the artichokes in acidulated water, then drain, slice and eat raw with vinaigrette or anchoïade (anchovy sauce), or sprinkle the slices with lemon juice and add to a leafy salad. Artichokes can also be braised until tender, or quartered and fried in olive oil with a little garlic, then served with a dash of lemon juice and a sprinkling of rock salt.

Medium artichokes If the stems are long, break them off close to the base – this will pull away the tough fibres from the heart. Remove any small or withered leaves from the base and rub the exposed surfaces with lemon juice. Put the artichokes into a very large pan of boiling salted water to which about 2 tablespoons of white wine vinegar or lemon juice have been added for every 1.2 litres (2 pints) of water. Set a wire cake rack or a double layer of muslin on top of them to hold them down and boil, uncovered, over a high heat for 30–45 minutes. They are ready when the leaves at the base can be easily removed and feel tender. Use tongs to transfer them to a colander, arranging the heads pointing down so the water drains out. Serve hot with melted butter, Hollandaise Sauce (page 233) or vinaigrette, or cold with vinaigrette or mayonnaise.

To eat artichokes Pull away the artichoke leaves one at a time, starting at the bottom. Dip the tender base into some butter or sauce, then draw the leaf through your teeth, squeezing out and eating the fleshy part. Discard the rest. When most of the leaves have been eaten, you will come to a few thin pale-coloured pointed leaves which can be pulled off in one piece. Nibble around these. This will leave a hairy mound like a haystack, topping a fleshy saucer-shaped heart – this is the most delicious part called the choke. Slide your knife between the hairs and the bottom and, holding both the knife and choke between finger and thumb, pull out the 'hay' in sections. Discard the hay and eat the heart.

The fleshy heart is often eaten by itself as a delicacy. It can be taken from the cooked artichoke once the leaves have been discarded, but can easily become overcooked and discoloured. To prevent this, I prepare them raw, which is the Italian and French way. Have ready a large bowl of acidulated water. Wash and drain the artichokes and break off the stems. Holding the artichoke by the head, bottom up, bend a lower leaf back on itself until it snaps, then peel it off towards the base, leaving the meaty part attached. Do this until you are left with a cone of fine central leaves which can be pulled out in one piece and removed with the choke. As you remove the leaves, rub the cut surfaces with lemon juice, then drop the hearts into acidulated water. Drop the hearts into boiling salted water to which the juice of a lemon and some olive oil have been added. Return to the boil and cook for 15–20 minutes until they can be pierced easily with the point of a knife.

Artichoke hearts taste good with hollandaise sauce, butter or vinaigrette, with a garlic or anchovy-flavoured sauce, or simply with thick natural yogurt sharpened with lemon juice. They can also be fried in butter, or sliced and added to salads, gratins and even scrambled eggs.

The fennel bulb has a high water content. It is low in calories and rich in the vitamins A and E. It is also a good source of calcium and potassium and aids digestion.

Sweet fennel, Italian fennel and Florence fennel are all romantic aliases for this decorative garden vegetable. The herb, common fennel, has a lineage stretching back to ancient times around the Aegean and the Mediterranean, where it grew wild and was used both for flavouring and medicinal purposes. In contrast, the vegetable's popularity is quite recent, stretching back no more than 300 years in Italy and to the 18th century in Britain.

Fennel, the vegetable, is grown primarily for its aniseed-flavoured bulb, which develops from the swollen base of the stalks. These broad, curved, fleshy leaf stalks overlap to form a firm pale green or white crisp head about 7–10 cm (3–4 inches) across. Growing out of these is a mass of bright green feathery foliage. The bulbs sit on top of the soil, their tiny roots filtering down into the earth and their feathery heads stretching sometimes to 60 cm (2 feet) tall. There are male and female bulbs. The short, squat ones are female, the more elegant, elongated variety the male. Baby fennel (opposite) are particularly attractive.

When buying fennel, choose firm bulbs which are pale in colour, have tightly packed leaf stalks and fluffy green foliage. Smaller bulbs are less wasteful as the outer leaves are less fibrous and not so much trimming is required.

Fennel is the perfect salad vegetable. It is crisp like celery, but with a clearer, more distinctive flavour. It does not discolour when it is cut and, if slightly limp, can be

fennel
Foeniculum vulgare

revived by steeping in a bowl of iced water for about 1 hour. To use the bulb whole or in halves, do not cut off the base because it holds the fleshy stalks together. Just tidy it up by shaving off a few slivers with a vegetable peeler. Rinse under cold running water, dry, then use as the recipe requires. To give a crisp texture through a leafy salad, cut the fennel across into thin rings. When it is to be used like celery and eaten with fruit and cheese or served as part of a platter of crudités, cut it downward into strips. Alternatively, it can be cut into wedges or just torn off into individual stalks, the base end trimmed, and served with fruit, Parmesan or pecorino cheese – a popular way of serving it in Italy. To include in a crisp salad, cut or chop it into smallish pieces. Any trimmings from the base or fibrous stalks can be removed and reserved for fish or chicken stock or soup. The stalks can also be cut off, chopped and used for stock, soup or stuffings, or dried and used to perfume the smoke of a barbecue fire – this is good when barbecuing fish and vegetables.

Fennel can be boiled whole, served with melted butter and garnished with chopped fennel heads. Puréed, it can be used for a soufflé or sauce. Blanched fennel can be tossed in butter until it begins to brown slightly, then finished with a little Pernod and cream and a sprinkling of chopped fennel. My own favourite is quite simple: par-boil, then sprinkle with Parmesan and brown under the grill. Raw or blanched fennel can be added to stir-fries or sautéed and added to stews. It is delicious as part of a selection of sautéed diced vegetables and is good with tomato-based sauces, garlic and olives. Cut into quarters, it is excellent grilled. Place the pieces, flat-side down, on a hot ridged cast iron grill pan and cook for about 5 minutes on each side. Don't fiddle with it or the sections will fall apart, and turn it carefully when ready.

the onion family

A source of vitamins A, B, C and E, calcium, phosphorus, potassium, iron, sodium, sulphur and copper in small amounts.

Onions are thought to have originated in the Middle East. Fresh and dried onions were eaten in Old Testament times, and the Bible records that they were one of the foods the Israelites longed for in the wilderness. They were common in ancient Egypt, and thought to be invested with supernatural powers. Onion bulbs and wooden models of onions have been found in tombs in the Valley of the Kings at Luxor and we are told that the main diet of the slave workers who built the pyramids at Giza consisted of radishes, garlic and onions.

Throughout the Middle Ages onions were unrivalled for both flavour and substance, in soups, broths and stews, but it was for their supposed medicinal value that they were most highly prized, and they were used to alleviate many ailments. By the 18th century, they were grown in almost every country garden in Britain. These days we know that onions pack a real vitamin and mineral punch, that they contain an antiseptic oil and an anticoagulant, and can help to lower cholesterol levels in the blood. There are over 300 different varieties.

onion
Allium cepa

Pickling onions Also known as baby onions and button onions, pickling onions are a small variety of yellow onion, bulbous, elongated and slightly flattened in shape. In some varieties the flesh is clearly tinged with yellow. They are used for home pickling, adding whole to stews, sautéing in butter and roasting. They can also be caramelized, used whole in tarts and threaded on skewers for barbecuing.

Red onions (opposite page) Sometimes called Italian or salad onions, these have a mild sweet flavour and are good for eating raw, thinly sliced or chopped in salads or salsas. They are very attractive, with ruby-red papery skin and pink-tinged flesh. They are of medium size and slightly squat, elongated or torpedo shaped.

Spanish onions (page 44) A large variety of yellow onion with a rich copper-coloured skin. Mild and sweet, they are excellent for general cooking and for using raw in salads. Their size makes them useful for baking.

Spring onions (page 48) Also known as scallions and green onions, particularly in north America, these are onions grown from seed and harvested very young before their green shoots have had time to mature and wither. They are white skinned with small, slightly flattened bulbs at the base of slim green stalks. They can have either a mild delicate flavour or a more pungent peppery taste and are generally eaten raw. Chopped (both the white and green parts), they are added to salads, salsas and dressings, cooked and stirred into mashed potatoes, added to egg dishes for colour and flavour and included in stir-fries.

Vidalia onions These are North America's version of the Spanish onion. They are large, pale and juicy, with a mild, sweet flavour. They are good roasted, excellent with a light creamy sauce and thinly sliced raw in salads.

Yellow onions The name is misleading because their skin is more golden brown than yellow. A good all-purpose onion, which comes in two sizes: large and medium/small. It is the variety that you will find everywhere throughout the year. They are thought to be the most pungent of the onions, but I find they vary slightly depending on type.

White onions These are available all year round in all shapes and sizes. The flavour varies from very strong to mild. The very small, mild onions with silver skins are called Paris Silver Skin and can be added whole to stews, or served in a creamy white sauce.

Onions are available all year round and, although they will change with the seasons, their characteristic flavour is always there. If you grow your own, they can be stored throughout the winter, or you can buy a string of onions and hang them up in a dark dry place for months, but they are so readily available that it is not really necessary to store them. When you buy them, make sure they are firm, with papery, dry and crackly skins. They should not have begun to sprout.

Once an onion is cut, it deteriorates rapidly as well as tainting everything near it, so don't store cut onions, even for a short time. Select the size you need so there will be no waste. The general preparation is the same regardless of the variety of onion. First remove the skin, unless you are intending to either roast the onion whole in its skin or add it to a stock where it will impart a rich golden colour. Remove the skin by pulling it away from the stalk end, then peeling it off in layers to expose the flesh. Trim the roots but do not cut them off at this stage; they will help hold the onion together while you either slice or chop it. Baby, pickling or silver skin onions have very tight skin, which can be difficult to remove in the normal way. For speed and convenience, drop these into a pan of boiling water and cook for 1 minute, then drain and refresh under cold water. Gently remove the skin. Trim off the root close to the flesh, but don't detach it completely or the onion will fall apart.

Onions can be cooked in a variety of ways. They can be fried in butter or oil, cut into rings, slices or dice, to be added to soups, stews, risottos, tians, omelettes and pilafs, sweated until meltingly tender and used as the filling for tarts, or puréed and made into a sauce. The frying can be slow, over a low heat to soften and tenderize without colour, or fast and furious, to caramelize and brown. Sautéed onions are an ideal accompaniment or garnish for fried or grilled meats. They can be sliced into rings, dipped in milk and flour or batter and then deep-fried. Small whole onions can be boiled and served in a white sauce or tossed in butter and sugar until caramelized. Small and medium onions can be roasted whole, with or without their skin, while larger onions can be stuffed and baked to make a substantial meal.

To slice an onion Peel the onion leaving the root attached, then slice either in whole rings the thickness that the recipe requires, or cut the onion in half lengthways through the root, then slice it into half rings, working towards the root.

To chop an onion Set the peeled onion on a board. With a sharp knife, cut the onion in half lengthways through the root, leaving the root attached. Set one half cut-side down on the board with the root facing the hand that is not holding the knife. Starting nearest to the board and working upwards to the rounded side, make a series of horizontal cuts from the shoot end of the onion towards the root but not through it. The closer you keep these cuts together the more finely chopped the onion will be. Turn the onion so the root is away from you. Working from the centre to the sides, make cuts down through the onion on to the board. Turn the onion back to its original position and slice across the onion from the shoot to the root, again keeping the cuts close together to obtain fine dice. The flesh will fall apart into small pieces and come away from the root, which can either be discarded or added to the stockpot. If necessary, chop through the onion to make finer dice. Repeat with the other onion half.

Onion juice Cut a peeled onion in half and scrape the cut surface with a broad-bladed kitchen knife over a bowl to release the onion juice. Alternatively, grate the onion on the largest section of a grater and, with the back of a spoon, squeeze the juice out of the grated flesh.

shallot

Allium cepa

Aggregatum group

Shallots are a good source of vitamins A, B, C and E. They contain small quantities of calcium, phosphorus, potassium, iron, sodium, sulphur and copper.

I have a cluster of shallots, a string of garlic and a bunch of bay leaves hanging on the dresser in my kitchen. To my mind the shallot is an icon of continental cooking. The French in particular have been noted for their use of shallots when making the sauces for which Cordon Bleu cuisine has become famous.

The shallot is not a baby onion. It is a member of the onion family, with very distinct characteristics. It grows in small, tight clusters like garlic, with anything from 2–6 bulbs grouped together and joined at the root. The single bulbs vary in shape, but are generally smaller, slimmer, flatter and, in some cases, pear-shaped and more elongated than the common onion. Its flavour is neither onion nor garlic, but it has similarities to both. It is definite and strong but without excessive fieriness, and its subtle mildness and lack of heavy smell makes it perfect for eating raw.

There are three main varieties of shallot. The most common is the bronzed, golden-yellow shallot (right), which is slightly larger than the others and keeps well. Then there is the *échalote rosé* (left), a small and pretty pinkish-red shallot, which to my taste has the best flavour.

The third kind is the smallish, grey-brown shallot, known by the French as *échalote gris*. This has a pronounced concentrated flavour and is mostly used for sauces.

Shallots should be firm without any green shoots, their outer skin crisp, papery and fresh. Most shallots are sold in small quantities in net bags, bunches or strings which can be hung up for storage, although they can also be bought loose. They keep for several months in a cool, dry, well-ventilated place.

The shallot is suited to the making and flavouring of sauces because of its subtlety of flavour and the way in which its tender flesh cooks to such softness. The most famous of the shallot sauces is bordelaise. Finely chopped shallots and Bordeaux wine are cooked together to concentrate their flavours before being used as a base for this rich and distinctive sauce, traditionally served with grilled entrecôte steak.

Like garlic and onions, whole shallots can be roasted with or without their skins until they are meltingly tender, or cooked around a roast. They can also be boiled in milk, or cooked gently in butter or oil. Mashed to a purée, the cooked shallot flesh can be used as the basis of a sauce or stirred into butter as a flavouring and garnish for grilled meats. Whole raw peeled shallots can be added to stews and casseroles to give extra flavour and texture, or they can be pickled. Finely chopped raw shallots can be blended with butter as a flavouring, eaten raw in salads, or used instead of onions when only a small amount is required. Young shallot leaves, finely chopped, can be used as a garnish for salads.

leek

Allium porrum

Contains small amounts of iron, potassium, vitamin C and protein.

Most shoppers today, given a choice between pre-packed, clean uniformity and unwashed, unpackaged vegetables, would probably choose the former for convenience. Unfortunately, they would then forego the pleasure of tasting really fresh leeks.

The leek has a very long history, stretching back well over 5,000 years to the ancient Egyptians, the Greeks and the Romans. It has been grown in Britain for the best part of 2,000 years and valued as a vegetable to provide bulk for the poor man's pot – it has been called the poor man's asparagus. In medieval times the leek was favoured for its medicinal value as a diuretic. Its association with the Welsh can be traced back over 1,400 years, when it was adopted as an emblem to commemorate a famous victory over the Anglo-Saxons.

Leeks can withstand wintry rain, frost and snow, and are the principal vegetable in the winter garden, standing alone when everything else has been harvested. Like the onion, the leek has a tight root structure at its base. It is long and elegant, between 20–30 cm (8–12 inches), and about 2–5 cm (¾–2 inches) across. In flavour it is milder than the onion and makes an excellent pot herb or onion substitute in many recipes.

When choosing leeks, opt for the smallest you can find and chose those of similar size, particularly if they are to be used whole. When picked small, leeks are tender and mildly aromatic. Make sure that the white part is really white, and that it feels firm. The leaves should be tightly rolled around each other and have a rich green colour.

If leeks have soil clinging to them, part-prepare them before storing. Cut off and discard any muddy roots, then trim away wilted or green tops, saving these in a plastic bag for the stockpot. Put the whole leeks in a loose-fitting plastic bag and store in the bottom of the refrigerator. Only wash leeks at this stage if they are very dirty, then dry them well. If storing pre-packed leeks, transfer them to a plastic bag in which they can breathe. Leeks deteriorate rapidly, so keep for only 3–5 days. They can taint other foods, so keep them away from butter, milk and cream.

Before cooking, all leeks need careful preparation because they tend to trap dirt and grit in their folds. Remove and discard the roots if this has not been done already, then remove the coarse, deep green ends of the leaves and the outer layer of white flesh along with its darker green tops. All of this is full of flavour and can be chopped and used for stock. If you are going to slice the leek across into rings, do so now, then wash them well in a colander under cold running water. If you need the white part only, with perhaps a little of the pale green leaves attached, cut off accordingly. If the leek is to be left whole, make a cut from the trimmed end halfway down its length, then hold leaf-end down under cold running water, gently opening out the leaves and allowing the dirt and grit to wash away. Shake well. Wash the leek, or chop first, then wash. If you are not intending to use all the leek at once, only wash the amount you require and store the rest, unwashed, in a plastic bag in the vegetable compartment of the refrigerator.

Trimmed whole leeks can be steamed or boiled in the minimum amount of water for 5–20 minutes, depending on thickness. They should be just tender, with a slight resistance when skewered with the point of a knife. Keep testing them as overcooked leeks are unappetizing and slimy. Leeks can be served simply with butter and seasoned with salt and pepper, coated with cream and herbs, or dressed while warm in a light vinaigrette and served cold as a salad. They can be part-cooked, coated in cheese sauce and cooked *au gratin* in the oven or under the grill, or layered with cheese and covered with cream, then baked in the oven and finished under the grill. Leeks can also be braised gently in butter or oil and perhaps a little wine or stock, with thyme or bay to season. This can be done in a heavy casserole or shallow frying pan with a tight-fitting lid and the leeks slowly cooked until tender. The juices can be made into a light sauce with the addition of butter, *beurre manié* or thick cream. Leeks are also compatible with lemon juice, paprika, caraway and coriander seeds.

Sliced across into pieces 5–7 cm (2–3 inches) wide, leeks can be gently fried in butter or oil until softened, then used in a gratin or gently stir-fried with garlic, chilli and grated fresh ginger before being moistened with a little water, dry sherry and soy sauce. They can be sliced across in rings (both the white and green parts), fried until soft in butter and oil without colouring and used as a base for a tart or quiche, gratin, sauce or soup. One of the traditional ways of using leeks is in stews and soups such as vichyssoise or cockie-a-leekie, while one of the most impressive ways of using them is as a garnish for roast or grilled fish or meat. Cut the leek into thread-like strips about 7 cm (3 inches) long, then deep-fry them until pale golden. The strands will curl and look like delicate pieces of straw.

garlic
Allium sativum

Contains small quantities of vitamin C and minerals, calcium, phosphorus, potassium and iron.

I well remember my larger-than-life art mistress at school inviting groups of us to her home. These were inspiring occasions, although the odour, a mix of perfume, face powder and garlic, was almost overpowering. She was certainly ahead of her time. Today, garlic's image is of a crucial flavouring for so many dishes now familiar to us from around the world, and as a medicinal warrior doing battle with harmful bacteria, bolstering the body's immune system and lowering cholesterol levels.

Garlic seems to have originated in Asia Minor, and it was held in awe by the Egyptians, Greeks and Romans as both food, medicine and talisman to guard against evil and misfortune – thousands of years before Count Dracula and his vampire cohorts slid across our cinema screens. Garlic bulbs have been found in ancient Egyptian tombs, and we know that the slave workers who toiled to build the pyramids demanded garlic in their diet. The use of garlic spread throughout continental Asia and the Mediterranean basin, and its popularity today is largely due to our relatively recent liking for Mediterranean, Indian and Asian cooking.

There are many different varieties, but they are all composed of a compact bulb, often described as a head, which grows below the soil and gives rise to fine green shoots. These can grow to a height of 90 cm (3 feet), finishing with a flourish in a mass of white blooms. The bulbs are white, pink or purple tinged, and comprise a number of almond-shaped segments called cloves. Each of these cloves is encased in a delicate paper-like skin, held tightly together by both a communal root structure and layers of skin. As a general guide, the bigger the garlic bulb the milder the flavour.

In this country, garlic bulbs are generally bought cured or semi-cured, that is dried. The bulbs are harvested when the tops are beginning to dry out, then hung up until the skin becomes papery. The individual cloves are still juicy and will keep in this condition for many months in a cool, dry place. Fresh garlic, also referred to as green or wet garlic, is available around June and July. This is newly pulled garlic, with large heads of cloves. It will still have its growing stem attached, will look a little green and have moist, pliable skin. Delightfully juicy and more delicate in flavour than dried garlic, it is good sliced in salads. Don't buy too much at a time as it does not keep very well. Dried garlic is available throughout the year and can keep for several months if stored in a cool, dry place. Garlic does not keep well in the refrigerator, because the damp air

causes it to sprout, but if kept in too warm conditions, the cloves will shrivel up and turn to grey powder. Whatever variety of garlic you buy, choose firm plump bulbs that feel heavy for their size. The skin of dried garlic should be clean, dry, crisp and unbroken. The bulbs should not have started to sprout.

To prepare garlic, remove the number of cloves you require from the bulb – these can vary in size and pungency depending on the type of garlic, so if they taste mild, you may want to add more than the recipe suggests. Peel away the papery skin surrounding each clove, then prepare according to recipe requirements. The more finely the garlic is sliced, chopped or crushed, the more juice is released and the stronger the flavour. When sliced it will be milder, when left whole, much less pungent. In fact, cooked whole garlic has a gentle, nutty flavour.

Raw chopped or sliced garlic can be added to salads and dressings and provides a mild, fresh taste. Whole, sliced, chopped or crushed, it can be stirred into stews or casseroles, soups and stocks. To soften its flavour, it can be fried first, but take care not to let it burn or it will be unpleasantly bitter. If frying onions which need to be browned, add the garlic once the onions are brown and fry only for a few minutes to soften without colouring.

Crushed raw garlic can be mixed with softened butter, finely chopped parsley and lemon juice, and seasoned with salt and pepper to create a wonderful garlic butter. This can then be served with vegetables or pasta, spread on bread to be baked, grilled or roasted, or used as the French

do to 'drown' snails. I use 6–12 garlic cloves to 50–125 g (2–4 oz) butter. A small knob of garlic butter tastes good melting over grilled salmon steaks.

Whole cloves of garlic or complete bulbs in their skins can be roasted in a preheated oven, 190°C (375°F), Gas Mark 5, for about 30 minutes until tender, either on their own, in a little oil or around a roast. Roasted garlic is sweet and succulent, with a mellow flavour. After roasting, the skins can easily be removed and the soft garlic segments released. Peeled cloves of garlic can be poached in milk or water to remove some of their fiery flavour, or if the tender cloves are required for a sauce or purée. It will take about 10 minutes to soften the cloves, which can then be crushed or processed to form a spreadable purée. The cooking liquor can be used to dilute the purée, added to soup, or enriched with egg yolk to make a sauce.

roots & tubers

The roots of beetroot are a good source of vitamins A and C, folic acid and potassium and they are high in sugar. The leaves are rich in iron, calcium and vitamins A and C.

Also known as red beet and beet, this all-year-round vegetable was enjoyed in ancient times – the Greeks ate the leaves and the root was included in the Roman diet. Nowadays it is grown primarily for its bulbous roots, but its leaves should not be ignored and can be prepared and eaten like spinach. The root can be round, globe-shaped, oval or tapered. In colour it can vary from ruby-red through golden yellow to white.

Pick or buy raw beetroot when small, about the size of a golf ball, then they will be tender and sweet. If the leaves are missing, make sure there is about 5 cm (2 inches) of stalk left on or the beetroot will lose colour and flavour during cooking. The skin should be smooth, firm and intact. Cut off the leaves to within 5 cm (2 inches) of the root, wash the earth off the root, gently scrubbing if necessary. Do not trim off the actual roots. Beetroot are also available boiled, often peeled and in vacuum packs. These are very convenient and ideal for quick salads. Check whether they are preserved in vinegar.

To cook whole raw beetroot, simmer in a pan of water with a good squeeze of lemon juice until tender, 1–2 hours depending on size. Or bake in a tightly covered roasting dish with 4–5 tablespoons water at 180°C (350°F), Gas Mark 4, for 2–3 hours. Individual beetroot can be tightly wrapped in foil and baked in the same way. The beetroot are cooked when they feel tender when pierced with a skewer, and when the skin is easily removed by pushing with the fingers. Cool slightly, then peel off the skin and top and tail.

Serve small boiled beetroot whole and hot, with lots of butter and a sprinkling of herbs like chives, parsley or dill, with aïoli, anchovy dip, sweet and sour sauce, natural yogurt or soured cream. Or slice or dice them and toss in a light garlic vinaigrette, or top with a creamy white sauce flavoured with horseradish. When cold, they marry well with orange segments, chopped apple, dates, dried apricots, sultanas, raisins, walnuts and pine nuts. Peeled cooked beetroot can be puréed, seasoned with salt, pepper and balsamic vinegar and served hot, on its own or mixed with an equal quantity of mashed potato.

beetroot

Beta vulgaris

Rich in vitamin C, calcium and niacin.

Turnip is a root vegetable belonging to the cabbage family, said to have been introduced into this country by the Romans. Although grown mainly for its root, the leaves of young turnips are tender, and have a peppery taste. In the southern states of America and in Europe these are called turnip greens, and are cooked like other leafy greens.

The root itself varies in size, shape and colour. It may be white, creamy white or streaked pinkish purple, yellowy green or green and white. Its shape is usually round or conical, 5–7 cm (2–3 inches) across, but some varieties, like the carrot-shaped French *vertus,* are longer. The young spring and summer turnips are often no larger than ping-pong balls and are sold tied up in bunches or laid out in boxes (above right), with their leaves still attached. French *navets* are small, round turnips tinged with pink or purple that have a sweet delicate flavour. The flesh of all turnips is generally white, but some may have a yellow tinge. The flavour is sweet and nutty when young and small; with age, it deepens in strength and loses some sweetness.

Choose turnips no larger than a tennis ball, with smooth, firm skin (page 56). These do not need to be peeled, just wash and scrub them. Cut any leaves off 1 cm (½ inch) away from the root, leaving some stalk intact. Store the leaves in a plastic bag in the refrigerator to use later as leafy greens. Larger turnips need to be peeled.

Boil turnips in just enough water to cover until just tender, this should take 10–15 minutes. Small turnips can be cooked whole, then tossed in butter, seasoned with salt and pepper and served just as they are or with ground cinnamon, ginger or mace. They can also be grilled and served with dipping sauces. When cooking large turnips, dice or slice them, then boil and finish in the same way as

turnip
Brassica campestrio
Rapifera group

small turnips, or combine them with carrots or parsnips. If dried well after draining, they can be mashed and seasoned with salt, pepper and nutmeg, on their own or with parsnips. Peeled, quartered and cubed, turnips can be added to soups and stews. They can be left whole, then peeled and cut into pieces and roasted. Blanch sliced turnips for 3–5 minutes, then fry in butter or oil flavoured with garlic. Blanched turnips make an excellent salad when tossed in a light or garlic vinaigrette.

swede
Brassica napus
Napobrassica group

purplish brown in colour with creamy yellow tinges, but some are yellow, purple and white. All swedes have pale orange flesh (in contrast to the white flesh of turnips) and their flavour is sweet and nutty, with slightly stronger cabbage undertones than the turnip.

Look for small specimens that are firm and smooth, solid and heavy for their size. Remove the skin with a firm serrated-edged knife rather than a potato peeler, then cut the flesh into slices, chunks, dice or fingers using a large, firm-bladed cook's knife. Take care if the swede is old because it can be very tough and resistant.

Swedes are ninety per cent water, and so need careful cooking. Steam or boil them in just enough water to cover until very tender. They are not pleasant to eat when even slightly undercooked, but take care because they can quickly go from undercooked to overcooked. Drain well, return to the pan and cover with kitchen paper. Allow to dry before tossing in butter with lots of seasoning. Nutmeg, cinnamon, mace and chopped parsley all taste good with swede, and they combine well with carrots and parsnips. Alternatively, mash them after drying, season well and serve as a rich purée. Cut into cubes or chunks, swede adds flavour to soups, broths and stews. They can also be roasted with a little oil and honey.

Swede is rich in vitamin C, calcium and niacin.

In Ireland, the vegetable we call 'turnip' is not a turnip at all but a swede. Confusion regarding names is widespread, even with the introduction of small turnips and sweet-tasting *navets*, so different in appearance to the much larger swedes. In Scotland, the 'bashed neeps' traditionally eaten with haggis are also swedes. However, there was a time about 300 years ago when there was only the turnip, for the swede is a relative newcomer, a mid-European hybrid cross between a turnip and kohlrabi. In the 18th century it was grown in Sweden, where it was and still is called rutabaga, then exported around Europe – as the swede.

Sometimes called turnip-rooted cabbage, the swede is a large winter vegetable belonging to the cabbage family, grown for both its roots and leaves. Although similar to the turnip, it is allowed to grow much larger so it has coarser skin, which can be quite knobbly. In shape the swede is round or slightly oblong, with a wrinkly neck made up of ridges, which are leaf scars. It is generally

taro

Colocasia esculenta

Taro has a high starch content and is also rich in B vitamins. It has some vitamin C, potassium and iron.

This tuber, which originated in East Asia thousands of years ago, is a staple food in tropical areas throughout the world, from China to the southern states of America. There are about 200 varieties, which explains its many different names – eddo and dasheen are Caribbean, while keladi is Indonesian and Malay, and it is also known as cocoyam, colocassi and elephant's ear. The varieties which we are most likely to come across in Britain are the large, barrel-shaped tubers resembling swedes, and the smaller, potato-shaped tubers. Both are dark brown in colour and have a rough, shaggy skin. When buying taro, choose small, even-sized specimens, and store in a cool dark place, where they will keep for a few weeks.

Taro is often confused with the yam but, unlike the yam, the bulbous taro has a ring of colour at the base of the stem and all of the plant is eaten – the root, stem, shoots and leaves. The leaves are called callaloo and are reminiscent of kale. The taro also has a more distinctive flavour than the yam and has been described by some as rather like that of a water chestnut. The tubers contain calcium oxalate below the skin – this is toxic and can only be eliminated by cooking. Therefore, when peeling taro, it is advisable to wear gloves as this prevents the toxins causing an allergic reaction. Taro can be boiled without peeling, the skin being removed after cooking.

Should you come across taro leaves (callaloo), these can be cooked in the same way as other leafy greens, but on no account should they be eaten raw because they too contain calcium oxalate.

Taro can be cooked in the same way as potatoes: boiled and mashed, roasted, fried, braised or made into fritters. As it readily absorbs the flavours of other ingredients, it is well suited to making soups, stews and casseroles.

A rich source of vitamin A, with significant amounts of B3, C and E and small amounts of calcium, phosphorus, potassium, sodium, zinc and iron. It is also a good source of fibre.

As a child I was told, along with probably every other child of my generation, that if I ate my carrots I would be able to see in the dark. I remember a visit to the pictures, walking into the auditorium and groping for my seat in the dark. In no time at all I could see quite clearly, which I assumed was due to my obedience in not leaving a single carrot on my plate. It was quite a few years later when I learned that there was a scientific basis for the medical claims for carrots, and that World War II pilots were encouraged to eat them to help with night flying.

The original carrot of Asia Minor must have been very unimpressive, described by Nika Hazelton in her book *Vegetable Cookery* as 'small, tough, pale fleshed and acrid', a far cry from the vibrant orange vegetable we know today. The Greeks and Romans certainly ate those early carrots, and prized them for their medicinal qualities, particularly for digestive ailments, but it was not until the coming of the Moors into Europe in the early Middle Ages that carrots appeared with any similarity to those of today, although the colour was then purple. In fact, the familiar orange colour is a Dutch invention of the late 18th century.

Carrots now come in numerous shapes, sizes and colours. Parisienne carrots are short, round and stubby, about 5 cm (2 inches) long and 4 cm (1½ inches) across, and slightly rusty orange in colour. They have a sweet earthy flavour and a texture between a crisp carrot and a soft parsnip. More familiar varieties range from 12 cm (5 inches) long and 1 cm (½ inch) wide to 20 cm (8 inches) long, finishing in a pointed or blunt end. Across the widest part they can be as much as 5 cm (2 inches). When young, they are sweet and deep in flavour, they are crisp and succulent and bright golden orange. These young carrots are often sold with their feathery leaves still attached (opposite page). Special varieties of very small carrots, no bigger than a little finger, are also available. These are sweet and succulent. Carrots generally range from bright orange to a more muted orange/brown, but there are also varieties which have white, yellow or purple roots.

Buy firm, smooth, well-shaped, even-sized carrots with a bright colour. Small to medium carrots generally have a sweeter flavour and more refined texture than large varieties, which may have more depth to their taste, but are inclined to be woody.

Very small carrots are best served raw or very lightly cooked. When serving them raw as part of a selection of crudités, leave a little foliage on or trim off the foliage to leave about 5 mm (¼ inch) stalk. The skin is so fine that it is not necessary to peel them, simply wash, scrub and dry. To cook very small carrots, steam or boil them in just enough water to cover for a few minutes until they are just tender and the water has evaporated. The delicate flavour of small carrots needs no more embellishment other than to be tossed in some melted butter and seasoned with salt, freshly ground black pepper and lots of finely chopped flat leaf parsley.

Carrots that are 10–12 cm (4–5 inches) long with tender skin can also be scrubbed and washed. Most of the precious nutrients are stored just under the skin, so only peel very large or older carrots with skin that is more textured or damaged. Medium and large carrots need to be trimmed top and bottom, then they can be cut into slices, sticks or dice and boiled or steamed. They will take 8–20 minutes, depending on their size and age. Carrots are heat sensitive and need to be steamed or boiled fast rather than simmered or they will never become tender. My favourite way is to just cover them with boiling water, add a knob of butter and a pinch of sugar and boil over a high heat with the lid on until almost tender. The lid is then removed and any remaining liquid reduced to a light syrup before adding lots of chopped parsley or chives and plenty of salt and freshly ground black pepper. These are known as Vichy carrots. After simply steaming or boiling, carrots can also be drained, dried and mashed, and they are good mashed with parsnips. They can also be made into a purée or mousse, or added to tarts, pancakes and puddings.

Large carrots can be cut into large chunks, par-boiled until they are just beginning to tenderize, then drained and roasted around a joint. Alternatively, diced large carrots may be mixed with other diced root vegetables and roasted with a little honey. It is these carrots that add an earthy flavour and substantial texture to robust stews and casseroles, and are indispensable in soups.

Raw carrots are equally valuable grated or cut into julienne as a major ingredient in salads, in which they taste excellent with either a mayonnaise or vinaigrette dressing. They combine well with many other ingredients, including cabbage, peas, dried fruit and citrus fruit, nuts and mustard. Herbs that go well with carrots include coriander, dill, chervil, tarragon and parsley; spices are nutmeg, cinnamon, caraway, coriander, turmeric and cumin.

carrot
Daucus carota

High in carbohydrate and rich in potassium, with some folic acid, zinc and B vitamins.

The yam could easily be described as the potato of Asia, now widely cultivated as a staple in tropical regions (it was originally spread by Iberian traders to Africa and the New World partly as a result of the slave trade). There are numerous shapes, colours and sizes, variously described as greater yams, water yams, sweet yams and Asiatic yams. Those that we see in our shops are generally thick, oblong tubers with skin that is brown, rough and a little hairy. The skin can vary from white to pink, yellow and dark brown, depending on the variety, and in some cases can also be smooth. The colour of the hard flesh can vary, from white right through to purple. As far as taste goes, yams are rather bland, but like that more famous tuber the potato, it is their ready availability and versatility that attracts cooks around the world.

When buying yams, choose those with firm unbroken skin. They will keep for several weeks if stored in a cool, dark place.

The skin of the yam contains the poison dioscorine, but this is destroyed during cooking. Small young yams can be cooked in their skins, but larger yams are best peeled. To boil yams, first wash them, then cook them in a saucepan of salted boiling water for 10–20 minutes. Yams can also be baked in their skins, or peeled, then roasted or mashed. They can be cut into cubes or slices and added to casseroles and curries, and they are excellent cut into chips and deep-fried. In West Africa boiled yams are made into *fufu*, a kind of porridge that is traditionally served with spicy stews and soups.

yam
Dioscorea

Rich in carbohydrate, Jerusalem artichokes are high in iron, with moderate amounts of vitamins B and C.

A hardy native of North America, imported to Western Europe in the 17th century, this is a real ugly duckling among vegetables – small, knobbly and irregularly shaped. This is a shame, because it has a wonderful nutty flavour and a meltingly tender texture. The name Jerusalem artichoke is said to stem from the Italian *girasol articocco* – *girasol* meaning 'towards the sun' and *articocco* because some people believe it has a smoky taste similar to that of the globe artichoke. Strangely, despite its name, it has nothing to do with Jerusalem.

When selecting Jerusalem artichokes, pick the least knobbly you can find, so that preparation is less tedious. A new, straighter variety is becoming more widely available, and is worth seeking out.

Sadly, this winter vegetable has long been neglected and underestimated, mainly because it has a reputation for causing wind in some people – unfortunate but true. Handling and cooking is similar to that of the potato. Scrub artichokes well to remove any soil or grit, then wash them. If the skin is smooth and fairly blemish free, peeling is unnecessary, and since most of the nutrients lie just under the skin it is best left on. If the artichokes are peeled, sliced or diced, keep them in water to which the juice of half a lemon has been added. The acidulated water

Jerusalem artichoke

Helianthus tuberosus

helps to preserve their pale colour, so too does adding a little milk to the water when boiling.

Jerusalem artichokes can be boiled or steamed, either whole, halved, quartered or sliced. I like their rugged appearance and cook them whole for 12–15 minutes until tender, then toss them in lots of butter and seasoning and sprinkle with chives or parsley. They also taste good tossed in a nut-flavoured oil, which emphasizes their own nutty flavour. To roast them, peel, par-boil for 8–10 minutes, then drain and roast in hot fat or oil until crisp and golden – just as you would potatoes.

Fried Jerusalem artichokes are equally tasty. Par-boil or par-steam them, then slice and fry in oil and butter. They are delicious mixed with strips of fried bacon and chopped herbs. They can also be dipped in flour, egg and crumbs or batter and deep-fried. When sliced very thinly and deep-fried, they make excellent crisps. Sliced cooked artichokes make tasty gratins with cream, herbs and cheese, and boiled artichokes can be mashed to a purée. They can be used to make soup, and eaten raw, grated and tossed into a salad with a little lemon juice or vinaigrette. They are also good cooked and sliced or diced in salads.

Rich in carbohydrate, beta carotene and vitamin C with moderate amounts of potassium.

Although this vegetable has the same name as our own favourite vegetable, it is from a completely different plant, a member of the 'morning glory' family. While some varieties look similar to our potato, most do not, and the overriding flavour characteristic is sweetness.

Originally from the humid regions of the Americas, probably the Andes, it was discovered by the Spanish in the 15th century and brought to Europe. However, it was never established outside the warmest regions because of its growing characteristics. There are many different varieties and many different names – kumara, ubi, keledek, ubi manis and Louisiana yam to name just a handful.

The skin can be smooth or rough textured, and ranges in colour across a wide spectrum from white through to pinkish purple and deep brown. The flesh also has a great

sweet potato
Ipomoea batatas

variety of colour: white, cream, yellow and bright orange among others. The texture varies from dry and mealy with a flavour reminiscent of chestnuts, to waxy.

Sweet potatoes can be prepared and cooked just like potatoes: boiled, mashed, sautéed, baked, roasted and fried. They can be boiled with or without their skins, but take care when cooking them in their skins as they are more delicate than the ordinary potato. They will discolour quickly after peeling and should be put into acidulated water. They make good soups and stews because of their distinctive flavour and ability to combine well with other ingredients. Eastern spices and flavours like lime, coconut milk, ginger and coriander marry well with sweet potatoes. Because of their sweetness, they are also widely used for sweet tarts, pies and pancakes.

parsnip
Pastinaca sativa

Parsnip has moderate amounts of vitamins A and E, small amounts of C and B, with some iron, calcium, phosphorus and potassium. It is high in carbohydrates.

Parsnips are thought to have originated as wild plants in Asia Minor, but there seems to be no evidence that the ancient Egyptians or the Greeks used them, though they seem to have been well established by Roman times. It appears that they spread through the northern parts of the Roman Empire into Gaul and Britain, where ideal winter growing conditions produced the characteristic sweetness caused by the conversion of starch into sugar. The old traditions of using crushed parsnips for making jam, desserts and fermented drinks like parsnip wine seem to date from the Roman period.

Parsnips are the edible underground roots of a plant related to parsley, fennel, celery and carrots. Some are stocky and bulbous, with slightly humped shoulders and an inverted leaf core, and some are more wedge-shaped with wide shoulders and a long root. Others have the wedge shape but are much longer and narrower from top to tail. There are also dainty miniature versions.

Although traditionally a winter vegetable, nowadays parsnips are available all year round. In the winter locally grown varieties are often available with leafy heads and soil still attached. Select medium-sized roots, firm and well-shaped. Avoid very large parsnips as they may be fibrous and woody. The younger the better, and the less preparation needed. If they are from the garden, cut the leaves off and discard, then scrub the parsnips under cold running water. Medium and large parsnips need the skin scraped or peeled with a vegetable peeler if they are coarse. Small and miniature parsnips have fine skin, and so need little or no peeling. Large parsnips need the woody core cut out: cut them in half or quarters lengthways, then cut out the core. Parsnips can be cut into chunks, slices, lengths, finger strips or dice; they can also be left whole if they are no more than 7 cm (3 inches) long and fairly narrow. Steam or boil them until just tender, for 10–20 minutes, then toss in butter or cream and season well. To roast parsnips, halve or quarter the thick end and leave the pointed sections whole. Cover them with cold water, bring to the boil and cook for 1 minute. Drain, then add to hot fat and roast for about 30 minutes. Parsnips make good chips, left as they are or dipped in batter, deep-fried or sautéed in butter and oil. In Ireland, one of the most popular ways of serving them is boiled and mashed with carrots, plenty of butter, salt and pepper. They can also be mashed with potatoes, and made into fritters, cakes and soufflés. Parsnips are delicious in robust winter stews. Their sweetness goes well with curry spices, parsley, chives, nutmeg and cinnamon.

radish
Raphanus sativus

High water content, moderate amounts of vitamin C with some calcium and iron. It has a little protein and is also low in calories.

The radish is an ancient food, favoured by the pyramid building Egyptian slave workers, the Greeks and the Romans, and recognized for its diuretic and cleansing properties since earliest times. In Britain it has been eaten as a salad vegetable for well over 1,000 years.

While the radish in popular imagination is small, with a deep reddish-pink skin, firm white flesh and neat vibrant green leaves, there are in fact many other varieties. Some are slightly more oblong in shape and blushed with white at their tip, these are known as the French breakfast radish, and have a more delicate taste than the standard red varieties like Cherry Belle and Scarlet Globe. Other varieties in this group may be pink, yellow or purple in colour, and either round or cylindrical in shape. These radishes are best eaten young and raw, either on their own with salt (they are good with drinks), in salads or as part of a selection of crudités. There is also a variety of radish known as the winter, Chinese or Spanish radish. This has white flesh and a skin colour that can range from black to purple, white and red. Its shape can also vary, from small and round to elongated, and it can weigh 500 g (1 lb) and over. One type of winter radish is the black radish (below left). It is large with firm, compact flesh. These kinds of radishes are commonly eaten raw, either sliced or grated and used in salads, but they can also be boiled as a vegetable like turnip, made into soup and added to casseroles and curries.

Mooli (below right) This large white Japanese or oriental radish, also known as daikon, is impressively long and about 5 cm (2 inches) in diameter with smooth skin. It generally has a mild flavour and is extremely popular in oriental cuisine, raw, cooked and pickled. It has a very crisp, juicy texture and is often served finely sliced or shredded raw as an accompaniment or garnish for Japanese foods. It also adds interest to soups and stir-fries.

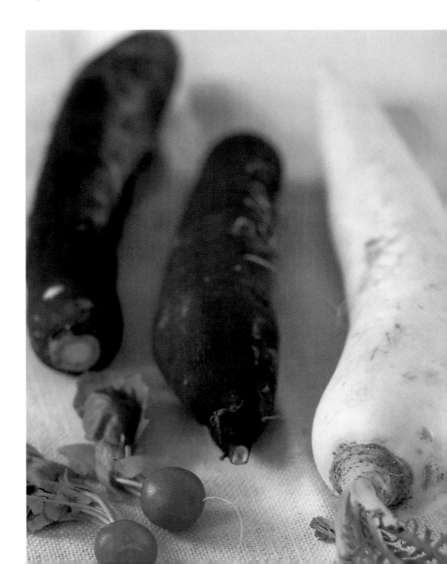

High in carbohydrates and low in fat. A good source of vitamin C with some vitamin B. A high mineral content with magnesium, potassium, iron, calcium, phosphorus and sodium.

The Irish didn't invent the potato, although it was once termed the Irish potato to distinguish it from the sweet potato. The potato has its origins in the high Andean plateaus of South America some 5,000 years ago. It was a staple of the Inca nation and was not discovered by Europeans until the time of the Conquistadors in the 16th century. Returning adventurers, including Francis Drake, brought the potato to Europe, but it was slow to catch on. It was the Irish who first grew it as their principal staple crop then, as emigrants, introduced it into North America in the early 18th century.

There are some 400 varieties of potato. Their cooking characteristics are dependent on the amount of water they contain. Floury potatoes are soft and break up easily, so are good for mashing, fluffy roast potatoes and chips. Waxy potatoes are firmer and keep their shape better than floury varieties; they are best for boiling (when they are to be served whole) and for using in salads. Potatoes are affected by light and turn green quite quickly, so store them in the cool and dark, but not the refrigerator because the extreme cold converts the starch into sugar.

Nutrients are contained in and just below the potato skin, so scrape or peel very finely, only if necessary. Alternatively, cook potatoes in their skins and peel after cooking if necessary. This is particularly suited to cooked potatoes for salads.

To boil potatoes, ensure they are of even size, or cut them into even-sized pieces. Cook, covered in boiling water, but don't boil too fiercely or the potatoes will break up. Timing depends on size and variety, but is generally 15–20 minutes. Steaming is more gentle and good for potatoes such as Kerr's Pinks, which tend to break up. Timing is 15–20 minutes. To bake, prick the skins with a fork and bake in a preheated oven, 200°C (400°F), Gas Mark 6, for 1½ hours. To roast, peel and cut into even-sized pieces, rounding off sharp edges. Put into a saucepan

of fast-boiling water, return to the boil and cook for 10 minutes. Drain, return to the saucepan to dry, and shake to roughen the surfaces. Place in a roasting tin with a little hot oil or fat and toss to coat. Roast in a preheated oven, 200°C (400°F), Gas Mark 6, for 40–50 minutes, turning and basting several times. To sauté, slice cooked potatoes and fry in a large heavy pan in a little hot oil for 15–20 minutes. To deep-fry, peel and cut into chips. Dry well, then gently lower into a pan of deep fat, preheated to 170°C (325°F). Cook for 8–10 minutes, until crisp and golden brown. Drain well before serving.

potato
Solanum tuberosum

podded vegetables

High in vitamin C with moderate amounts of vitamin B. Also contains calcium, iron, potassium and trace elements.

Okra originated in North Africa, and possibly Egypt. It is thought to have spread east to Saudi Arabia, where it is known as *bamia*, and then to India, where it flourishes in the sub-tropical south and is known as *bhindi*. It was introduced to the Caribbean and the southern states of America around the 17th century. Robbed of their homeland and identity, slaves carried with them into bondage the seeds of familiar plants – and okra was one of them. A bi-product of this period in history is that okra became an important ingredient in Creole cooking.

Also known as ladies' fingers and gumbo, okra is the fruit pod of a tropical plant, five-sided, elongated and slightly pointed in shape. It looks a little like a lantern with a conical cap, an elegant lady's finger, hence its alternative name. Dull green in colour with slightly hairy skin, it has rows of tiny seeds inside the pod. The unique quality of okra is the gooey, mucilaginous substance which exudes when the pod is cut or exposed to heat during long slow cooking. This last characteristic is particularly valued for thickening soups and stews and is perfectly illustrated in an American-Indian dish called gumbo, a cross between a soup and a stew with a thick, gluey consistency. Gumbos are now the hallmark of Creole cooking.

Always buy small, young, crisp pods – mature okra is fibrous. The ideal length is about 5–9 cm (2–3½ inches).

okra

Hibiscus esculentus

Scrub the pods well under cold running water, then trim off the stalks. If you are going to use the okra whole, leave the conical caps on and carefully pare around them to neaten their appearance, otherwise slice the okra, cutting off the caps with the stalks. When very young, small and tender, okra can be eaten raw in salads, either whole or sliced, otherwise they need to be cooked.

Boil or steam okra for 8–10 minutes until just tender. Drain, then toss in butter, season with salt and pepper and serve as an accompanying vegetable. Okra has a particular affinity with garlic, lemon or lime juice and sweetcorn. It also goes well with Spicy Tomato Sauce (page 232). Leave the okra whole, then fry them in a little butter or oil for a few minutes, pour the tomato sauce over and cook gently for 20–30 minutes until the okra is tender. Season well, then sprinkle with finely chopped flat leaf parsley and serve hot with flat bread, or cold with natural yogurt and finely chopped mint.

Frying whole okra seems to prevent them becoming slimy. Heat a few tablespoons of oil in a frying pan, add a little garlic and chilli and fry until soft but not coloured. Add the whole okra and toss for 1–2 minutes until just tender, a few minutes more if you prefer them to be crisper. Remove the okra from the pan with a slotted spoon, set aside to drain on kitchen paper and serve as a nibble or as a vegetable accompaniment to curry. For a slightly crunchy texture, whole okra can be tossed in flour, beaten egg and cornmeal and fried in about 2.5 cm (1 inch) of vegetable oil. Whole or sliced okra can be added to any type of soup or stew. They marry well with chicken, ham, bacon, lamb, prawns, tomatoes, onions, garlic, chilli, peppers, ginger and Indian spices – a truly versatile vegetable.

runner bean

Phaseolus coccineus

High in protein, carbohydrate and fibre. Moderate amounts of vitamins C and A, betacarotene and iron.

The runner bean is one of the many New World beans, a native of Central America and thought to have been a food crop for over 2,000 years. The 'scarlet runner', a climbing bean, was introduced into Britain in the early 17th century as an ornamental plant, grown for its pretty scarlet flowers and delicate leaves around gazebos, arbours and arches, over trellises and walkways, as well as in flower beds. It was also used in posies and bouquets. It was not until the end of the 19th century that the runner bean began to be used as a vegetable, but its wonderful flavour was soon recognized and it became an important feature in cottage gardens throughout the country.

Runner beans are long and flat with a slightly rough skin and purple seeds within the pods. To best enjoy their distinctive fresh flavour, eat them when they are in season from July to October. They are at their best when small, young and tender. For this, you need to grow your own, or have a friendly gardening neighbour. Unfortunately, it is rare to see small runner beans in the shops, and frozen varieties can be bland and wilted. At their best, runner beans should be firm and snap easily. To be sure of this, they should be picked just before cooking.

To prepare runner beans, wash and dry them, then top and tail. Many of today's varieties are stringless, but check for any strings and remove if necessary. If the beans are thin, short and young, they can be eaten raw in salads, either whole or sliced. They can also be stir-fried, steamed or boiled until tender, allowing 5–7 minutes, then drained and tossed in melted butter or olive oil and a dash of balsamic vinegar. Larger beans can be cut into thin, elongated diagonal pieces and treated the same way. Sometimes I toss cooked runner beans with a light sesame oil and lemon juice, or I finish them with a few tablespoons of double cream, along with plenty of seasoning and finely chopped parsley. Or I make a thick spicy tomato sauce and either cook the beans in it or toss them in it just before serving. Sometimes I use a pepper sauce instead. Another favourite way is to stir boiled runner beans into a mixture of thinly sliced fried onions, garlic and chanterelles with plenty of seasoning, finely chopped parsley and a dash of balsamic vinegar.

French bean

Phaseolus vulgaris

Rich in protein, carbohydrate, vitamins B and C. Also includes potassium, folic acid, betacarotene and high amounts of the essential amino acid lysine.

The French bean, a native of South and Central America, was introduced into Europe by the Conquistadors in the 16th century. The name 'French bean' is just one of many given to a type of bean in this large family of New World beans. Others include bobby bean, Kenyan bean, string bean, green bean, dwarf bean, haricot vert, haricot bean, wax (yellow) bean and Thai bean.

The beans can be flat, oval or round in shape, and range from 6–7 cm (2½–3 inches) to 23 cm (9 inches) in length and 5 mm–1 cm (¼–½ inch) across. Their skin and flesh may be green, yellow, purple or marbled, and their seeds are colourful or mottled. They are grown for their immature pods, which are eaten whole with the tiny seeds still inside. Once they ripen and mature, they are dried, and the seeds are then eaten as haricot beans. Perfect winter nourishment.

Look for fleshy beans, irrelevant of their shape or colour. They should be firm, crisp and snap easily (hence another of their names). The preparation and cooking of all varieties is the same. Wash and dry, then top and tail. If the pods are very large, cut them in half or into 4 cm (1½ inch) lengths.

French beans taste so fresh and distinctive that they require little embellishment. Their crunchy texture is good when raw in a crudités selection or salad of mixed leaves or crisp vegetables. Their taste and colour is preserved with quick cooking such as stir-frying in a little oil for a few minutes, on their own, with garlic or with other vegetables. They can also be steamed or boiled in the minimum amount of water for as short a time as possible. Cook for 5–7 minutes, just until tender, but do not cover the pan or the beans will lose their bright green colour. Drain, return to the pan and toss with a little butter or olive oil. Season well before serving, and add a splash of balsamic vinegar. This family of beans also marries well with fried onions and a seasoning of chopped parsley and thyme. For a more substantial dish, they can be cooked in a well-flavoured tomato sauce. If you have an excess of beans, they can be added to a mixed vegetable soup.

High in protein, carbohydrate, vitamins B and E, potassium, calcium and phosphorus.

The culinary history of the pea is an ancient one. Pea seeds have been found in the tombs of ancient Egypt, and certainly the Romans cultivated them. The dried pea was a major source of protein throughout the Dark Ages and into Medieval times, but it was not until the 16th century that we find the first references to the green pea.

The garden pea is harvested from the end of May, and it is at this time, and for several months, that fresh peas are sold in their pods. When they are plump, small and bright green, they are tender and sweet with an incomparable flavour. If they have been allowed to get big and their pods a little wrinkly, they are not worth eating, and frozen peas are a better choice. If you grow your own, pick them just before you need them, and either eat them raw or cook them immediately after shelling. Raw peas taste great in a mixed leaf salad.

To boil peas once shelled, put them in a saucepan and cover with about 2.5 cm (1 inch) of boiling water. Add a sprig of fresh mint. Return to the boil, cover with a lid and cook until just tender, 3–5 minutes. Drain and top with a knob of butter and a few chopped mint leaves, or return the peas to the pan and toss with a little thick cream and seasoning to make a light sauce. For me, there is only one other way to serve fresh peas and that is *'à la française'*,

pea
Pisum sativum

combining two summer vegetables which glut at the same time – lettuce and peas. Finely shred several small lettuce hearts, put them in a heavy casserole dish and add a few finely chopped spring onions, about 500 g (1 lb) freshly shelled peas, a knob of butter and a little water. Cover the casserole dish with a piece of greaseproof paper and the lid and cook for about 20 minutes. By this time the peas will be tender, the lettuce wilted and most of the liquid evaporated. Season well and serve immediately.

Fresh garden peas make an excellent addition to a meat or vegetable stew, added about 5 minutes before serving. Puréed, they make a wonderful soup or sauce for poached chicken or fish, or the base for a soufflé. When cooked, they can be stirred into quiche fillings, omelettes and rice dishes such as risotto, or into a white sauce with cooked ham and chicken to make a savoury tart or pie filling. Topped and tailed fresh young pods can be boiled and tossed with melted butter, or used to make a soup or purée, either on their own or combined with shelled peas.

Mangetouts and Sugar Snaps

These are also members of the Pisum sativum family. They have a similar appearance to the garden pea, but the mangetout has a much flatter pod, which tapers at both ends and is about 7 cm (3 inches) long and 1 cm (½ inch) across. The tiny peas (seeds) are just visible through their almost translucent pod. The entire pod is eaten, accounting for its French name, which means 'eat all'. Like sugar snaps, mangetouts have a wonderful crunchy texture. The sugar snap, also known as sugar pea and snow pea, is fatter, and falls somewhere between the garden pea and the mangetout. Its flavour is more pronounced and sweeter than that of the mangetout, tasting more like a raw garden pea.

When choosing mangetouts or sugar snaps, look for crisp pods which have a bright green, juicy appearance. Some are sold ready topped and tailed, but if not, simply cut a little off each end and remove the string from along the edge.

Both mangetouts and sugarsnaps can be eaten raw, allowing you to enjoy their fresh taste and crisp texture. Use them whole with other vegetables in a plate of crudités, sliced in a mixed green leaf salad, or sliced and combined with garden peas, celery and some other crisp vegetables, lightly moistened with vinaigrette. Orange goes well with mangetouts, so sometimes I include some orange segments in a salad and sharpen the vinaigrette with orange juice.

To cook these peas, either boil or steam them as quickly as possible to preserve their texture and colour, about 3–5 minutes. They should be only just tender, with no hint of sogginess. Drain and toss quickly in melted butter. They cool down very quickly, so serve immediately, piping hot. You can toss them with chopped fried bacon, fresh herbs and salt and pepper, or stir-fry them with other vegetables, either whole or sliced lengthways along the diagonal. Cook them very quickly, adding them almost at the end of cooking, just to warm through and combine with the other ingredients. Both mangetouts and sugar snaps make excellent soup.

High in protein, carbohydrate and fibre. A good source of calcium, potassium and iron, also vitamins A, B, C and E.

Also called fava beans and horse beans, broad beans are one of the first vegetables of the spring, appearing in May and June. Their season is very short, so be sure not to miss them. They have rich green, velvety pods that can grow to over 30 cm (12 inches) in length, but when they reach this size are only good for soups, purées and stews.

They are at their sweetest and most tender when no longer than 7–10 cm (3–4 inches). Both seeds and pods should be bright green. The best way to have a ready supply is to grow them, because they are not often seen like this in the shops. Pick or buy them just before use because the pods go limp very quickly after picking, the sweetness diminishes and the texture alters. The broad bean is one of the least altered by freezing, so either pick them and freeze them immediately or buy commercially frozen beans – both are very good.

Very young, small beans can be eaten whole. Wash, dry and top and tail, then serve them raw as part of a crudité selection, dressed with a light garlic vinaigrette, or with cured ham, salami or cheese. To cook broad beans, either boil them in the minimum amount of water or steam them for 4–5 minutes until tender, then drain, season and serve with melted butter, or toss in a little thick cream which has been reduced by boiling.

broad bean

Vicia fava

As the pods get larger, shell the beans and either serve them raw in salads, or cook and serve them as for the young pods. The French add a little savory to the boiling water and scatter some of the chopped herb over the beans before serving. Cooked broad beans combine well with spices such as chilli, nutmeg and cinnamon, and with garlic, courgettes, tomatoes, spring onions, celery, other beans, ham, bacon, chicken and cured meats.

For luxurious service, drain the beans after cooking, cool slightly under cold water, then slit the skins and squeeze the beans out. Toss the succulent jewels in warm butter, cream or sauce and serve hot, or toss in a light vinaigrette and serve cold or use in salads. This is the perfect treatment for older beans. When young, the whole pods can be cut into pieces between the beans and braised with flavouring vegetables, pork, bacon or pancetta.

sweetcorn

Zea mays

High in carbohydrate and fibre, sweetcorn is rich in vitamins A, C and some B. It also contains potassium, magnesium sulphur and iron.

Maize, or corn as it is better known, is the third most important cereal in the world, with a history of cultivation stretching back to its origins as an edible grass in the Andean foothills. It was revered as the core of life in the golden civilizations of the Americas – the Inca, the Maya and the Aztec – and was a staple of the indigenous tribes of North America. Discovered by Columbus, it was brought to Europe and used mainly as cattle fodder. It is only recently that sweetcorn has been eaten as a vegetable.

From the moment the sweetcorn cob is picked, the natural sugars change into starch, causing a loss of sweetness. So use them as soon as you get home or, if you grow your own, pluck and cook them immediately. Sweetcorn should have bright green husks that snuggle around the kernels. The silk at the end of the husk should appear feathery and be turning dark brown at the tip. The kernels should be tightly packed, plump and juicy. Baby sweetcorn, which is picked when still immature, should look lively and creamy yellow, with juicy kernels.

Corn-on-the-cob To boil, strip off the husks and silks, then rinse the cobs. Cook in fast-boiling unsalted water for 7–10 minutes until the kernels are tender. Test frequently after 7 minutes, taking care not to overcook. Drain and serve with butter and seasoning.

To grill, strip off the husks and silks, or leave the husks on and strip out the silks. Soak the cobs in cold water for at least 30 minutes, then drain and pat dry. If the husks have been removed, brush the kernels with a little oil. Grill on the barbecue for 15–20 minutes, turning frequently. The cobs can be cut into chunks, 1–2.5 cm (½–1 inch) thick, soaked, then skewered and grilled in the same way.

To roast, prepare as for grilling, then wrap in thick foil. Roast in the hot coals of a barbecue or on a baking sheet in a preheated oven, 200°C (400°F), Gas Mark 6, for 20–30 minutes. Oven roasting can be done without foil; simply brush the cobs with a little oil.

Whole baby sweetcorn are best eaten raw with a dip or light sauce or mixed into salads. I sometimes stir-fry them, which retains their qualities better than boiling.

Sweetcorn kernels Remove the husks and silks from raw cobs, then wash and dry. Scrape the kernels off with a sharp knife, then drop the kernels into fast-boiling water and scrape the cob over the pan to squeeze out the milky juices. Cover and cook for 3–5 minutes. Drain, toss in butter or cream and season well. The kernels can also be boiled in milk or cream. They can be added to soups and stews, used in fritters, pancakes, omelettes, frittatas and salads, and used in fillings for pies or tarts.

fruiting vegetables

Rich source of vitamin C. Also contains vitamins A, B1, B2 and E, and small amounts of potassium and folic acid. Excellent source of fibre.

There are certain objects which I am drawn to, attracted by colour or shape and texture. The urge to touch and to pick up is irresistible, the feel in my palm and against my fingers a sensual pleasure. There is a vegetable which fulfils this sense more than any other – the sweet pepper or pimiento, whose vibrant colours remind me so much of early childhood and my first bright paints. Peppers are a vital ingredient in much of my cooking, one of a quintet of ingredients for healthy, Mediterranean-style eating – olive oil, garlic, tomatoes, sweet peppers and red wine.

Poor old Columbus. In 1492 he didn't succeed in his objective to discover a sea route to the fabulous Orient, nor did he perchance discover the American mainland. He returned to his Spanish patrons with no gold, no precious stones and no silks. Instead he brought back evidence of the rich plant life he had discovered, amongst which were members of the capsicum family – sweet peppers and their kinsmen, chilli peppers.

Peppers are positively bursting with colour – yellow, orange, red, green, deep violet-purple and black. Their flavour varies slightly, depending on the colour. The green pepper, although mature, has been picked rather than being left to ripen on the bush. It has a slightly sharper, more savoury, flavour than the red pepper, which is fully ripe with sweet-tasting flesh. The yellows and oranges are

pepper

Capsicum annuum

also more sweet than savoury, but not as rich or mellow as the deep, almost ruby-red varieties. The white, black and violet-purples are more akin to green peppers in taste.

The most common peppers are bell-shaped, hence one of their names 'bell pepper' (another is bullnose pepper). They have 3–4 lobes, which widen slightly towards the stalk end and are then pulled into the centre of the hollow fruit, creating slightly humped shoulders. Some peppers are long, tapered and pointed, others short and wide or heart-shaped.

Peppers should be firm and very smooth, with a bright glossy sheen. They should have thick flesh and feel heavy. The green stalks should still be intact, an indication of freshness. They first need to be washed or wiped, then dried. If the pepper is to be sliced in strips or diced, it can be cut in half lengthways and the stalk, pith, core and seeds pulled or cut out, along with any tough membrane. If you are going to cut the pepper into rings or stuff it whole, cut around the stalk to release it from the flesh, then pull it out along with the seeds and core. Then turn the empty shell upside down and tap it on the work surface to dislodge any remaining seeds.

If the pepper is to be roasted or grilled whole, leave the seeds, core and stalk intact and remove them after cooking. This gives the pepper more flavour because it cooks in its own juices in a sealed parcel. If the pepper is to be roasted or grilled after being cut in half, remove the seeds, core and stalk before cooking.

Roasting and peeling sweet peppers alters the whole appearance and structure of the vegetable, reducing any sharpness to a rich softness. In the case of red peppers, it gives them a concentrated sweetness, almost as though they have had sugar added. Lightly rub the whole pepper with oil, then put in a heavy roasting tin or dish and roast in a preheated oven, 220°C (425°F), Gas Mark 7, for 30–40 minutes until the skin is blistered and charred black in places. This charring gives a smoky flavour to the flesh. Alternatively, the pepper can be impaled on a heavy metal skewer with a wooden handle and roasted over an open gas flame until it blisters and softens. This is quicker than the oven method, but it requires constant turning for 10–15 minutes. The skin can also be charred and blistered under a fierce grill, over a barbecue or among the hot ashes or coals of a barbecue or open fire. Once the peppers are cool enough to handle, the skin should peel away

easily. If you have difficulty, seal them in a plastic bag for about 10 minutes, then remove them and peel the skin away. Cut the peppers in half and remove the seeds along with the core and any pulpy ribs. Some people wash the seeds out, but I don't like to lose any of the precious juices or wash the flavour away.

Roasted and peeled peppers can be sliced or diced. My favourite way is to cut them into wedges or thick strips and marinate them in olive oil, garlic, parsley, thyme and savory for a few days before serving in a salad with olives and anchovies, or rolling them up, securing with skewers and serving with drinks. They are also delicious stirred through lightly cooked egg dishes, such as omelettes or scrambled eggs, or mixed with fried onions and used to fill pies and tarts. They can also be used as a base for dishes like Goat's Cheese with Peppers & Pine Nuts (page 135).

Sliced or diced raw or roasted peppers can be fried in olive oil and served as an accompaniment, added to stews and braised dishes and used in dishes such as ratatouille, peperonata, pipérade, soups, sauces and purées.

Because of their shape, peppers make ideal containers for stuffing, served raw or cooked. Remove the stalk, core and seeds by cutting out at the stalk end, or cut off a slice containing the stalk to make a lid and remove the core and seeds from it. The vegetable can then be stuffed and baked if required. If baking, drop the pepper into boiling water for 1 minute, then drain and refresh before stuffing. This keeps the taste sweet and shortens the oven cooking time.

An excellent source of vitamins A and E.

Chillies are members of the capsicum family. They bring colour, fire and zest to cooking, and kick even the blandest foods into life. There are literally hundreds of varieties. Some are small and round like cherries, others are shaped more like sweet peppers, but are smaller and puffier like little bonnets. Some are long, thin, tapering cones, while others are slightly fuller, wrinkly and more stubby. In colour, they range from green through yellow to red.

The heat-producing element in chillies is a volatile oil called capsaicin. It is measured in Scoville units, which range from 0 for sweet peppers to over 300,000 for the habañero. A medium-hot chilli is around 600 units. Capsaicin is concentrated in the seeds and pith, so these need to be removed unless you want to add excessive fire to your dish. This volatile oil has a burning effect on the skin and eyes, so when handling chillies, take care not to rub your eyes or touch your face or mouth.

Add chillies gradually to your cooking to get the degree of heat you want. Generally, the smaller the chilli the more fiery, likewise the dark green chillies, and those that are thin and sharply pointed. Ancho chillies look similar to sweet peppers, but are much smaller. They are relatively mild, with an underlying sweetness. Anaheim are longer than ancho, about 10 cm (4 inches), thin and with a rather blunt end. They are red or green, generally with a mild,

chilli pepper
Capsicum frutescens

sweet taste. Jalapeño, probably the best known chilli, are quite short and blunt. They start dark green and eventually turn red. Chipotle are smoked jalapeño. Bird's eye or bird chillies, also known as Thai or pequin chillies, are small and pointed, red, orange, green or cream, and very hot. Serrano are Spanish chillies that are small and thin. Red or green, they can be mild or hot. Poblano chillies are small and dark green. They generally have a mild, spicy flavour, but may also be scorching hot, it is hard to tell. In Spain they are eaten in tapas bars, either roasted or grilled whole. They are also widely used in Mexican dishes. Habañero are pretty, like tiny, shiny, sweet peppers, but their appearance is deceptive – they are the hottest chillies in the world. Scotch bonnets are cousins of the habañero chilli.

Chillies give spice, heat and a distinctive flavour to otherwise bland ingredients such as rice, beans and lentils. They can be added to meat and vegetable stews, poultry and fish, and are extensively used in soups and sauces. Some varieties are even stuffed and eaten whole.

cucumber

Cucumis sativus

Mostly water, but a good source of potassium and some vitamins A and C.

The cucumber's wild forebear is many thousands of years old with origins in Asia. It was favoured by the Greeks and Romans, eaten cooked and raw for its high water content and refreshing effect, even though it was considered to be indigestible and the cause of excessive wind. Even today, this characteristic causes some people to avoid it.

The classic cucumber is long and green, about 4 cm (1½ inches) in diameter and with a slightly ridged skin, but there are other varieties which are shorter, more squat and yellow in colour.

When buying cucumbers, ensure they are firm, bright in colour and unblemished. Cucumber is generally considered to be a salad vegetable to be eaten raw. It is generally sliced thinly into rounds for salads, but it can be chopped or shredded, as it is for many Middle Eastern dishes and the Indian side dish Cucumber & Mint Raita (page 216), in which it is mixed with yogurt and served with curries for its cooling effect. It is the main ingredient in the chilled Spanish soup gazpacho, and makes a refreshing cold or iced soup in its own right. When cooked and combined with cream, herbs and spices, cucumber is delicious, and goes particularly well with fish dishes. It is seldom that anyone has afternoon tea these days, so the cucumber sandwich belongs to a bygone age, kept alive only in some traditional homes and hotels.

Good source of vitamin A, with some C and small amounts of B. Small quantities of folic acid, potassium and iron.

The pumpkin's name derives from *pepen*, the Greek word for melon. It was brought to Europe after the discovery of the Americas by European adventurers, and was soon established as a bulking substance in stews and soups.

Pumpkins grow to some size, up to 27 kg (60 lb). I find the best between 3–5 kg (7–11 lb), no bigger than a beach ball. Sometimes they are more oblong than round, and the colours range from warm buff to bright orange. Some are even grey. The skin can be smooth, rough or ribbed. The flesh is usually orange, with a mild, slightly sweet flavour.

Select pumpkins that are clean, heavy and bright. They should sound hollow when knocked. The skin should be thick and firm, free from bruises and cracks. If buying wedges or halves, make sure the flesh is moist and well wrapped. Pumpkins improve with keeping, the flavour concentrates and they are said to have 'cured'. They will keep for months in a cool, dry place. Once cut, cover the exposed surface and store in the refrigerator for up to 2 weeks. Excess flesh can be puréed and frozen.

Pumpkin skin is very hard and inedible and needs to be removed if raw flesh is required. Cut the pumpkin into wedges like a melon, then remove the seeds and fibres. Saw

pumpkin
Cucurbita maxima

off the skin from each piece, then cut the flesh according to recipe requirements. Like this, pumpkin can be boiled or steamed until tender, drained and tossed in butter and served as an accompaniment. It is particularly good seasoned with cumin, coriander, garlic or ginger. It can be used to make soups and stews, baked with cream, cheese and spices to create gratins, and roasted in large chunks. It can be used in risottos, or dipped into batter and deep-fried.

Pumpkin can also be baked. Cut it in half across the widest part and pull out the seeds and fibres. Cross-hatch the flesh, taking care not to pierce the skin. Rub the flesh with oil and lay each half, cut-side down, in a roasting dish. Cover loosely with foil and cook in a preheated oven, 200°C (400°F), Gas Mark 6, for 1–2 hours until the flesh is tender. When cool enough to handle, cut the flesh into cubes or scoop out the flesh and purée in a food processor.

courgette
Cucurbita pepo

Reasonable source of vitamins A and C, with small amounts of calcium and potassium. Low in calories.

Courgettes are simply small immature marrows. The word courgette is the diminutive of the French word *courge* for marrow. The history of the courgette is similar to that of the marrow, another member of the squash family, Cucurbita pepo. Courgettes were introduced to Europe from North America during the 19th century. They are classified as summer squash and belong to the gourd section of that family.

Delicacy and size are important and small really is beautiful, 7–20 cm (3–8 inches) in length and 1–5 cm (½–2 inches) across. Look also for tiny 'baby' courgettes no wider than 5 mm (¼ inch) and 5–6 cm (2–2½ inches) long. The most common courgette has deep green skin with faint ribbing. The yellow courgette is slightly straighter than the green, and the Italian courgette is very long, thin and pale lime green. You can also find round and bulbous varieties of courgette. The skin should be brightly coloured and glossy, thin, soft and smooth. The colour, texture and flavour of the flesh is largely the same in all varieties.

Courgettes require just a quick wash and wipe dry and trimming top and bottom. To cook whole baby courgettes, blanch them in boiling water for 10 seconds, then drain and toss with melted butter and perhaps a little softened garlic for a few minutes. If they are no more than 10 cm (4 inches) long, they can be cut into thin rounds or matchsticks and eaten raw in a salad or tossed in vinaigrette. They can also be grated, or very thinly sliced lengthways on a mandolin to serve in a vegetable carpaccio. Medium courgettes 10–15 cm (4–6 inches) long can be sliced across in rings of any thickness or cut on the diagonal, then tossed in butter and served with lemon juice and seasoning. They can be cooked in a rich tomato sauce, added to ratatouille

or moussaka, or baked with butter, rosemary, cream and egg in a gratin. Strips or sticks can be stir-fried or grilled. Grated or diced courgettes can be used in omelettes, risottos, tians or scrambled eggs, or puréed to make a sauce or soufflé. They can also be coated in batter or egg and breadcrumbs and deep-fried. As courgettes get larger, they can be hollowed out, stuffed and baked in the oven.

Courgette flowers

The wonderfully shaped, yellow-orange flower heads of courgettes are edible, and can be used in both salads and cooked dishes. They do not keep well, and need to be used soon after picking. Wash them well and gently shake dry. They can be added to salads as they are, shredded and stirred into an omelette or scrambled eggs, or used to garnish soup. They can also be stuffed.

marrow

Cucurbita pepo

Composed mainly of water, marrow has some carbohydrate and few calories. It contains small amounts of minerals and vitamins A and C.

A summer-maturing member of the squash clan, all of which originated in North America, the marrow came to Britain in the middle of the 19th century.

The best-tasting marrows are no more than 30 cm (12 inches) long, with a firm feel, but still a little 'give' when pressed with the thumb. They should be well round-ed with a glossy, bright, unblemished skin.

Marrows make reasonable soup if combined with well-flavoured stock and robust ingredients such as carrots, parsnips and potatoes, lots of herbs like parsley, sage and oregano, or oriental spices to give them a lift. The same applies if you want to use them for jam or chutney, which is one of the best ways of using marrow. Good additions are garlic, chilli, red and green peppers, stem ginger, apples and dried fruit. In both cases the preparation is the same. Wash or wipe the skin, top and tail, then cut in half length-ways and remove the seeds and pith. Cut off the skin, then cut the flesh according to recipe requirements.

To cook marrow, cut the flesh into 1 cm (½ inch) dice, blanch in boiling water for 1–2 minutes, then drain and pat dry. Toss in a pan in a little butter or olive oil with a hint of garlic until browning slightly. Serve with grated Parmesan cheese, or layer in a gratin dish with Parmesan and Gruyère, some nutmeg and chopped parsley. Cover generously with double cream and bake briefly in the oven.

I like to stuff and bake marrow. The stuffing needs to be well flavoured, spicy and highly seasoned. Add a touch of sweet chilli sauce or harissa to make the mixture taste more lively. Rice will help to absorb the moisture in the marrow, and a rich tomato sauce served with baked marrow is very tasty.

To prepare rings, cut the marrow across into 4 cm (1½ inch) slices. Remove the seeds and pith, leaving a hole for the stuffing. To prepare boats, cut the marrow in half lengthways. Scoop out the seeds and pith, then remove the remaining flesh to form a boat with 2.5 cm (1 inch) thick walls. Chop the flesh and mix it with the other stuffing ingredients. Blanch in boiling water for 3–4 minutes, drain and pat dry. Set the marrow in a lightly oiled roasting dish. Pack the rings tightly together and pile stuffing in the holes, heaping it up so that it will soak up the watery juices from the marrow. Fill boats generously with stuffing. Put 2–3 tablespoons water or stock around the marrow, dot the stuffing with butter and cover with foil. Bake in a preheated oven, 200°C (400°F), Gas Mark 6 for ¾–1 hour.

squash
Cucurbita pepo

Squash have a high water content, with varying amounts of vitamins A, B and C and minerals. They are low in calories.

The squash family is of New World origin. The word squash comes from the native American *askutasquash*, which means 'eaten raw'. Whether or not this is how they were first tasted by the Pilgrim Fathers when they were coming to terms with the bleak reality of survival in the early 17th century is not sure, but those harsh early days are now commemorated each November in the traditional Thanksgiving dinner. The pumpkin has an honoured place at the table with the turkey and cranberries.

Squash are classified according to the season as either summer or winter squash. Summer squash are best eaten fresh and young before the seeds have had time to develop, while winter squash are allowed to mature on the plant to be harvested in autumn so they have thicker, harder skins than their summer cousins and the flesh is more fibrous. They benefit from being stored in the light and warmth for a few weeks after harvesting to 'cure'.

Shades of green, soft creams, honeys, harvest russets, empire suns and sunset reds demand exciting flavours to complement such colour. Enrichment with butter, cream or olive oil is a starting point. Mingling with savoury flavours like garlic, herbs, spices and strongly flavoured cheese is transforming. For dessert, ingredients such as cinnamon, nutmeg, sugar, honey and ginger are a delight. In general, squashes can be baked, boiled, roasted, steamed or fried. They are ideal for stuffing, make excellent purées and are delicious in warming soups and stews. They can also be pickled, made into chutneys or delicious preserves and, to round off the menu, can be transformed into a range of desserts from traditional pumpkin pie to mousses and compotes, and used as a flavouring for breads and cakes.

Acorn (opposite page, right) A small heart-shaped winter squash, similar to a large acorn. Acorn squash have ridged beautiful deep green or orange skin, or a mixture of both, and firm, bright orange flesh. Like pumpkin, acorn squash can be peeled and wrapped in foil and baked, the flesh then used as required. I like it diced, tossed in butter and served with cheese. It also makes wonderful soup.

Butternut (page 80) A winter squash resembling a giant pear with a hard, buttery coloured skin. It has deep orange flesh, which is firm, nutty and slightly sweet. It is excellent for soup or any pumpkin recipe. Baking really seems to concentrate its flavour.

Crookneck Named after its awkwardly shaped neck, this summer squash is bright yellow-gold in colour and is best used when it is about 10 cm (4 inches) long. Prepare it as you would Pattypan. Or cut it in half lengthways, brush with butter and sprinkle with cheese, then bake in a hot oven for 10–15 minutes.

Hubbard As can be seen from its other names of golden hubbard and blue hubbard, this winter squash has a wide range of possible colours from bright orange through yellow to blue. It is large and has a thick hard shell with a bumpy texture. The flesh is slightly grainy, particularly when the squash is very large. Hubbard are best boiled or roasted and prepared like pumpkin.

Kabocha squash (opposite page, left) Originating from New Zealand, this attractively coloured squash makes an ideal accompaniment to any meal either boiled or mashed. It has a firm texture and is full of flavour. To boil, first peel and remove the seeds, then cut the flesh into 2.5 cm (1 inch) dice and add to a saucepan of boiling water. Bring back to the boil, then simmer fot 5–6 minutes. Kabocha squash can also be roasted. Cut the flesh into 5 cm (2 inch) dice, baste in hot fat and roast in a preheated oven 200°C (400°F), Gas Mark 6, for 40–50 minutes.

Little gem (page 89, back right) This winter squash is small, round and dark green. When picked, it looks like a baby watermelon, the size of a tennis ball. As it matures it turns a rich yellow colour. Its flesh is pale yellow and has a delicate nutty flavour. Boil or steam whole for about 20 minutes. Cut in half, remove the seeds and serve with butter and freshly milled black pepper. It mixes well with other ingredients, such as garlic, onions and tomatoes.

Onion squash This handsome winter specimen is bright reddish-orange in colour, round and onion shaped. It has a close texture and mild honey flavour that is not unlike pumpkin. It can be used for most pumpkin recipes.

Pattypan (page 89, front left) Also known as custard marrow and scallop squash, this is an attractive summer squash. It is small and dainty with a fine skin in a variety of delicate colours, pale matt cream, green and crocus yellow. Pattypan are almost round, but look as if they have been slightly squashed to form a curved, heavily scalloped edge. They have an elegant green stalk protruding from one end and a little top-knot on the other. In flavour they are very similar to courgettes and can be used in the same way – sliced across and fried in butter and oil, with a hint of garlic. They can also be steamed whole (this will take about 20 minutes), the top cut off and a little of the centre scooped out and filled with melted butter and plenty of seasoning. Prepared this way, an even greater portion of the flesh can be removed and added to a light savoury stuffing of herbs, cream and mild cheese. They can also be used to make soups, soufflés, fritters and gratins. For best results, buy when the skin is tender and the specimen is no larger than 10 cm (4 inches) across.

Spaghetti squash A most unusual summer squash that has earned its name from the resemblance of its cooked flesh to spaghetti. It is also called vegetable spaghetti, spaghetti marrow and noodle squash. In flavour, however, it bears no similarity. It looks rather like a marrow and has the same ability to grow to an enormous size, but it is best no more than 20–25 cm (8–10 inches) long and around 1 kg (2–2½ lb) in weight. It ranges from pale creamy white through varying shades of yellow and sometimes has a greenish tinge. It has a very distinctive fragrant flavour, and is at its best when boiled or steamed and served with butter, pepper, a little chopped garlic or spring onions, a tomato or pesto sauce and perhaps some Parmesan cheese. It can also be baked.

To cook, pierce the end with a skewer, then boil, steam or bake whole for 30–45 minutes. Drain, then cut in half lengthways. Remove the seeds and then the flesh, using a fork to comb the spaghetti-like strands out of the shell.

Turk's turban This is one of the most decorative and beautiful of all the squashes. It is a winter squash, multi-coloured, shaded and striped, deep orange, yellow, cream and green in varying hues. It looks like a small pumpkin with a smaller one pressed halfway into the centre. Hence the reference to turban, because that is what it looks like. It has a firm yellowish flesh and a nutty taste. It can be stuffed and baked.

tomato

Lycopersicon esculentum

Rich in vitamins A and C, with some vitamin B and some potassium and folic acid. High in fibre.

One bright morning our neighbour arrived with a bag of baby tomatoes – all golds, reds and greens – fresh from the greenhouse. We didn't wait until lunch, but ate them like the fruits they are with slices of mango and papaya for breakfast, sitting outside in the early September sunshine. The sea was a deep Mediterranean blue, the yachts were rocking gently in the harbour – and those pop-in-the-mouth, sun-ripened tomatoes tasted as tomatoes should, sweet and juicy with just a hint of sharpness.

The tomato is a colourful member of the nightshade family, in company with the potato, aubergine, pepper and tobacco. Its origins can be traced back to South America and the Andean foothills before the time of Christ. By the time the Conquistadors arrived in the 16th century, tomatoes (*tomatl* to the Aztecs) had spread throughout Central America into Mexico and the north. The first tomatoes were yellow, and they received a very cautious reception in Europe, especially in the north, where the plants only became popular as a trailing decoration in gardens. The early Italian name was *pomo d'oro* (golden apple), which the French corrupted to *pomme d'amour* (love apple), and for a time the fruit was thought to be an aphrodisiac. Tomatoes were used extensively in Spanish and Italian cooking during the 17th and 18th centuries, but it was not until the end of the last century that they began to be widely used in British cooking.

The tomato is the fruit of a vine, a berry fruit, which has pulpy flesh and seeds rather than stones. It can be bright pillar-box red, vibrant yellow, orange-gold, acid green, or striped variants of these. It may be round, oval, plum or pear shaped, and it can be big, up to 1 kg (2 lb) in weight and over 10 cm (4 inches) in diameter, or tiny like a cherry, no more than 2.5 cm (1 inch) across. Its delicate juicy flesh can be red, blush pink, orange or pale gold, and its flavour when at its best a perfect balance of sweetness and acidity. Home-grown tomatoes, sun-ripened on the vine and picked just after the sun has been on them, have the best flavour.

Round or salad tomatoes are the standard commercial crop available all year. They are about 5 cm (2 inches) round, orange-red and fairly juicy, with plenty of seeds and no particularly distinctive taste. This is because they are generally picked and ripened off the plant, which affects their flavour, but this can be improved by seasoning with salt, pepper, a pinch of sugar and a little balsamic vinegar. Some of the most flavoursome are Ailsa Craig, Alicante and Moneymaker. Vine-ripened tomatoes still attached to the stalk have an excellent flavour. They are deep red and slightly smaller than the common round tomato.

Cherry tomatoes are grown for their concentrated sweet flavour and dainty size. They are available in a choice of red or yellow, round, oval, plum or pear shapes. Some of the best are Tiny Tim, Phyra, Cherry Belle, Gardener's Delight and Sweet 100.

Large or beefsteak tomatoes can be up to 6 cm (2½ inches) tall and 10 cm (4 inches) in diameter. They are pulled in slightly to the centre where the stalk and calyx sit rather like the top of an indented beret. The skin is ridged and deep red or orange. The flesh is solid and substantial with only a few seeds. The flavour is generally reasonable

and can be very good if they have been ripened in the sun. Some of the best include Super Beefsteak, Delicious, Dombello, Marmande and Oxheart Giant.

Plum tomatoes are richly flavoured, fleshy Italian tomatoes with lots of juice, few seeds and a rich red colour. They need plenty of sun to ripen and develop their flavour. For growing, the best variety is Roma VF.

Sun-dried tomatoes have been dried in the sun or the light for several weeks until they have curled up and lost their moisture but none of their flavour. They can be bought in their natural dry state or preserved in oil. Their flavour is very concentrated.

Choose tomatoes with a bright colour and firm unblemished skin. I like to buy them with the calyx attached. If the tomatoes are not fully ripe, set them in a

bright, warm, sunny place to ripen (or put them in a brown paper bag) before storing them in the refrigerator. Remember to return to room temperature to recapture their flavour before use. If you want to freeze them, it is best to make them into a sauce, purée or soup. Because of their high water content, whole tomatoes break down on freezing and cannot be used later for slicing or salads.

Before using tomatoes, wash and wipe them dry. If using raw, cut across their width into thick or thin slices. This is particularly appropriate if they are going to be served with slices of cheese such as mozzarella and dressed with a light vinaigrette. In some salad combinations they are best cut lengthways, then into quarters or wedges. Sometimes they need to be skinned, deseeded and finely diced, especially for use in dishes such as scrambled eggs, omelettes and stuffings. More coarsely prepared, they are used in soups, sauces and purées. Tomatoes are excellent in stews and casseroles particularly when combined with other sun-drenched vegetables like aubergines, courgettes and peppers. Their acidic taste combines well with starchy vegetables like potatoes, dried beans and chickpeas, and they are enhanced by fragrant herbs such as sweet basil, oregano, marjoram, thyme, rosemary and bay. Tomatoes taste good peeled and sliced, dipped in beaten egg and breadcrumbs or polenta and shallow-fried, or cut in half, topped with butter, herbs, garlic and toasted crumbs and grilled. They can be stuffed and served cold, or baked in the oven. Beefsteak tomatoes are just right for this and make a perfect meal on their own.

A good source of vitamins C and A and high in potassium, with some iron, calcium and magnesium.

Whenever I see this odd-looking vegetable, it puts me in mind of some heavily camouflaged tropical lizard waiting in the undergrowth for its prey. Its skin is warty and it changes colour as the fruit matures – from silvery white to rich deep green then vibrant orange-red. It is a member of the bitter gourd family, a fruiting vegetable that grows on a vine, and bitter gourd, bitter cucumber, balsam pear, African cucumber and karela are all related. Originally from tropical Asia, it is very popular in Chinese and Indian cooking because of its characteristic bitter flavour.

The fruits are generally picked young and small to avoid excess bitterness. When they are more mature, remove any extreme harshness by cutting the flesh or scraping the skin, then salting it. Its bitterness can also be lessened by chopping it into cubes and blanching in salted water before use. Remove the seeds and central spongy section of mature fruit before cutting it into cubes or slices.

Chinese bitter melons are used in soups, curries, stir-fries and other oriental dishes, as well as being stuffed with meat, fish, onions and spices.

Kantola This is another bitter gourd, widely used in Indian and oriental cooking. Like Chinese bitter melons, kantolas need salting or blanching before use to remove any bitterness, then they can be sautéed or deep-fried, or added to stir-fries or curries.

Chinese bitter melon
Momordica charantia

avocado

Persea americana

An excellent source of vitamins A, C, B and E. Particularly rich in potassium and magnesium, phosphorus, calcium and iron. A good source of protein and fibre. It is cholesterol free, low in sodium and easily digested.

Avocado has long been enjoyed for its buttery, creamy flesh and the easy way it mixes with other flavours. Now we know that it is one of the most complete foods we can eat, packed with a unique combination of nutrients.

This sub-tropical berry fruit has been a staple in Central America for many centuries. It was prized by the Mayans and also the Aztecs. Despite wide planting throughout Central America, it was not until the early 20th century that the avocado was first planted in California, but now it is established right across the globe, as far afield as South Africa, Australia, around the Mediterranean, and especially Israel.

There are three main varieties. Hass are medium to small in size, with a distinctive pear shape and a rough dark skin. Fuerte are medium-sized with an elongated shape and a rich green, slightly roughened skin. Ettinger tends to be larger than the other varieties, with a smooth and shiny thin green skin.

All varieties have a large stone in the middle of delicately coloured pale green flesh, and they all have a gentle, slightly nutty flavour. They are hardly ever 'just ripe' for eating when bought, but will soon ripen in the warmth of a kitchen. The perfect avocado should yield slightly when gently pressed with a finger and thumb. An important point to remember is that the flesh discolours very quickly when cut. To help prevent discoloration, rub or toss all cut surfaces with lemon juice.

Cut the avocado in half down the centre through to the stone, twist the two halves apart and remove the stone to create two avocado halves with a central cavity in each. Fill the cavities with a dressing like vinaigrette, or with something more substantial. Diced avocado is good in salads, sandwiches and salsas, while mashed avocado is the main constituent of the creamy Mexican dip guacamole.

Containing ninety per cent water, chayote is low in calories with some vitamin C and trace elements.

Towards the end of last year, some very good friends went to South-East Asia and Australia. Knowing they were about to have many exotic gastronomic experiences, I asked them to take note of the unusual vegetables and fruit they came across. One of the vegetables which struck them as peculiar was called *labu siam*. They described it as looking like a pear with ridges along the skin. Travelling on to the sub-tropical region in North Australia, they came across the same vegetable, this time called *choko*. In

describing it to me I recognized it by another name, chayote, familiar from the greengrocers stalls in the Portobello Road area of London, imported from the West Indies. It is known by various other names, amongst them vegetable pear, chocho, chow-chow, christophene, chaka and pepinello.

This vegetable is a type of gourd. It originated in sub-tropical Central America, its most common name chayote being a corruption of the Aztec word, *chaytol*. Like many plants from this region, it now flourishes in hot and humid regions around the world. The vegetable grows on a vine, and in the humid growing conditions of the sub-tropics, the rate of growth is phenomenal. Although the ridged green skin is the most common variety of chayote, there are others, including some with spiny, smooth and even white skins. I am always reminded of the avocado, with its different skin textures depending on variety. The chayote is bland, almost nondescript in flavour. It has a firm and juicy flesh, rather like that of a cucumber or marrow, which lends itself to many different cooking methods and flavour additions.

It is best eaten young and small. When very young, it is excellent raw, either diced or sliced in salads, in much the same way as cucumber is used. Young chayote can also be cooked whole, skin and all, like small courgettes. It works well in combination with tomatoes and strong flavours like peppers, chillies, garlic and curry spices. As the fruit gets larger, it is best stuffed and baked like its cousin the marrow, or used to make stews, curries and chutneys. In Caribbean and Central American cookery the chayote is a well-known ingredient in desserts, sweet tarts, pies and cakes. I am told that in Mexican cuisine it is often used to add extra bulk to an apple pie.

chayote
Sechium edule

aubergine
Solanum melongena

Low in calories and rich in vitamins B and C, aubergine provides small amounts of iron and calcium.

A member of the nightshade family, the aubergine is strictly a berry fruit, grown on a bush. It has a very long pedigree from over 5,000 years ago in India. Its main migration was westwards into the Middle East, although it was grown 2,000 years ago in China and there has been a long tradition of eating certain varieties in Thailand and Japan. From the Middle East it spread into Spain, Italy and around the Northern Mediterranean and North Africa.

The most well-known aubergine is the long plum aubergine, slightly oval in shape. This variety is stunningly beautiful, with its rich purple-black lustrous skin, so glossy it looks like it has been waxed. It is generally 15–16 cm (6–6½ inches) long and is topped with a green calyx and stalk, which remind me of an elf's cap. There are also mini sizes (above right), which look very decorative char-grilled, or halved, stuffed and baked. There are many other shapes and colours – lilac-purple with creamy white marbling, purple-maroon, white and white-green, plus there are small and plump ivory-white aubergines like large oval eggs (hence the American name eggplant). The Japanese or Asian aubergine is much straighter, longer and narrow. It ranges from a variegated lilac-purple and white to solid purple. Thai aubergines are often small and round (the tiny ones are called pea aubergines), some are dark green, some cream and green, others oval and golden yellow.

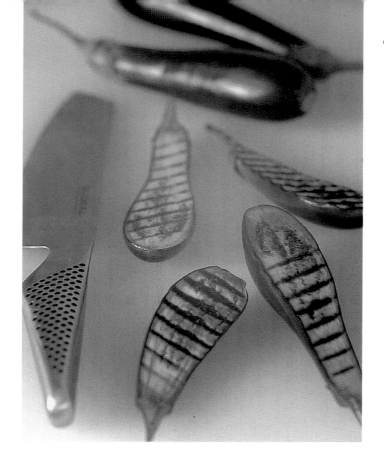

Aubergines should feel heavy and be firm but supple. The skin should be smooth with a high gloss. Pick small to medium aubergines as their flavour will be milder than that of larger specimens. After slicing or dicing, some people believe it necessary to draw out the bitter juices from aubergine flesh by sprinkling it with salt and leaving it to degorge before rinsing and drying. After years of experience I find degorging makes little difference to the flavour or amount of oil absorbed when frying, and it does nothing to improve the texture.

Aubergines absorb any flavour which is added to them. Their texture is substantial and gives depth and distinction to mixed stews like ratatouille, caponata and moussaka. They combine well with tomatoes, peppers and chillies, but they need to be cooked to absorb these flavours. To do this they can be fried, grilled, stewed or baked, but avoid boiling, poaching or steaming, as they will absorb the water like a sponge. Aubergines can be cut into slices about 1 cm (½ inch) thick and coated in batter or egg and breadcrumbs and deep-fried, or cut into slices, spheres or cubes to be fried in oil and served hot.

mushrooms

cultivated mushrooms

Cultivated mushrooms contain essential minerals, potassium, iron, sulphur, magnesium and phosphorus. Low in calories, they are a source of B vitamins and vegetable protein.

Mystique surrounds the mushroom. Its reputed magical powers, elusiveness and the fact that some are poisonous – indeed deadly – have always been a fascination. The Romans had specially made dishes to hold them, and although the French were first to cultivate mushrooms in Europe from the beginning of the 18th century, the Chinese and Japanese were many centuries ahead with their cultivation of shiitake mushrooms.

Whatever the type of cultivated mushroom, they should look fresh, have a clear bright colour and a dry texture. They should also be clean. Store in the refrigerator in a paper bag (a plastic bag will make them sweat and soggy) where they should keep fresh for a few days.

Mushrooms are pretty full of moisture so they should not be soaked in water. A wipe with a damp cloth should be enough by way of preparation. Trim tough stalk ends if applicable and slice stalks and large caps for ease of cooking. Peeling should hardly ever be necessary.

The textures and flavours of different mushrooms are a delight to enjoy. Some have a very subtle flavour, while others enjoy a more noticeable aromatic quality which can add depth of flavour to even the most simple of dishes. They are so versatile and can be prepared in a variety of ways. I find that the best way to cook mushrooms is by frying or sautéing in a little butter or olive oil, or a mixture of the two. They can also be dipped in batter or egg and breadcrumbs and deep-fried. Large mushrooms can be grilled or baked in the oven, with or without a stuffing.

stronger flavour is required. They are good in pasta sauces, casseroles and stews with strong flavours such as onions, garlic, tomatoes and herbs. They keep their shape well.

Oyster mushroom (Pleurotus osteatus, page 98) This mushroom can be found in the wild growing on rotten wood, but it is now also widely cultivated and so available in supermarkets. It has a flappy appearance, and the stalk, gills and cap are all the same colour, ranging from pink to grey. Oyster mushrooms have a good flavour and a soft, silky texture, which makes them a welcome change from ordinary white and button mushrooms. Ideally they are best eaten when young. They have a high water content, however, so care is needed when cooking them, especially in combination with other ingredients – they taste good in stir-fries and have a special affinity with garlic.

Shiitake mushroom (Lentinus edodes, opposite page). A variety of 'tree' mushroom originally from China and Japan, the shiitake is now widely cultivated and easy to obtain at supermarkets (although quite expensive). It is dark brown in colour, with a rich meaty flavour and robust texture, ideally suited to vegetarian casseroles, stews and oriental stir-fries. Dried mushrooms sold in oriental shops are almost always shiitake, although they may not be labelled as such. See Dried Mushrooms (page 103).

White and button mushrooms (Agaricus bisporus) These are by far the most common cultivated mushrooms, accounting for 60 per cent of the world's production. Consequently, they are available throughout the year. They are sold at three stages of development: small (button), mid-size (closed cap) and large (open cap). Although fairly bland, they absorb other flavours well. They provide good bulk in stews and are excellent for soups and sauces where their flavour can be enhanced. They can be stewed, grilled or fried, and are good raw in salads, either sliced or whole.

Chestnut mushroom (Agaricus brunnescen, above) With thick stems and brown caps, these have a little more flavour and a meatier texture than their white cousins. Use them in place of white mushrooms, in dishes where a

Wild mushrooms contain essential minerals, potassium, iron, sulphur, magnesium, and phosphorus. Low in calories, they are a source of B vitamins and vegetable protein.

Only pick your own wild mushrooms if you are absolutely sure of their identity and safety before using. All wild mushrooms should be brushed or dusted before storing, or 'dried' for storage and used later. Any leftovers are much too valuable to waste, so slice them and dry them on a baking sheet. Choose a warm, well-ventilated place such as an airing cupboard with the door ajar and leave them for a couple of days, or in the oven on a low heat for a couple of hours.

Cep (Boletus edulis) This grand, fat-stemmed mushroom has a cream colour and a bun-like cap. It is called *porcini* in Italy, and is renowned for its sheer versatility. It is at home in soups, sauces, stews and stuffings and is very frequently dried (opposite page). When young, it can be eaten raw, and makes a flavoursome addition to a salad.

Chanterelle (Cantharellus cibarius, right) This firm-fleshed, curvaceous trumpet smells faintly of apricots. It is my favourite wild mushroom. Chanterelles range in colour from cream to golden orange-yellow and keep both their colour and texture when cooked. They are excellent in risottos, sauces and egg dishes, and just a few will add a special flavour to the simplest dish. Because of their small gills they need careful cleaning. Dried chanterelles are well worth buying if you cannot obtain fresh.

wild
mushrooms

Field mushroom (Agaricus campestris) This mushroom has a great deal more flavour than its cultivated cousin (Agaricus bisporus). Its large white dome or later open cap is still a fairly common sight in autumn fields. A good all-rounder, but I like it best when fried in butter or oil for a leisurely Sunday breakfast.

Giant puffball (Langermannia gigantea and Lycoperdon giganteum) It is always a great surprise when you come across this mushroom. It is a phenomenal size, as big as a football, with white marshmallowy looking flesh. It is good to eat, fried or cut into strips and added for bulk to stews. One puffball is enough for several meals, but don't keep leftovers too long because they turn yellow and become inedible.

Horn of plenty (Craterellus cornucopioides) A little offputting in appearance because it is grey. In France they call it *trompette des morts* or 'trumpet of death'. I have occasionally found these mushrooms amongst chanterelles, which they resemble in shape. They go well with fish and white meats, and are a colourful contrast in white sauces.

Morel (Morchella esculenta and Morchella vulgaris) With its cone-shaped sponge like a dark, pitted hollow cap, this mushroom looks rather like something picked up from a coral reef. It appears in spring rather than autumn and is considered to be one of the great edible fungi. Morels need to be very carefully cleaned. Wash them under cold running water; no brush can get right into their tiny recesses.

Pied de mouton (Hydnum repandum, below) Also called the hedgehog mushroom because of its spiny gills, this mushroom does not have a particularly distinctive flavour, but it is relatively easy to find and it has a good, firm texture. It is best used in combination with other wild mushrooms, in egg dishes, especially scrambled eggs and omelettes, risottos and sauces for pasta. The gills are best removed before cooking.

Dried mushrooms

Many varieties of mushrooms are now widely available dried – cep, chanterelle, morel and shiitake being the most common. Before using, cover with boiling water and soak for 15 minutes. Remove from the water and chop or slice as the recipe requires. The soaking liquid makes excellent stock, but strain it before use to make sure there is no grit or dirt from the mushrooms.

High in protein, mineral salts potassium and phosphorus, truffles also contain magnesium and calcium. Up to nine essential amino-acids have been detected in truffles. Their nutritional value is higher than that of cultivated mushrooms, largely owing to a lower water content – ninety per cent in mushrooms, seventy-five per cent in truffles.

The truffle is the most sought after and most elusive of mushrooms, and therefore also the most expensive. It grows underground around the roots of trees (usually oak), hence the traditional need for dogs or pigs to sniff it out. The flavour is so powerful that even a very thin sliver or shaving is enough to transform the simplest of dishes. To prepare truffles, simply brush them gently with a vegetable brush to remove any grit, peel them if you like (the peelings can be used in soups, sauces and stocks), then slice the truffle as thinly as you possibly can or finely shave it with a vegetable peeler. There are three varieties.

truffle

Black truffle (Tuber melanosporum, right) This is the most famous truffle from France, sometimes also called the Périgord truffle because it is found in the Périgord region in the south-west. It is a deep ebony black with a hard, knobbly skin and can grow up to 12 cm (5 inches) in diameter, although most are 2.5–5 cm (1–2 inches). Slivers or shavings of black truffle can be eaten raw, but they are more often used in cooking. They are good with eggs, in stuffings, braises and sauces (especially with Madeira), and they impart the most wonderful flavour to the flesh of chicken when inserted beneath the skin before roasting.

Summer truffle (Tuber aestivum) This truffle grows in beech woods in Britain and is harvested in late summer, but unfortunately it is something of a rarity. It has a similar appearance to the white truffle (below), but has a wart-covered skin. The flesh is a solid brown colour, with white veins running through. It can be used in the same way as white or black truffles.

White truffle (Tuber magnatum) Also sometimes called the Piedmont truffle, because it is exclusive to the Piedmont region in northern Italy. It is knobbly and like a potato in appearance. The skin and flesh range from cream to pale brown, and the flesh is very firm in texture. The white truffle has an exceptionally intense aroma and is the ultimate flavour prize, to be added raw at the last moment, finely shaved or grated, to risottos, polenta, pasta and egg dishes.

recipes

soups

chilli bean & pepper soup

A fiery soup inspired by the rich colours and contrasting moods and flavours of Latin America. A devillish meal in itself, cooled by the subtle smoothness of an avocado salsa.

1 Heat the oil in a large saucepan and fry the onion and garlic until soft but not coloured. Stir in the red peppers and chillies and fry for a few minutes. Stir in the stock and tomato juice or passata, the tomato purée and paste, chilli sauce, kidney beans and coriander. Bring to the boil, cover and simmer for 30 minutes.

2 Cool slightly, then purée in a food processor or blender until smooth. Return to the pan and taste and adjust the seasoning, adding a little extra chilli sauce if necessary. Bring to the boil and serve in warmed soup bowls, topped with avocado salsa and coriander sprigs and accompanied by tortilla chips.

Serves 6

2 tablespoons sunflower oil

I large onion, finely chopped

4 garlic cloves, finely chopped

2 red peppers, cored, deseeded and diced

2 red chillies, deseeded and finely chopped

900 ml (1½ pints) vegetable stock

750 ml (1¼ pints) tomato juice or passata

I tablespoon double concentrate tomato purée

I tablespoon sun-dried tomato paste

2 tablespoons sweet chilli sauce, or more to taste

I x 400 g (13 oz) can red kidney beans, drained

2 tablespoons finely chopped coriander

To Garnish:

Avocado Salsa (page 211)

coriander sprigs

tortilla chips

Chilli Bean & Pepper Soup is shown on the preceding page

pumpkin soup
with crusty cheese topping

This substantial eatin' and drinkin' soup can be served in small hollowed-out pumpkin or squash shells. Indeed, pumpkin soup is an ideal way to use up the scooped-out flesh of a pumpkin, the result of making a festive lantern. Heat the shells in a very hot oven for about 10 minutes before using.

2 tablespoons sunflower or olive oil
1 large onion, finely chopped
3 garlic cloves, crushed
2 celery sticks, chopped
750 g (1½ lb) pumpkin flesh, roughly chopped
750 ml (1¼ pints) light vegetable or chicken stock
pinch of freshly grated nutmeg
1 bay leaf
a few parsley stalks
65–150 ml (2½–5 fl oz) double cream
1–2 tablespoons finely chopped parsley
salt and pepper

To Garnish:
1 small French stick
125–175 g (4–6 oz) Gruyère or fontina cheese, grated
4 flat leaf parsley sprigs

1 Heat the oil in a saucepan and fry the onion and garlic until soft but not coloured. Add the celery and pumpkin flesh and fry for 10–15 minutes to draw out the flavours. Stir in the stock and nutmeg. Tie the bay leaf and parsley stalks together with string, add to the pan and bring to the boil. Reduce the heat and simmer for about 30 minutes until the vegetables are soft.

2 Remove the bouquet of herbs and purée the soup by pushing it through a fine vegetable mouli or using a food processor or blender. Return the purée to the saucepan, bring to the boil and season with salt and pepper. Stir in the cream and parsley, return to the boil, then reduce the heat and keep the soup warm while preparing the garnish.

3 Cut the French bread into twelve 1 cm (½ inch) slices, place on a baking sheet and toast under a preheated grill until pale golden on both sides. Leave the grill on.

4 Pour the hot soup into 4 deep ovenproof bowls. Arrange 3 pieces of French bread on top of each one, overlapping them slightly. Sprinkle the soup generously with grated cheese. Set the bowls on the baking sheet and cook quickly under the grill until golden brown and bubbly. Garnish with parsley sprigs and serve immediately.

Serves 4

courgette & dill soup

A flavoursome soup, perfect in the height of summer when there is a glut of courgettes. It is excellent served chilled and freezes well. Fresh dill gives a refreshing tang, but if it is not available, use fresh garden fennel or just a pinch of dried dill. For an entirely different flavour, use fresh basil leaves.

1 Heat the oil in a large saucepan and gently fry the onion and garlic until soft but not coloured. Add the courgettes, cover tightly with greaseproof paper and cook over a low heat for 10–15 minutes until tender. Add the stock, cover with a lid and simmer for a further 10–15 minutes.

2 Using a slotted spoon, transfer the courgettes and a little of the stock to a food processor or blender. Purée until smooth, then pour into a clean saucepan. Add the remaining stock and the dill, season to taste with salt and pepper, then bring to the boil.

3 Serve in warmed soup bowls, each one garnished with a swirl of cream and fresh dill fronds.

Serves 8

2–3 tablespoons sunflower or light olive oil

1 large onion, chopped

2 garlic cloves, crushed

1 kg (2 lb) courgettes, sliced or roughly chopped

1.2–1.5 litres (2–2½ pints) vegetable or chicken stock

2–4 tablespoons finely chopped dill

salt and pepper

To Garnish:

125 ml (4 fl oz) single cream

dill fronds

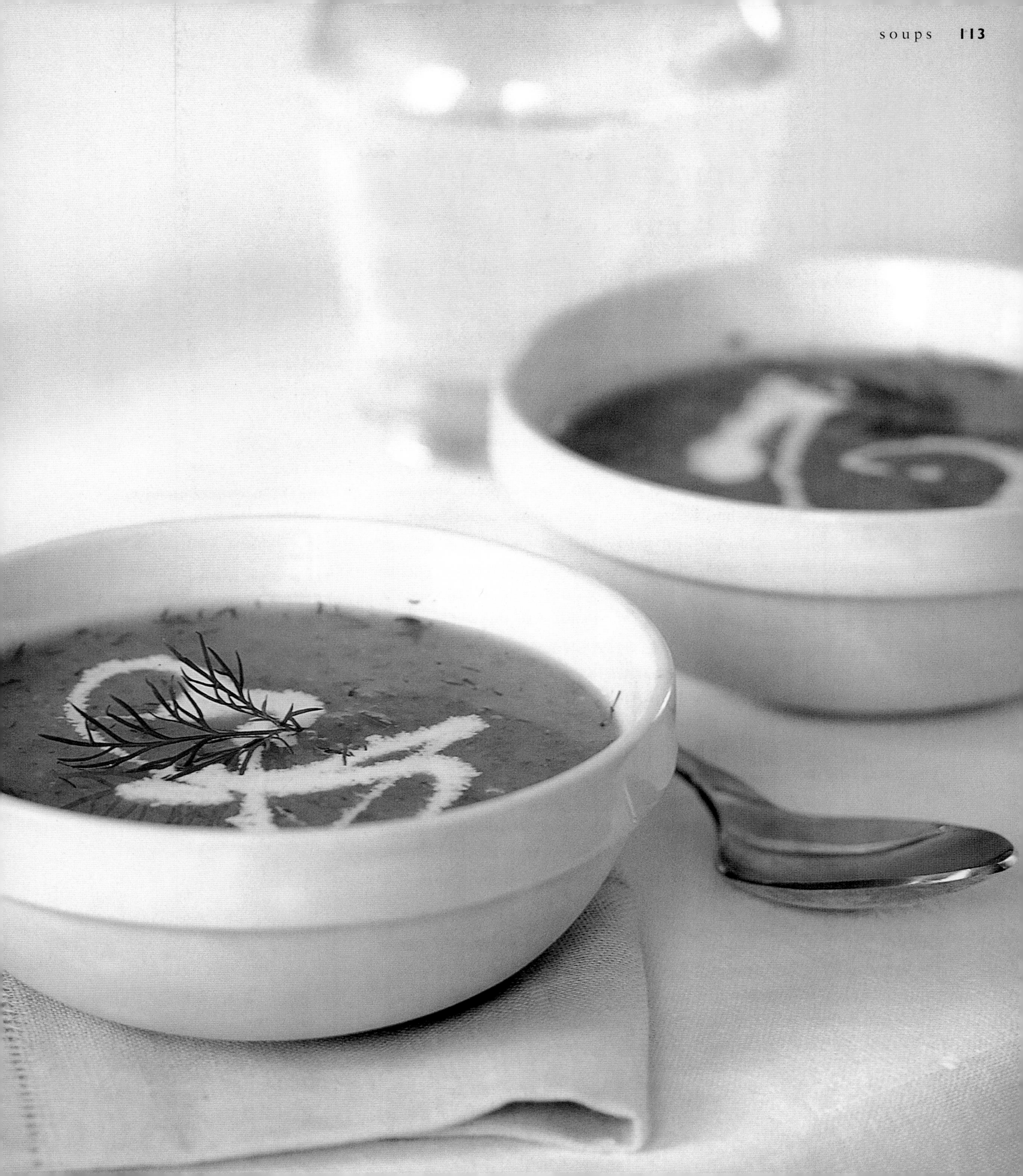

beetroot borscht
with soured cream & chives

This vibrant, blood-red soup has a tangy, sweet and sour taste. There are many versions, ranging from a simple beetroot juice to a complex combination of meat and beetroot stock enriched with fresh and salted beef, pork and shredded cabbage. Traditionally finished with soured cream, borscht can also be accompanied by lavish helpings of fried chipolata sausages, sliced boiled meats, small meat dumplings and Piroshki (page 247). For many years I enjoyed this soup in the home of my friend Gran Kanareck, whose family were Polish. This is her recipe.

1 Scrape young beetroot, or peel older ones with a potato peeler, then grate the flesh on a coarse grater into a large saucepan. Grate the carrot and onion into the pan. Add the garlic, stock, lemon juice and sugar and season with salt and pepper. Bring to the boil. Cover the pan, reduce the heat and simmer for 45 minutes.

2 While the soup is cooking, prepare the garnish. Cut the whole cooked beetroot into 3 mm (⅛ inch) slices, then into 3 mm (⅛ inch) sticks about 4 cm (1½ inches) long. Cover and refrigerate until required.

3 When the vegetables for the soup are tender, strain the contents of the pan through a sieve lined with muslin. Discard the vegetables. At this stage the beetroot juice can be cooled and stored in the refrigerator until required. It will keep for several days. It can also be frozen.

4 Put the beetroot juice into a clean pan along with the beetroot sticks. Gently bring to the boil, then simmer for a few minutes to warm the beetroot through. Taste and adjust the seasoning as necessary, ladle into warmed soup bowls and serve with a spoonful of soured cream and a sprinkling of snipped chives.

Serves 6

CHEF'S TIP This soup can be thickened slightly with egg before adding the beetroot sticks. Lightly beat 2 eggs in a bowl. Whisking continually, pour a cup of hot (not boiling) beetroot juice on to the eggs. Pour this into the soup, whisking all the time to blend with the rest of the beetroot juice. Add the beetroot sticks and reheat very gently without boiling.

750 g (1½ lb) fresh raw beetroot, washed
1 carrot
1 onion
2 garlic cloves, crushed
1.5 litres (2½ pints) well-flavoured beef or vegetable stock
juice of 1 large lemon
2 tablespoons sugar
salt and pepper

To Garnish:
1 large cooked beetroot
150 ml (¼ pint) soured cream
1 teaspoon snipped chives

gazpacho Andaluz

This cold, tomato-based vegetable soup, often referred to as 'liquid salad', is one of the most refreshing of all summer soups. Originally from Andalucia in Spain, there are now many different versions. This is my 'quick' recipe, which keeps well in the refrigerator for several days and also freezes well. If full-flavoured fresh red tomatoes are not available, you will get a better colour and taste by using canned chopped tomatoes – use three 400 g (13 oz) cans.

1 Reserve about 4 tablespoons each of the onion, green and red peppers and cucumber for the garnish. Put the remaining diced vegetables into a food processor or blender with the fresh and canned tomatoes, garlic and tomato purée and work to a smooth purée.

2 Add the tomato juice, water, sugar, oregano and wine vinegar, then process again until well mixed. Season with salt and pepper. Transfer to a large bowl or measuring jug, cover and chill for at least 2 hours.

3 Just before serving, divide the reserved diced vegetables between 7–8 chilled soup plates, pour the cold soup on top and garnish with the garlic croûtons and snipped chives.

Serves 7–8

125 g (4 oz) onion, finely diced
125 g (4 oz) green pepper, deseeded and finely diced
125 g (4 oz) red pepper, deseeded and finely diced
375 g (12 oz) cucumber, peeled and finely diced
750 g (1½ lb) well-flavoured red tomatoes, peeled, deseeded and coarsely chopped
1 x 400 g (13 oz) can chopped plum tomatoes
3–4 garlic cloves, crushed
2–4 tablespoons double concentrate tomato purée
500 ml (17 fl oz) tomato juice
150–300 ml (¼–½ pint) water
1–2 teaspoons soft brown sugar
1 teaspoon finely chopped oregano
5 tablespoons red wine vinegar
salt and pepper

To Garnish:
75 g (3 oz) garlic croûtons (page 249)
1 tablespoon finely snipped chives

sweetcorn chowder

This is real comfort food, just the thing for a fireside supper on a cold wintry night. Chowder was originally a soupy stew from Brittany. It was taken to Newfoundland by the Breton fishermen, and then travelled down the Atlantic coast to New England.

1 Melt the butter in a large saucepan, add the onion and garlic and fry over a gentle heat without colouring until soft. Add the diced potato and cook for a few minutes. Add the milk, sherry and stock, season with salt and pepper and bring to the boil. Reduce the heat to a simmer and cook for 10–15 minutes.

2 Add the sweetcorn, return to the boil and simmer for 10–15 minutes. Meanwhile, prepare the sage garnish. Heat the oil in a deep-fryer to 220°C (425°F), drop in the sage leaves and deep-fry for 20–30 seconds until crisp. Drain on kitchen paper and keep warm.

3 When the soup is ready, pour three-quarters of it into a food processor or blender and purée until smooth. Add the purée to the soup remaining in the pan and return to the boil.

4 Season with salt and pepper and stir in the cream and lime juice, adding a little extra stock if necessary to obtain the desired consistency. Heat the chowder thoroughly and stir in the chives. Serve immediately, garnished with the sage leaves and accompanied by cheesy crisps.

Serves 6

VARIATIONS Just before serving, add one or more of the following and heat through: thin strips of cooked chicken breast and roasted red pepper; diced green chillies; diced plum tomatoes.

Instead of the sage leaves, garnish with skinned and mashed roasted red pepper mixed with lightly whipped cream.

Roasted cumin seeds or hot spices, such as chilli, cayenne and paprika, can be fried with the onion and stirred in before adding the stock, or sprinkled on top of the finished chowder.

50 g (2 oz) butter
1 large onion, finely diced
3 garlic cloves, finely chopped
125 g (4 oz) potato, finely diced
300 ml (½ pint) milk
75 ml (3 fl oz) medium sherry
600 ml (1 pint) vegetable or chicken stock
750 g (1½ lb) fresh or frozen sweetcorn kernels or 2 x 340 g (11½ oz) cans sweetcorn kernels, drained
65 ml (2½ fl oz) single cream
2 teaspoons lime juice
2 tablespoons finely snipped chives
salt and pepper

To Garnish:
vegetable oil, for deep-frying
12 sage leaves
Cheesy Crisps (page 243)

celery & lovage soup
with herb cream & croûtons

Lovage is a herb with a flavour somewhat similar to celery, but much stronger. It is easy to grow and widely available in nurseries and garden centres in seed or plant form. Once established in the garden it is a prolific grower which can reach 60 cm–2 metres (2–6 feet) in height. It is most attractive during the spring and summer, dies back in the autumn and has vanished by winter, but sends out new shoots in the spring. If fresh lovage is not available, use 1 teaspoon crushed celery seeds instead.

1 Melt the butter in a large heavy saucepan. Add the celery, onion, leek and potatoes, cover closely with greaseproof paper and sweat over a gentle heat for 10–15 minutes until soft but not coloured.

2 Stir in the lovage leaves and pour in the stock and milk. Season with salt and pepper and bring to the boil, then cover the pan and reduce the heat to a simmer. Cook for 20–25 minutes.

3 Purée the soup in batches in a food processor or blender until smooth. Return to the pan, adjust the seasoning and consistency as necessary, and bring to the boil.

4 Mix the cream with the chopped herbs, reserving a few. Pour the hot soup into warmed soup bowls, spoon a little herb cream on top of each one and sprinkle with the reserved herbs, celery seeds and croûtons.

Serves 6

50 g (2 oz) butter
375 g (12 oz) celery sticks, chopped
1 large onion, roughly chopped
1 small leek, white part only, sliced
125 g (4 oz) potatoes, cubed
14 large lovage leaves, chopped
750 ml (1¼ pints) vegetable or
  chicken stock
300 ml (½ pint) milk
salt and pepper

To Garnish:
150 ml (¼ pint) double cream, lightly
  whipped
1 tablespoon each finely chopped
  lovage, parsley and chives
¼ teaspoon celery seeds
75 g (3 oz) croûtons (page 249)

minted green pea soup
with hot paprika & croûtons

Green pea soup made with the first tender young peas of the season is one of the most delicious offerings from the spring vegetable garden. In this recipe I have combined them with the velvety leaves of mint, the sharp fresh flavour of lime and the heat of paprika to produce a colour and flavour which is hard to equal. If you are not able to get freshly picked garden peas, use good quality frozen petits pois. These produce a result which is equally good and can be enjoyed throughout the year.

1 Heat the oil in a large saucepan and fry the onion and celery until soft but not coloured. Stir in the paprika and fry for a few minutes. Bring the stock to the boil in another saucepan and add to the pan with the peas, mint and lime juice. Bring to the boil, then reduce the heat and simmer for 15–20 minutes until the peas are tender. If using frozen peas, cook for only 5–8 minutes. Don't overcook the peas or the soup will lose its bright green colour.

2 When the peas are soft, blend the soup in a food processor or blender until smooth. If you prefer a very finely textured soup, pass the purée through a sieve or vegetable mouli. Return the purée to the saucepan, bring to the boil and season to taste. Remove from the heat and stir in two-thirds of the cream or crème fraîche, then add a little extra stock, if necessary, to give the desired consistency. Warm through gently.

3 Serve the soup in shallow soup plates. Whip the remaining cream until it just holds its shape and add a spoonful of it or some crème fraîche to the centre of each plate. Sprinkle a little paprika on top of the cream and finish with a sprig of mint. Serve the croûtons separately.

Serves 6

1 tablespoon olive or sunflower oil
1 onion, chopped
2 celery sticks, sliced
1–2 teaspoons hot paprika
**900 ml (1½ pints) vegetable or
  chicken stock**
750 g (1½ lb) fresh or frozen peas
3 mint sprigs
juice of ½ lime
**150 ml (¼ pint) double cream or
  crème fraîche**
salt and pepper

To Garnish:
a little hot paprika
6 small young mint sprigs
75 g (3 oz) croûtons (page 249)

tomato & orange soup
with basil cream

A refreshing soup for a hot summer's day when tomatoes are sweet and ripe and basil heavily perfumed. If you want to make this soup at other times of year when fresh tomatoes have a less intense colour and flavour, it is best to use four 400 g (13 oz) cans of plum tomatoes.

1 Heat the oil in a large saucepan and fry the onion and garlic until soft but not coloured. Add the tomatoes along with their seeds and juice and stir in the tomato purée, stock, orange rind and juice and basil. Bring to the boil, reduce the heat, then cover and simmer gently for 20–25 minutes until the vegetables are soft and pulpy.

2 Let the soup cool slightly, then purée in batches in a food processor or blender and push through a plastic sieve into a clean saucepan to remove the seeds. Season with salt, pepper and a little sugar. This will help counteract the acidity of the tomatoes without actually making the soup sweet. Return the pan to the heat and bring to the boil, then add a little extra stock or tomato juice, if necessary, to achieve the desired consistency.

3 To serve, fold the chopped basil gently into the whipped cream. Pour the hot soup into warmed soup plates, spoon a little basil cream on each one and top with tiny basil sprigs and orange julienne.

Serves 6

ORANGE JULIENNE With a vegetable peeler, remove a thin paring of rind from an orange. There should be very little white pith with the rind. Cut the rind into very thin strips (julienne) and drop them into a pan of boiling water for 30 seconds. Drain and refresh under cold water. Drain again and pat dry.

2 tablespoons olive or sunflower oil
1 onion, roughly chopped
2 garlic cloves, crushed
2 kg (4 lb) ripe tomatoes, peeled and chopped
2 tablespoons tomato purée
450 ml (¾ pint) vegetable or chicken stock
grated rind of 1 large orange
75 ml (3 fl oz) freshly squeezed orange juice
4 basil sprigs
1–2 teaspoons brown sugar
salt and pepper

To Garnish:
2–3 tablespoons finely chopped basil
150 ml (¼ pint) double cream, lightly whipped
6 small basil sprigs
orange julienne (left)

creamed celeriac
& Parmesan soup

Celeriac makes a rich, well-flavoured and creamy textured soup, and it is particularly good when combined with a strong cheese such as the Parmesan in this recipe. If you prefer, you can replace the Parmesan with 125 g (4 oz) strong blue cheese, such as Stilton or Cashel, and use snipped chives for the garnish instead of parsley. Alternatively, the cheese can be omitted altogether and the soup finished with a drizzle of truffle oil and a scattering of toasted pine nuts. Although truffle oil is expensive, a little goes a long way and it adds a wonderful flavour.

1 Melt the butter in a large saucepan and fry the onion, garlic and celeriac over a gentle heat for 4–5 minutes to draw out the flavours without colouring. Add the stock and bring to the boil. Reduce the heat to a simmer, cover and cook for 25–30 minutes until the celeriac is tender.

2 Let the soup cool slightly, then blend in a food processor or blender, in batches, until smooth. Return the purée to the pan and add half of the cream and Parmesan. Reheat and simmer gently for a few minutes, stirring to blend.

3 To serve, whip the remaining cream until it just holds its shape. Put 1 tablespoon of the remaining Parmesan in the bottom of each warmed soup bowl and pour on the hot soup. Add a spoonful of whipped cream to each bowl and garnish with a grind of black pepper and a sprinkling of chopped parsley. Serve with the scones.

Serves 6–7

25 g (I oz) butter
2 large onions, roughly chopped
I garlic clove, crushed
875 g (1¾ lb) celeriac, to give about 500 g (I lb) when peeled and roughly chopped
1.25 litres (2¼ pints) vegetable or chicken stock
300 ml (½ pint) double cream
50–125 g (2–4 oz) Parmesan cheese, freshly grated
salt and pepper

To Serve:
2 tablespoons finely chopped parsley
Cheesy Leek & Herb Scones (page 240)

roasted pepper soup
with tomatoes, garlic & fragrant herbs

Roasted vegetables of all varieties have a very distinctive flavour but the rich sweetness of charred red peppers is one of the most exquisite. The quantity of stock needed may vary depending on the amount of juice created by the vegetables during roasting. You may also need to add a little concentrated tomato juice if the fresh tomatoes are lacking in flavour. This soup is also excellent cold, when it should be garnished with thin strips of roasted red pepper and some freshly chopped herbs instead of the cream.

1 Put the oil into a large roasting tin, about 35 x 25 x 6 cm (14 x 10 x 2½ inches), and heat on the top of the stove. Add the peppers, tomatoes, onions, carrots, celery, garlic and chillies and toss to mix. When they are sizzling hot, transfer to a preheated oven, 200°C (400°F), Gas Mark 6, and cook for 1 hour, stirring occasionally. Remove the tin from the oven, stir in the tomato purée and leave the vegetables to cool.

2 Transfer the vegetables to a food processor or blender and process until very smooth. This may need to be done in batches. Push through a plastic sieve into a clean saucepan to remove any remaining skin and seeds. The purée will be thick and rich with a brilliant orange-red colour and a magnificent taste. In this form it can be used as a sauce for fish or stirred into other vegetable dishes.

3 Put the thyme, basil and parsley into the food processor or blender with about 150 ml (¼ pint) of the purée and process until well blended. Add to the rest of the purée in the saucepan. Dilute with the vegetable stock to the desired consistency. Season with sugar, salt and pepper and a little Tabasco sauce if you feel the need for a hotter chilli flavour. Serve in warmed soup bowls, garnished with a spoonful of crème fraîche and a sprig of basil or parsley.

Serves 7–8

4 tablespoons olive oil
5 large red peppers, total weight 1–1.25 kg (2–2½ lb), cored, deseeded and roughly chopped
1 kg (2 lb) red tomatoes, halved lengthways
2 large onions, roughly chopped
2 carrots, roughly chopped
2 celery sticks, chopped
10 large garlic cloves, peeled
1–2 small red chillies, deseeded and finely chopped
2 tablespoons double concentrate tomato purée
2 teaspoons finely chopped thyme
3 tablespoons finely shredded basil
2 tablespoons finely chopped flat leaf parsley
1.25–1.5 litres (2¼–2½ pints) hot vegetable stock
1–2 teaspoons brown sugar, to taste
Tabasco sauce, to taste (optional)
salt and pepper

To Garnish:
250 ml (8 fl oz) crème fraîche
7–8 basil or flat leaf parsley sprigs

Jerusalem artichoke soup

This soup has an earthy, almost smoked, flavour and an attractive texture and colour. Choose young artichokes that are not too misshapen and of a reasonable size — between 5–10 cm (2–4 inches) — so they can be used without peeling. If you don't want to make the chips for the garnish, use croûtons instead, or slivers of toasted almond.

1 Melt the butter in a large heavy saucepan and fry the onion, garlic and celery gently until soft but not coloured. Add the artichokes, then tightly cover the vegetables with a piece of greaseproof paper to 'sweat' them and draw out their flavour. Cook over a low heat for 10 minutes.

2 Stir in the vinegar and flour, then gradually add the stock, stirring to blend all the ingredients together. Season lightly with salt and pepper. Bring to the boil, reduce the heat, then cover and simmer for about 30 minutes until the vegetables are tender.

3 Let the soup cool slightly, then purée in a food processor or blender until smooth. Return to the pan and bring to the boil. Adjust the seasoning, stir in the cream and reheat the soup thoroughly. Add a little extra cream or stock, if necessary, to achieve the desired consistency. Serve hot, garnished with artichoke chips, chopped parsley and parsley sprigs.

Serves 9–10

75 g (3 oz) butter

1 large onion, finely chopped

2 garlic cloves, crushed

125 g (4 oz) celery, roughly sliced

1 kg (2 lb) Jerusalem artichokes, well scrubbed and sliced

1 teaspoon white wine vinegar

15 g (½ oz) plain flour

1.5 litres (2½ pints) vegetable or chicken stock

about 175 ml (6 fl oz) single cream

salt and pepper

To Garnish:

Jerusalem Artichoke Chips (page 248)

2 tablespoons finely chopped flat leaf parsley

flat leaf parsley sprigs

starters

vegetable carpaccio
with Parmesan shavings

This vegetable recipe was inspired by the famous dish made with thin slices of raw fillet of beef, created by Guiseppe Cipriani at Harry's Bar in Venice. Here I have used thinly sliced vegetables moistened with olive oil and finished with Parmesan cheese shavings. Any fresh crisp vegetables can be used, but choose those which will create an interesting variety of texture, colour and taste.

1 Trim the radishes and cut into thin circles. Cut the peppers in half, remove the seeds and white membrane and cut the flesh into short julienne strips. Peel the carrots and cut into very thin diagonal slices. Remove any coarse strings from the celery and cut into thin slices to form semi-circular pieces. Cut the fennel into thin slivers.

2 Divide the vegetables between 4 large plates and arrange in attractive mounds in the centre. Drizzle with enough olive oil to lightly moisten the vegetables. Scatter the Parmesan shavings around them and finish with a few grindings of black pepper. Serve with crispy bread.

Serves 4

12 small crisp red radishes
1 green pepper
1 red pepper
2 small tender young carrots
2–3 celery sticks
1 very small fennel bulb, or
 1 x 125 g (4 oz) piece of fennel
2–3 tablespoons extra virgin olive oil
pepper
25 g (1 oz) Parmesan cheese, cut into
 thin shavings

Vegetable Carpaccio is shown on the preceding page

crudités

Allow 125–150 g (4–5 oz) assorted vegetables per person with a selection of 3–4 dips, salsas and sauces (pages 208–235)

This is the general term given to a collection of crunchy raw vegetables and salad leaves eaten with the fingers and served with dips. Middle Eastern hummus made from chickpeas and tahini (sesame seed paste) is good with crudités, so too is guacamole, an avocado dip from Central America, and tapenade, a Provençal olive paste. Pesto, a classic Italian sauce of sweet basil, is also served with crudités, as are numerous uncooked tomato-based sauces and relishes from Mexico called salsas. Crudités are the perfect start to any meal because they are light and refreshing and can be eaten informally with drinks or at the dining table. They also make a healthy lunch or snack with crusty bread as well as excellent party or finger food.

1 Choose firm, crisp vegetables, such as carrots, celery, cucumber, fennel, chicory, peppers, spring onions and lettuce hearts. These can be cut into finger-length pieces or sticks. Tight-headed vegetables, such as broccoli or cauliflower, can be broken into florets and small whole vegetables like cherry tomatoes, mushrooms, mangetouts, green beans and radishes can be left just as they are.

2 Wash and dry the vegetables well, then arrange them on a serving platter or individual plates.

3 Serve the dips, salsas and sauces separately.

vegetable beignets

Serve these crisp, puffy vegetable fritters with either Aïoli (page 223) or Sweet & Sour Sauce (page 228). The key to success, apart from using a varied selection of fresh vegetables, is the batter. After experimenting with many recipes, I believe this Japanese tempura batter is just right.

1 Cut the peppers lengthways into 3–5 mm (⅛–¼ inch) strips. Cut the courgettes into flat batons about 2 x 4 cm x 3 mm (¾ x 1½ x ⅛ inch) and the aubergines into slices on the diagonal about 3 mm (⅛ inch) thick. Cut the sweetcorn in half lengthways, the onions into rings and the French beans into 4 cm (1½ inch) lengths. Cut the cauliflower into florets and parboil them for 2 minutes. Drain and refresh. Leave the mushrooms whole if small, or cut in half or in quarters if large.

2 About 20 minutes before cooking, prepare the batter. With a small wire whisk, beat the egg well in a large bowl. Still beating, add the lager in a thin stream. Sift the flour, baking powder and a pinch of salt into another bowl, stir in pepper to taste and tip on top of the egg and lager. Stir with the whisk, barely enough to mix. Don't overbeat. Cover and leave to stand for about 10 minutes.

3 Heat the oil in a deep-fryer to 190°C (375°F). Dip the vegetables in the batter, one type at a time. Fry no more than 6 pieces at once or the temperature of the oil will drop and make the batter greasy. Courgettes, onions, cauliflower, baby sweetcorn and mushrooms take 3–5 minutes; peppers, aubergines and beans about 3 minutes. The batter should be puffy, crisp and golden, the vegetables just tender.

4 Transfer the vegetables to an ovenproof dish or tray lined with kitchen paper and keep warm in a preheated oven, 190°C (375°F), Gas Mark 5, until they are all cooked. They will hold quite successfully for about 30 minutes.

5 Arrange the beignets on a large platter around a bowl of sauce, or pile about 9 beignets in the centre of each individual plate and put a few spoonfuls of sauce on the side. Garnish with herbs or salad leaves and serve immediately.

Serves 6–8

750 g (1½ lb) assorted vegetables,
  such as peppers, courgettes,
  aubergines, baby sweetcorn, onions,
  French beans, cauliflower, mushrooms
sunflower oil, for frying
fresh herbs or salad leaves, to garnish

Batter:
1 large egg
200 ml (7 fl oz) lager, very well chilled
125 g (4 oz) plain flour
½ teaspoon baking powder
salt and pepper

vegetable pakoras

The size of these spicy Indian fritters can vary depending on whether they are to be served as a starter or cocktail snack. Served with cucumber raita, salad and relishes they are also delicious as a main course. Any combination of finely sliced or chopped vegetables can be used, as long as the total weight is 375–475 g (12–15 oz) for the amount of batter given here.

1 Make the batter. Sift the gram flour into a bowl, add the chilli powder, salt, baking powder, dry spices and thyme along with the crushed garlic and ginger. Gradually blend in the water to form a smooth batter of dropping consistency. Stir in the oil.

2 Add the prepared vegetables to the batter and stir to combine.

3 Heat the oil in a deep-fryer to 160–190°C (325–375°F). When ready, drop dessertspoons or teaspoons of the prepared vegetables directly into the hot oil. Keep the wire basket in the pan but don't use it except to lift the pakoras out. Fry about 6 pakoras at a time, depending on their size, for about 4–5 minutes until crisp and golden. Remove from the oil and drain on kitchen paper.

4 Garnish with lemon wedges and coriander leaves and serve immediately, with cucumber and mint raita.

Makes 25–30 large pakoras to serve 5–6 as a starter, or 50–60 small pakoras to serve 16–20 as a cocktail snack

75 g (3 oz) onion, finely chopped
75 g (3 oz) potato, peeled and finely diced
75 g (3 oz) cauliflower, broken into tiny sprigs
75 g (3 oz) red pepper, cored, deseeded and finely chopped
vegetable oil, for deep-frying

Batter:
300 g (10 oz) gram (chickpea) flour
1–2 teaspoons chilli powder
1–2 teaspoons salt
1 teaspoon baking powder
3 teaspoons ground cumin
3 teaspoons ground coriander
3 teaspoons pepper
3 teaspoons dried thyme
3 garlic cloves, crushed
1–2.5 cm (½–1 inch) piece of fresh root ginger, peeled and grated
250–300 ml (8–10 fl oz) cold water
2 teaspoons vegetable oil

To Serve:
lemon wedges
coriander leaves
Cucumber & Mint Raita (page 216)

leek & spinach
filo triangles

These are a variation on burek, the deep-fried pastries filled with minced meat or cheese from the Middle East. They make excellent finger food to serve with pre-dinner or party drinks or, as in this recipe, with fromage frais as a first course. The preparation of filo pastry is long and complicated, so ready-made frozen filo is generally used. It is widely available from Greek and Middle Eastern shops and supermarkets. Once defrosted, it quickly dries out and becomes brittle, so work with one sheet at a time, keeping the rest covered with clingfilm and a damp cloth.

1 Wash and pick over the fresh spinach and remove any tough central stalks. Shake off the surplus water, leaving only that which clings to the leaves.

2 Heat half of the butter in a large saucepan and fry the onion, garlic and leek until soft but not coloured. Add the spinach and stir to combine. Cover the pan tightly with greaseproof paper and a lid and cook over a moderate heat for 5–8 minutes until the spinach has wilted and is tender and all the liquid has evaporated. Shake the pan occasionally to prevent it sticking and burning.

3 Squeeze the spinach to remove any excess moisture, leave to cool, then stir in the feta and ricotta, nutmeg, pepper and beaten egg.

4 Melt the remaining butter and work with 1 sheet of pastry at a time, brushing each one with butter before peeling it off the pile. If you are using the smaller filo sheets, fold each one in half lengthways and place 1 heaped tablespoon of the spinach mixture on one of the short ends. Fold the left corner over the filling and continue folding until you have a pastry triangle with a small flap to tuck underneath. Brush with a little more butter and place on an oiled baking sheet. Repeat to make 14 triangles. If you are using the large sheets of filo, put 2 sheets on top of each other then cut into five 8 cm (3½ inch) strips, each 30 cm (12 inches) long. Brush with butter, fill and roll in the same way to form triangles. Repeat with the remaining pastry to make 15 triangles.

5 Bake in a preheated oven, 190°C (375°F), Gas Mark 5, for 25–35 minutes until golden brown. Garnish with chervil or parsley sprigs and serve warm or at room temperature, with fromage frais or thick natural yogurt.

Makes 14–15 triangles, enough to serve 7

250 g (8 oz) fresh spinach, or 125 g
  (4 oz) frozen spinach, defrosted
75 g (3 oz) butter
65 g (2½ oz) onion, finely chopped
2 garlic cloves, finely chopped
75 g (3 oz) leek, thinly sliced
40 g (1½ oz) feta cheese, crumbled
40 g (1½ oz) ricotta cheese
pinch of freshly grated nutmeg
1 small egg, beaten
14 sheets fresh filo pastry, each 31 x
  18 cm (12½ x 7 inches), or 6 sheets
  frozen filo pastry, each 46 x 30 cm
  (17½ x 12 inches), defrosted
pepper

To Serve:
chervil or flat leaf parsley sprigs
fromage frais or thick natural yogurt

goat's cheese
with peppers & pine nuts

If you don't want to go to the trouble of coating the cheese before baking, you can leave it plain, or simply roll it in toasted breadcrumbs. For a speckled coating, add some chopped fresh herbs to the nut and breadcrumb mixture.

40 g (1½ oz) pine nuts, toasted
(below right)

15 g (½ oz) fresh breadcrumbs,
toasted

½ tablespoon finely chopped basil

1 small garlic clove, finely chopped

2 x 60 g (2½ oz) crottins de Chavignol
cheeses, halved

1 tablespoon pine nut or hazelnut oil

4 small roasted red peppers
(page 83), peeled, deseeded and cut
into slivers

1 quantity Vinaigrette (page 231)

To Garnish:

12 small basil leaves

8 whole chives

1 Chop 15 g (½ oz) of the toasted pine nuts and combine them with the bread-crumbs, chopped basil and garlic. Brush each piece of cheese lightly with oil, then coat evenly in the nutty crumbs. Set on a lightly oiled baking sheet and bake in a preheated oven, 200°C (400°F) Gas Mark 6, for 8–10 minutes until the cheese is warmed through and beginning to melt at the edges.

2 Arrange the pepper slivers on 4 large serving plates. Carefully lift the cheese off the baking sheet and set on top of the peppers. Shake the dressing and drizzle a little over each serving. Garnish with the reserved whole toasted pine nuts, the basil leaves and chives and serve immediately.

Serves 4

TOASTED PINE NUTS Spread the pine nuts on a heavy baking sheet and toast under a preheated hot grill, tossing frequently until an even golden colour. Don't overbrown the nuts or they will taste bitter.

grilled asparagus

Cooked on a ridged cast iron grill pan or barbecue, asparagus has an entirely different taste and texture from boiled or steamed asparagus, particularly if it has been allowed to singe and brown a little, which gives it a rich deep flavour. Choose fine asparagus spears or sprue about 1 cm (½ inch) in diameter.

1 Melt the butter with the oil in a small saucepan over a low heat. Lay the prepared spears on a preheated very hot grill pan or barbecue, and brush with the oil and butter mixture. Reduce the heat slightly to allow the asparagus to cook through without burning, and cook for about 5 minutes without moving. Turn the asparagus, brush again with the oil and butter and cook for a further 5 minutes until the asparagus is tender, well seared and slightly wilted.

2 Remove the asparagus from the grill with tongs, and serve on a warmed plate. Season with the rock salt and black pepper, and garnish with the lemon. A little fine quality olive oil or melted butter can also be drizzled over the asparagus if liked, and few fresh Parmesan cheese shavings also make an excellent addition.

Serves 1

25 g (1 oz) butter
1–2 tablespoons light olive oil
6–8 fresh asparagus spears, trimmed
rock salt and black pepper
¼ lemon, to garnish

Grilled Asparagus is shown on page 256

mushroom
& green herb pâté

This succulent, earthy pâté can be made with one type of mushroom, such as the white button mushrooms available everywhere, or the large open cap variety which have a more definite flavour. If expense is no object, a few fresh or dried wild mushrooms will give the pâté a more intense, fuller flavour. Serve with fingers of toast, warm pitta bread, crostini or savoury crackers. For a more elegant presentation, mould the pâté into four 125 ml (4 fl oz) ramekin dishes lined with clingfilm, leave to set, then turn out to serve. Sliced sautéed mushrooms can be sandwiched between a bottom and top layer of pâté in the ramekins, or mushrooms piled on top when the pâté is unmoulded.

2 tablespoons light olive oil

50 g (2 oz) unsalted butter

I small onion, finely chopped

I–2 garlic cloves, crushed

250 g (8 oz) mushrooms, sliced

I teaspoon ground coriander

I teaspoon mushroom ketchup
 (optional)

dash of Worcestershire sauce

125 g (4 oz) low-fat cream cheese

I tablespoon fine brown breadcrumbs

2 tablespoons finely chopped
 coriander

2 tablespoons finely choppped flat
 leaf parsley

2 tablespoons clarified butter
 (below right)

salt and pepper

1 Heat the oil and butter in a large frying pan and fry the onion and garlic over a gentle heat until soft but not coloured. Increase the heat and add the mushrooms. Fry until all the moisture has been driven off and the mushrooms are a rich toasty golden brown colour. This will take about 15 minutes.

2 Add the ground coriander and fry for a few minutes to develop the flavour. Add the mushroom ketchup (if using) and the Worcestershire sauce, stirring to remove any sediment from the base of the pan. Allow to cool slightly, then turn into a food processor or blender. Add the cream cheese, breadcrumbs, coriander and parsley and process until well blended, stopping and starting the machine several times to scrape the mixture well down on to the blades. The pâté can be processed until very smooth or left with a little texture, depending on taste. Season with salt and pepper.

3 Pile the pâté into either 1 large or 4 individual bowls, level the surface and pour a little clarified butter on top. Cover with clingfilm and refrigerate until required. Allow the pâté to return to room temperature about 1 hour before serving, otherwise the flavours will be masked by the cold.

Serves 4

TO CLARIFY BUTTER Melt the butter in a saucepan over a low heat. Using a spoon, skim off the froth from the surface and discard. Set a sieve lined with muslin over a bowl and carefully pour through the clear, melted butter and leave to settle. Gently pour into another bowl, leaving the milky sediment behind. The clarified butter is now ready for use.

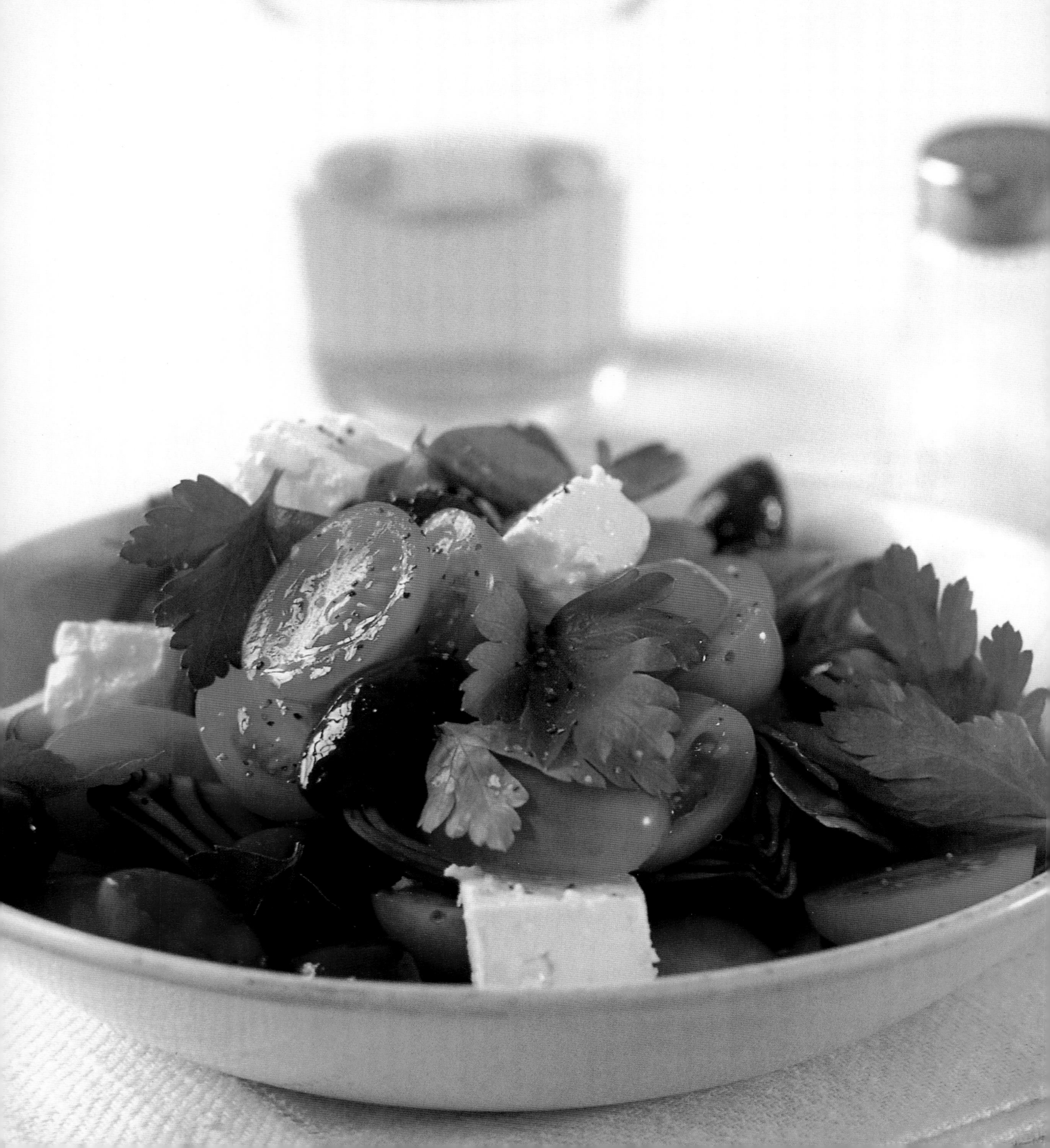

rustic Greek salad

There are a few classic combinations of ingredients that are so perfect they require no embellishment. This peasant salad, known as horiatiki in Greece, is one of them. To capture it at its best, use only the finest quality ingredients.

500–800 g (1 lb–1 lb 10 oz) tomatoes (large, cherry or miniature plum)

200–250 g (7–8 oz) feta cheese, drained and cut into 1 cm (½ inch) cubes

1 small red onion, peeled

16 black kalamata olives, pitted if preferred

25 flat leaf parsley leaves

2 tablespoons lemon juice

4–5 tablespoons light extra virgin olive oil

salt and pepper

warm pitta bread, to serve

1 If using large tomatoes, cut them in half lengthways, then cut each half into 3 wedges. If using baby tomatoes, cut them in half lengthways. Put into a large bowl with the feta.

2 Cut the onion into quarters, then cut each quarter into 4 sections. Scatter over the tomatoes and cheese. Add the olives and parsley leaves.

3 Pour over the lemon juice and toss very gently to coat. Use 2 wooden spoons or your fingers so as not to break the tomato flesh or the cheese. Pour over the oil and toss again, seasoning with salt and pepper. Serve the salad immediately, with warm pitta bread.

Serves 8

eggs Florentine

A divine combination of lightly cooked egg and meltingly tender spinach finished with a topping of crème fraîche, Cheddar and Parmesan cheeses. Perfect as a first course, light lunch or snack. Frozen spinach can be used if fresh is not available, in which case allow 500 g (1 lb).

1 Wash and pick over the spinach, discarding any tough central stalks and damaged or discoloured leaves. Rinse and drain, leaving only the water that clings to the leaves.

2 Melt half of the butter in a large saucepan, add the spinach, cover tightly and sweat until the leaves have wilted, the spinach is tender and any liquid has evaporated. Transfer to a large sieve or colander and squeeze out any liquid that remains. Return to the pan and season with nutmeg, salt and pepper.

3 Brush six 175 ml (6 fl oz) gratin dishes with the remaining butter. Divide the spinach between them, making a well in the centre for an egg and leaving a 1 cm (½ inch) space at the top.

4 Mix the crème fraîche and cream. Break an egg into the centre of each gratin dish and dust with salt and pepper. Spoon the cream mixture evenly over the eggs and sprinkle with the Cheddar and Parmesan.

5 Set the gratin dishes on a heavy baking sheet and bake in a preheated oven, 220°C (425°F), Gas Mark 7, for about 10–12 minutes until the whites are set but the yolks are still runny.

6 Remove the dishes from the oven and place under a preheated hot grill until the topping is bubbling and the cheese golden brown. Serve immediately.

Serves 6

1 kg (2 lb) fresh spinach
40 g (1½ oz) butter
a little freshly grated nutmeg
salt and pepper
6 large eggs

Topping:
150 ml (¼ pint) crème fraîche
50 ml (2 fl oz) double cream
40 g (1½ oz) Cheddar cheese, grated
40 g (1½ oz) Parmesan cheese, freshly grated
salt and pepper

spinach & ricotta gnocchi

These bright green savoury dumplings from Tuscany are usually eaten as a first course. They are also excellent as a main course, served simply with lots of melted butter and Parmesan cheese as in this recipe, or dressed with a thin, creamy béchamel or tomato sauce and a dusting of cheese, then grilled until bubbling and golden.

1 Wash and pick over the spinach, discarding any tough central stalks and damaged or discoloured leaves. Rinse and drain, leaving only the water that clings to the leaves. Cover and cook for a few minutes until the leaves are wilted and tender. Increase the heat to drive off any remaining water. Squeeze dry and leave to cool.

2 Put the spinach, ricotta, egg yolks, Parmesan, nutmeg, sage leaves and salt and pepper into a food processor and work to a smooth purée. Turn into a bowl, sift over the flour and mix to form a dough. Cover with clingfilm and leave in the refrigerator for about 15 minutes.

3 Meanwhile, prepare the dressing. Melt the butter and gently fry the chilli in it until soft. Keep warm.

4 Using well-floured hands, take 15 g (½ oz) pieces of the gnocchi mixture and shape them into small ovals or egg shapes. As each gnocchi is made, place it on a lightly floured tray until ready to cook.

5 Bring about 3.6 litres (6 pints) salted water to the boil in a large wide pan, reduce the heat to a simmer and poach 6 gnocchi at a time for 4–5 minutes until they are puffy and have risen to the surface. Remove with a slotted spoon and pile into warmed individual dishes.

6 Pour over the chilli butter, sprinkle with the Parmesan cheese and shredded sage leaves and serve immediately.

Makes 24, to serve 8 as a starter or 4 as a main course

750 g (1½ lb) fresh spinach
175–250 g (6–8 oz) ricotta cheese
2 egg yolks
50 g (2 oz) Parmesan cheese, freshly grated
¼ teaspoon freshly grated nutmeg
2 sage leaves, finely chopped
50 g (2 oz) plain flour
a little extra flour, for shaping
salt and pepper

To Serve:
75 g (3 oz) butter
1 small red chilli, deseeded and finely chopped
125 g (4 oz) Parmesan cheese, freshly grated
6–8 sage leaves, shredded

potato gnocchi
with pesto sauce

Gnocchi are light, airy little dumplings from the north of Italy. In Genoa, where this recipe comes from, they are served with pesto. The secret of making successful gnocchi is in the quality and dryness of the potatoes (King Edward or Maris Piper are both good), the proportion of flour to potato, light mixing and handling, and careful cooking.

1 Bake the potatoes in a preheated oven, 200°C (400°F), Gas Mark 6, for about 1 hour until tender. Leave to cool slightly.

2 Peel the cooled potatoes and weigh the cooked flesh, you should have about 750 g (1½ lb). Mash or press through a potato ricer while still hot. Season well with salt, pepper and nutmeg. Sift on the flour, add the beaten egg and, using a wooden spoon, bring together as lightly as possible to form a soft dough. Do not overwork or the gnocchi will be tough and heavy.

3 Divide the dough into quarters. Lightly dust your hands and work surface with a little flour and roll each into a sausage 2 cm (¾ inch) in diameter, then cut into 1 cm (½ inch) pieces. Dust lightly with flour and put the gnocchi pieces on a floured tray. Cover with clingfilm and chill for 30 minutes.

4 Press each gnocchi on to the prongs of a fork, to make a ridged pattern, then set on a floured tray ready for poaching. The ridges provide grooves to hold the butter or sauce which will coat them.

5 Brush a shallow baking dish with the melted butter. Fill a large saucepan three-quarters full of unsalted water and bring to the boil. Add one-third of the gnocchi and simmer gently until they float to the surface (this will take about 3 minutes), then cook for a further 20–30 seconds.

6 Lift the gnocchi out of the water with a slotted spoon, drain and put into the buttered dish. Keep warm while cooking the remaining gnocchi in batches. Pour a little of the remaining butter over the gnocchi between each batch.

7 Make the sauce. Melt the butter in a pan, stir in the pesto and heat gently until it bubbles. Divide the gnocchi between warmed plates and coat with the pesto. Garnish with the basil and serve, with grated Parmesan.

Serves 8

I kg (2 lb) floury baking potatoes
200 g (7 oz) self-raising flour
I–2 teaspoons salt
pepper
pinch of freshly grated nutmeg
I medium egg, beaten
a little extra flour, for rolling
I5 g (½ oz) butter, melted

Sauce:
50 g (2 oz) butter
I50 ml (¼ pint) Pesto (page 234)

To Serve:
fresh basil sprigs
25 g (I oz) Parmesan cheese, freshly grated

asparagus
& white wine risotto

Risotto with asparagus is one of my favourite dishes, and perfect for a light first or main course lunch or supper in spring. It is easy to make, and you will achieve perfect results if you follow my method – and use the correct rice of course. I like to use arborio rice.

1.5 litres (2½ pints) light vegetable stock or water

500 g (1 lb) young green asparagus (whole stems), trimmed and peeled, with trimmings reserved

1 bay leaf

2 large onions, 1 quartered and 1 finely chopped

125 g (4 oz) unsalted butter

425–500 g (14–16 oz) risotto rice

300 ml (½ pint) dry white wine

50 g (2 oz) Parmesan cheese, thinly shaved

salt and pepper

1 Bring the stock or water to the boil, put in the asparagus trimmings, the bay leaf and onion quarters and boil for 20 minutes. Strain into another pan and return the stock to the boil.

2 Meanwhile, cut the asparagus tips into 2.5–4 cm (1–1½ inch) lengths. Cut half of the remaining stems into similar-sized pieces and chop the rest very finely. Cook the asparagus tips and pieces of stem in the boiling stock for 3–4 minutes depending on their thickness, until just tender. Transfer the asparagus to a colander with a slotted spoon and refresh under cold running water until completely cold. Drain and reserve. Keep the stock simmering.

3 Melt half of the butter in a large heavy pan over a low heat. Add the chopped onion and cook gently until soft and transparent but not coloured. It is important to cook gently or the butter will burn and brown. Stir in the dry unwashed rice and cook, stirring constantly, until the rice becomes opaque. Add the wine and boil for 1 minute, stirring all the time.

4 Add a ladleful of simmering stock and stir until it is absorbed, then add another ladleful and repeat the process until nearly all the stock has been absorbed and the rice is almost cooked. This will take about 15 minutes. Stir constantly to prevent the rice sticking and ensure even cooking.

5 Add the asparagus with the remaining stock and continue cooking, stirring carefully until the asparagus is tender and the rice creamy. Stir in the remaining butter and season with salt and pepper. Serve immediately in soup plates, topped with Parmesan shavings.

Serves 4

CHEF'S TIP Leftover risotto can be mixed with a little beaten egg and the mixture dropped in tablespoonfuls into hot butter in a frying pan and pressed into little cakes. Cook for a few minutes until golden brown on each side.

stews

spicy beef koftas
in pizzaiola sauce

Serve as a main course with noodles or rice and a crisp mixed leaf salad. Or make miniature koftas and serve as a cocktail savoury on sticks, with the sauce considerably reduced and served as a dip. The sauce is also good with pasta and gnocchi. Chicken or lamb can be used for the meatballs instead of the beef.

1 First make the koftas. Beat the egg in a large bowl, stir in the breadcrumbs and add the beef and onion. Season with salt and pepper. Work together until well combined. You will find that your hands are best for this. Divide the mixture into 8 portions, shape each one into a ball and roll in a little flour. Heat the oil in a large frying pan and fry the koftas until evenly browned, turning frequently. This will take about 10 minutes.

2 Meanwhile, prepare the sauce. Heat the oil in a saucepan and fry the onion and garlic until soft but not coloured. Add the remaining ingredients, except half of the olives. Bring to the boil and cook over a high heat for 10 minutes to concentrate the flavours and slightly reduce the liquid.

3 Using a slotted spoon, lower the koftas into the sauce. Cover and cook gently for about 30 minutes until the meat is cooked through and the sauce rich and pulpy. Remove about 50 ml (2 fl oz) of the sauce and a few olives and process to a thick purée in a food processor or blender. Stir into the sauce. Taste and adjust the seasoning, if necessary, and garnish with the parsley sprigs and remaining olives before serving.

Serves 4

Koftas:
1 medium egg
50 g (2 oz) coarse breadcrumbs
500 g (1 lb) lean minced beef
75 g (3 oz) onion, grated
2 tablespoons plain flour
2 tablespoons sunflower or olive oil
salt and pepper

Pizzaiola Sauce:
1–2 tablespoons sunflower or olive oil
1 large onion, finely chopped
2 garlic cloves, crushed
1 red chilli, deseeded and finely chopped
1–2 red peppers, cored, deseeded and chopped
1 x 400 g (13 oz) can plum tomatoes
300 ml (½ pint) beef stock
2 tablespoons double concentrate tomato purée
2 tablespoons finely chopped basil
1 teaspoon finely chopped oregano
pinch of sugar
1 tablespoon chopped flat leaf parsley
50–125 g (2–4 oz) black Kalamata olives, pitted
flat leaf parsley sprigs, to garnish

Spicy Beef Koftas are shown on the preceding page

Breton beans
with cheese & herb crust

Any combination of vegetables and beans can be used to make this dish, and it makes an excellent main course served with a mixed leaf salad. Alternatively, prepare the vegetable stew without the cheese & herb crust and serve it as an accompaniment to roast or braised leg of lamb.

3 tablespoons olive oil

2 large onions, finely sliced

2–3 garlic cloves, chopped

2 large courgettes, about 500 g (1 lb), cut into 1 cm (½ inch) dice

2 red peppers, cored, deseeded and diced

2 x 400 g (13 oz) cans chopped plum tomatoes

1 tablespoon double concentrate tomato purée

2 x 400 g (13 oz) cans butter or other white beans, drained

150 ml (¼ pint) vegetable stock

1 tablespoon finely chopped basil

1 bay leaf

1 teaspoon sugar

salt and pepper

Cheese & Herb Crust:

1 small French stick, very thinly sliced

2 tablespoons olive oil

2 tablespoons finely chopped basil

1 tablespoon finely chopped parsley

50 g (2 oz) Parmesan cheese, finely grated

1 Heat the oil in a large saucepan or flameproof casserole and fry the onions and garlic until soft but not coloured. Add the courgettes and continue to fry for a few minutes until beginning to colour. Add all the remaining ingredients, except salt, and stir well to combine. Bring to the boil, reduce the heat, cover and simmer until the tomatoes are thick and pulpy and the flavours blended. This will take about 30–40 minutes. Taste and adjust the seasoning, adding salt if necessary.

2 Uncover the stew. Brush the bread slices with oil, arrange on top of the stew and scatter with the herbs and Parmesan. Toast under a preheated grill until the bread is golden brown and crisp. Serve immediately.

Serves 6

saffron-spiced
vegetable couscous

Couscous combines delicate velvety grains and fragrant spicy stew. It is traditionally made of meat, generally lamb or chicken, with several different types of vegetables. In this recipe I have concentrated solely on the vegetables. Couscous is a wonderful combination of tastes, textures, colours and smells, and, although the list of ingredients may look daunting, the dish itself is as simple to prepare as any stew.

1 Put the couscous into a large bowl and cover with the water. Leave to soak for 10 minutes, then fork through and leave for a further 10 minutes.

2 Meanwhile, prepare the sauce. Heat half of the oil in a large saucepan. Fry the onions until beginning to brown, then add the garlic and ginger. Stir in the ground spices and cinnamon stick and fry for a few minutes. Add the soaked saffron to the pan with the stock, tomatoes, tomato purée and chilli sauce. Bring to the boil.

3 Add the carrots and turnips to the sauce, reduce the heat, cover and cook for about 10 minutes. Meanwhile, heat the rest of the oil in a large frying pan and fry the fennel wedges until lightly coloured. Transfer to the sauce with a slotted spoon. Fry the aubergine and courgettes until browning, adding a little extra oil if necessary. Drain and add to the sauce. Cook gently for 15–20 minutes until the vegetables are tender and the sauce rich and thick. During this final cooking, steam the couscous.

4 To serve, pile the couscous in a large dish, fleck with pieces of butter and stir in with a fork. Stir the chopped coriander into the stew. Serve a mound of couscous to each person, spoon the vegetable stew on top and garnish with coriander sprigs.

Serves 6

375–500 g (12–16 oz) pre-cooked couscous

300 ml (½ pint) water

250 g (8 oz) carrots, cut into 2 cm (¾ inch) chunks

250 g (8 oz) small turnips, cut into 2 cm (¾ inch) chunks

1–2 large fennel bulbs, each cut into 6 wedges

1 large aubergine, cut into 2 cm (¾ inch) cubes

250 g (8 oz) courgettes, cut into 2 cm (¾ inch) slices

50 g (2 oz) butter

2–3 tablespoons finely chopped coriander

salt

coriander sprigs, to garnish

Sweet Spicy Sauce:

8 tablespoons extra virgin olive oil

2 large onions, cut into wedges

4 garlic cloves, crushed

2.5 cm (1 inch) piece of fresh root ginger, peeled and grated

1 tablespoon each ground cumin and coriander

1 teaspoon each turmeric, paprika and black pepper

5 cm (2 inch) piece cinnamon stick

1 teaspoon saffron threads, soaked in 2 tablespoons warm water

750 ml (1¼ pints) vegetable stock

2 x 400 g (13 oz) cans chopped tomatoes

2 tablespoons tomato purée

2 tablespoons sweet chilli sauce

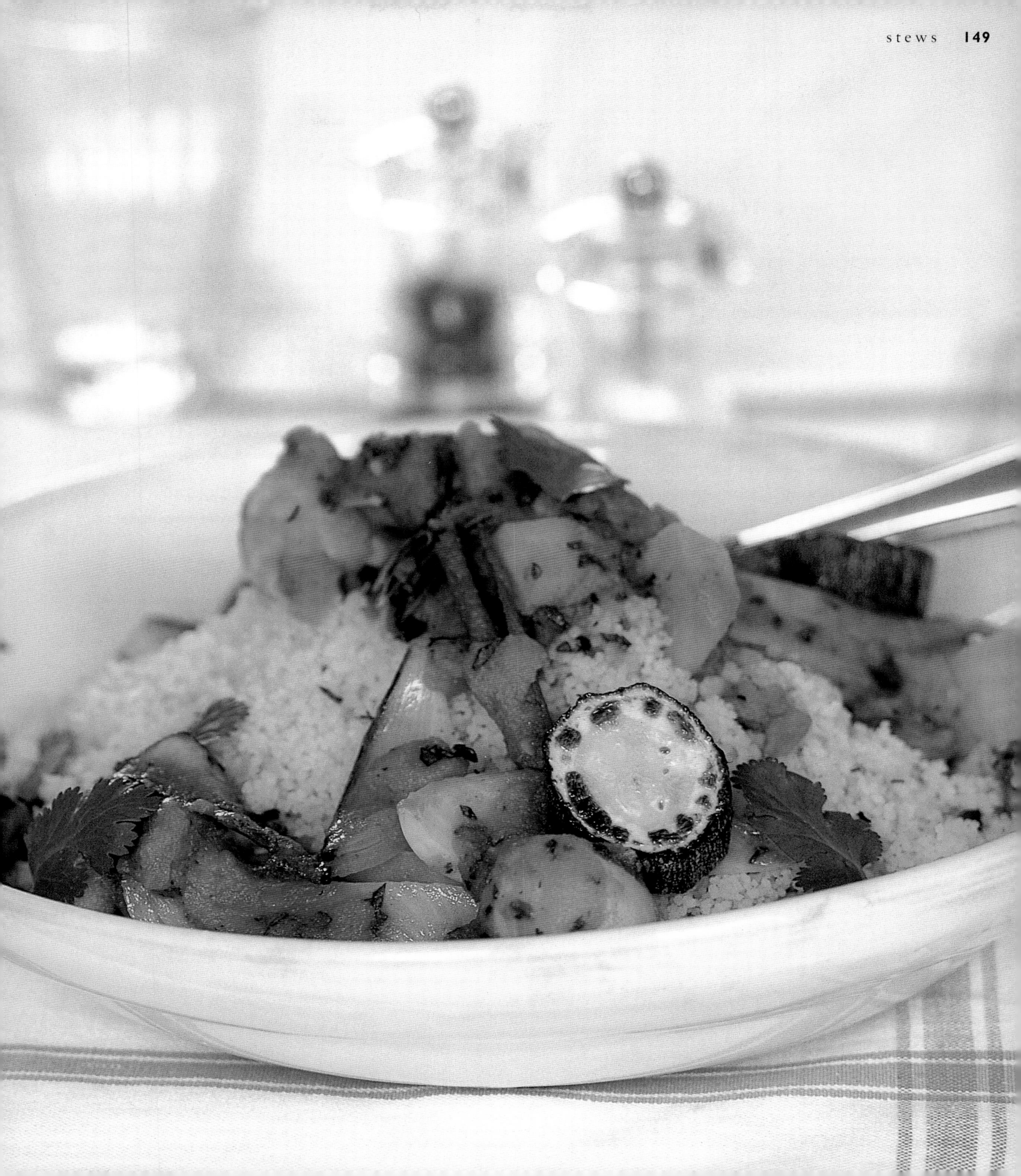

Mexican bean stew
with avocado & tomato salsa

A fiery stew of mixed vegetables and beans, an updated version of the classic chilli con carne without the meat. Vegetables such as onions, red and green peppers, carrot and celery give an excellent texture and variety of colour. They are then spiked with garlic and chilli peppers, enriched with two varieties of kidney bean – red and black – and cooked in a sauce of tomato, coriander and lime until rich and thick. Serve with tortilla chips and/or basmati rice for a main meal or party dish.

1 Heat the oil in a large saucepan and fry the onions, garlic and chillies for about 10 minutes until soft but not coloured. Add the vegetables, half of the coriander, the lime juice, tomato purée, tomatoes and vegetable stock. Stir well to combine, bring to the boil and cook for 30 minutes.

2 Add the beans, cover and simmer for 15 minutes until the vegetables are tender and the sauce thick and pulpy. Ten minutes before the end of cooking, add the diced peppers.

3 Remove 2 soup ladlefuls of the cooked stew and purée in a food processor. This will give extra body and substance to the stew. Return to the pan, stirring to combine. Add the sugar, season with salt and pepper and add the remaining chopped coriander. Serve immediately in large soup plates, each portion topped with 1 tablespoon fromage frais, a little of the salsa and a sprig of fresh coriander.

Serves 6–8

2–3 tablespoons sunflower oil
2 large onions, finely chopped
2 garlic cloves, crushed
2 green chillies, deseeded and chopped
500 g (1 lb) mixed vegetables, such as 2 celery sticks, 2 medium carrots, 1 large courgette, 1 medium parsnip, all cut into 1 cm (½ inch) cubes
3 tablespoons finely chopped coriander
1 tablespoon lime juice
2 tablespoons double concentrate tomato purée
2 x 400 g (13 oz) cans chopped tomatoes
450 ml (¾ pint) vegetable stock
1 x 400 g (13 oz) can red kidney beans, drained
1 x 400 g (13 oz) can black kidney beans, drained
2 large red peppers, cored, deseeded and diced
a pinch of sugar
salt and pepper

To Serve:
6–8 tablespoons fromage frais
Avocado & Tomato Salsa (page 212)
6–8 coriander sprigs

spinach & chickpea stew

The combination of fresh tangy green spinach and the rich nutty flavour of pale golden chickpeas give this rustic stew a most delicious flavour. It is a very useful standby dish because it can be quickly made from storecupboard ingredients. Serve with thick natural yogurt and a mixed leaf salad.

1 Blend half of the chickpeas in a food processor or blender, adding enough stock to give a smooth paste.

2 Wash and pick over the spinach, discarding any tough central stalks damaged or discoloured leaves. Rinse and drain, then put the spinach into a large saucepan with only the water that clings to the leaves. Cover tightly with a piece of greaseproof paper and a lid and cook gently until tender, turning and shaking occasionally. This will take about 4 minutes.

3 Heat the oil in a large saucepan and fry the onions and garlic until soft but not coloured. Add the cumin and paprika along with the whole chickpeas and fry for a few minutes, stirring well. Add the spinach, tomatoes, tomato purée, chickpea purée and oregano. Season with salt and pepper. Bring to the boil, reduce the heat and simmer for 5–10 minutes until the flavours are blended and the stew rich and pulpy.

4 Stir in half of the Cheddar cheese until just melted, then divide between four to six 300–375 ml (10–13 fl oz) gratin dishes. Mix the remaining Cheddar and Parmesan cheeses together and sprinkle over the stew. Flash under a preheated grill until the cheese is bubbling and forms a golden crust. Serve immediately.

Serves 4–6

2 x 400 g (13 oz) cans chickpeas, drained
125–150 ml (4–5 fl oz) vegetable stock
500 g (1 lb) fresh spinach
2–3 tablespoons olive oil
1–2 large onions, finely chopped
2–4 garlic cloves, crushed
2 teaspoons ground cumin
2 teaspoons paprika
2 x 400 g (13 oz) cans plum tomatoes
1 tablespoon double concentrate tomato purée
2 teaspoons finely chopped oregano
50 g (2 oz) mature farmhouse Cheddar cheese, grated
25 g (1 oz) Parmesan cheese, freshly grated
salt and pepper

green vegetables
with Thai-spiced coconut sauce

Any combination of crunchy seasonal green vegetables can be used, as long as they offer variety in shape and texture. For a non-vegetarian alternative, finger strips of raw chicken breast can be added to the sauce with the vegetables. Serve with boiled rice.

175 g (6 oz) mangetouts, topped and tailed and halved on the diagonal, if large

2 large courgettes, cut into 5 mm (¼ inch) slices

125 g (4 oz) shelled peas

250 g (8 oz) broccoli florets, trimmed

Coconut Sauce:

3 tablespoons vegetable oil

1 large onion, finely chopped

4 garlic cloves, finely chopped

3–4 teaspoons green Thai curry paste

2 teaspoons turmeric

2 teaspoons brown sugar

2 x 400 g (13 oz) cans coconut milk

juice of ½ lime

3 tablespoons desiccated coconut

175 ml (6 fl oz) vegetable stock

1 tablespoon cornflour

50 ml (2 fl oz) double cream

4 tablespoons chopped coriander

salt and pepper

1 First make the sauce. Heat the oil in a large saucepan and fry the onion and garlic until soft but not coloured. Stir in the curry paste, turmeric, sugar, coconut milk, lime juice, desiccated coconut and stock, mixing well to blend. Bring to the boil and cook quickly, stirring frequently, for 10–15 minutes to reduce the sauce slightly and concentrate the flavours.

2 Blend the cornflour with the cream to make a smooth paste, add to the sauce and cook for a few minutes to thicken, then stir in half of the coriander. Add the mangetouts, courgettes and peas and simmer gently.

3 Steam the broccoli for 4 minutes, then add to the sauce and cook for a few minutes until all the vegetables are tender. Season to taste, sprinkle with the remaining coriander and serve immediately.

Serves 4

fragrant mixed vegetable stew

This rich vegetable stew in tones of orange, green and gold was inspired by the exotic blend of spices used in Indian cooking, more often fragrant than hot and fiery. The vegetables chosen have a variety of taste, colour and texture, but any balanced selection could be used. I suggest limiting the number to six plus the onion so that the stew does not become a confusion of flavours and tastes. Serve with white or brown basmati rice, natural yogurt or Cucumber & Mint Raita (page 216) and Mung Dhal (page 251).

1 Heat the oil in a large saucepan and fry the onions and garlic until golden. Stir in the curry paste and fry, stirring, for a few minutes to develop the flavours. Stir in the tomato purée. Mix the coconut cream with the boiling water and add to the pan with the lime juice and sugar. Bring to the boil and cook for about 20 minutes to reduce and concentrate the flavours.

2 Add the carrot, new potatoes and sweet potato and stir well. Bring to the boil, then reduce the heat and simmer for 25 minutes until the vegetables are almost tender.

3 Add the beans and cauliflower (if using), cover and cook over a low heat for 10–20 minutes until the vegetables are almost tender. Add the broccoli (if using) and cook for 4–5 minutes. Taste, season with salt as necessary and stir in the chopped coriander. Serve immediately, garnished with coriander sprigs.

Serves 6

4 tablespoons vegetable oil

2 large onions, finely chopped

6 garlic cloves, finely chopped

4 tablespoons mild curry paste

½ teaspoon double concentrate tomato purée

2 x 200 ml (7 fl oz) cartons coconut cream

450 ml (¾ pint) boiling water

2 tablespoons lime juice

1 tablespoon brown sugar

250 g (8 oz) carrot, cut into 2.5 x 2 cm (1 x ¾ inch) chunks

250 g (8 oz) small new potatoes, halved lengthways

250 g (8 oz) sweet potato, cut into 1 cm (½ inch) cubes

250 g (8 oz) green beans, trimmed and halved

250 g (8 oz) cauliflower or broccoli, cut into florets

2 tablespoons finely chopped coriander

salt

coriander sprigs, to garnish

fricassée of mushrooms

This simple stew of wild and cultivated mushrooms in its rich garlic and herb sauce is one of the countryside's great gifts to the enthusiastic cook. Any edible mushrooms can be used, but my favourite combination is chanterelles, ceps, trompettes des morts, puff-balls and a few field or button mushrooms. It is a quick and easy dish to prepare and has many different uses. In late summer and early autumn I've served it perched on a croûte of fried potato bread and topped with a fried egg. I've also enjoyed it as a light lunch or supper dish piled on crostini, bruschetta or fingers of toast. For a cocktail savoury, I chop the mushrooms more finely, pile them into miniature pastry cases and serve them hot or cold with drinks. In this recipe, I suggest serving the fricassée with grilled polenta cakes for a substantial main course. For a first course to serve six, allow 2 polenta triangles per person.

125 g (4 oz) unsalted butter
1 large onion, finely chopped
2 garlic cloves, finely chopped
1 kg (2 lb) mixed mushrooms, brushed, cleaned and sliced if large
2 tablespoons finely chopped parsley
175 ml (6 fl oz) red wine
1 egg yolk
1 teaspoon arrowroot
4 tablespoons double cream
2 tablespoons finely snipped chives
salt and pepper

To Serve:
Polenta Cakes (page 250)
125 g (4 oz) rocket leaves

1 Melt the butter in a very large frying pan and fry the onion and garlic until soft but not coloured. Add the mushrooms and cover with a lid or sheet of foil. Cook over a gentle heat for about 10 minutes to draw out their juices – at this stage the mushrooms should stew rather than fry.

2 Add the parsley and red wine to the mushrooms. Bring to the boil, then cook gently over a low heat for a few minutes. Blend the egg yolk with the arrowroot and cream and use to thicken the wine and mushroom juices. Stir in the chives and season with salt and pepper.

3 Arrange the mushroom fricassée on warmed plates with 3 polenta triangles to accompany each serving. Garnish with rocket leaves and serve immediately.

Serves 4

hot spiced stew with
potatoes & cauliflower

Stews made with vegetables can be light and subtle or richly spiced and substantial. The possibilities are endless. In this simple but flavoursome stew, potatoes, cauliflower, lentils and spices are combined to produce a colourful and tasty main course.

1 Rinse the lentils or split peas under cold running water, drain and put into a large saucepan with half of the stock. Bring to the boil, then reduce the heat and simmer for 30 minutes until the lentils or split peas are soft and all the liquid has been absorbed.

2 While the lentils or split peas are cooking, prepare and cook the vegetables. Heat the oil in a large saucepan, add the onions and fry over a low heat for about 8 minutes, stirring frequently. Add the potatoes and cauliflower to the pan with the garlic and cook for 1 minute. Stir in the turmeric, mustard and fennel seeds and the chopped chillies, turning and tossing them in the pan. Add the remaining stock and the soaked saffron and bring to the boil. Reduce the heat and cook gently for 10–15 minutes until the vegetables are almost cooked.

3 When the lentils or split peas are cooked, mash them with a potato masher to form a thick purée, leaving a few whole through the mixture. Add the coconut cream and stir well to mix. Add this thick purée to the vegetables and stir well to combine. This will make the stew rich and thick. Season with salt and pepper and cook gently until the vegetables are completely tender and the flavours combined. Stir in the coriander and serve immediately.

Serves 6

375 g (12 oz) whole lentils or split yellow peas, rinsed and soaked in water to cover for 15 minutes

1.8 litres (3 pints) vegetable stock

3 tablespoons vegetable oil

2 large onions, cut into wedges

1–1.25 kg (2–2½ lb) potatoes, cut into chunks

1 cauliflower, cut into florets and stalks removed

3–4 garlic cloves, crushed

2 teaspoons turmeric

2 tablespoons black mustard seeds

1–2 tablespoons fennel seeds

1–2 small fresh green chillies, deseeded and chopped

1 teaspoon saffron threads, soaked in 2 tablespoons warm water

1 x 125 g (4 oz) carton coconut cream

2 tablespoons chopped coriander

salt and pepper

Mediterranean lamb stew
with tomatoes, olives & pasta

In this recipe I have used leg of lamb because of its sweet taste and the fact that it isn't too fatty. The cubed lamb is simmered in a rich broth of onions, garlic, tomatoes and herbs until all the flavours have blended and the meat is meltingly tender. Luscious black olives and freshly cooked pasta are stirred in before serving to create a perfect one-dish meal. Serve with salad and garlic bread or pieces of grilled polenta (page 250).

1 Put the lamb into a non-metallic bowl and cover with the wine. Leave to marinate at room temperature for about 1 hour.

2 Heat 2 tablespoons of the oil in a large frying pan and fry the onions and garlic in batches until beginning to brown. Transfer to a casserole and add the chopped chilli.

3 Remove the meat from the marinade, reserving the marinade, and drain on kitchen paper. Fry in the remaining hot oil until browned all over, in batches if necessary. Transfer to the casserole using a slotted spoon.

4 Add the tomatoes, tomato purée, lamb stock and wine marinade. Tuck the bouquet garni down the side, stir in the olives and bring the mixture to the boil. Reduce the heat, cover closely with greaseproof paper and a lid and simmer very gently on top of the stove or in a preheated oven, 150°C (300°F), Gas Mark 2, for ¾–1 hour until the meat is almost tender. Keep checking after 30 minutes; overcooked meat will be tough and stringy.

5 While the lamb is cooking, make beurre manié to thicken the stew by kneading the butter and flour together to form a paste. Cook the pasta in a large pan of boiling salted water for 7 minutes or according to the packet instructions. Drain and refresh in cold water until completely cold.

6 When the stew is cooked, remove the bouquet garni, season well with salt and pepper and thicken with the beurre manié. Do this by stirring little pieces into the hot stew until you feel it is the correct consistency. Add the pasta and cook for a few minutes to heat through. Serve in warmed large soup plates, sprinkled with the herbs and Parmesan.

Serves 6

1 kg (2 lb) leg of lamb, trimmed and cut into 4 cm (1½ inch) pieces
400 ml (14 fl oz) dry white wine
4–6 tablespoons extra virgin olive oil
2 large onions, sliced
2 garlic cloves, chopped
1 red chilli, deseeded and chopped
2 x 400 g (13 oz) cans chopped tomatoes
2 tablespoons double concentrate tomato purée
150 ml (¼ pint) rich lamb stock
1 bouquet garni (2 bay leaves tied together with 2 parsley stalks, 1 sprig each thyme and rosemary and 1 piece of celery stick)
175 g (6 oz) black olives
2–3 tablespoons softened butter
2–3 tablespoons plain flour
175 g (6 oz) dried cavatellucci, garganelli, romagnoli or other small pasta shapes
salt and pepper

To Garnish:
2 tablespoons finely chopped flat leaf parsley
2 tablespoons finely chopped mint
50 g (2 oz) Parmesan cheese, freshly grated

vegetable stew
with mustard & herb dumplings

A spicy and versatile stew finished with light-as-air dumplings. Any seasonal vegetables can be used in any combination — in addition to the ones I have used here, parsnips and courgettes are particularly delicious. A perfect dish for an autumn day.

2 tablespoons olive or sunflower oil

I large onion, sliced

2 large carrots, cut into 2.5 cm (I inch) chunks

3–4 celery sticks, cut into 2.5 cm (I inch) chunks

175 g (6 oz) turnip, cut into 2.5 cm (I inch) chunks

500 g (I lb) potatoes, cut into 2.5 cm (I inch) chunks

I x 400 g (13 oz) can plum tomatoes

750 ml (1¼ pints) vegetable stock

2 tablespoon tomato purée

I tablespoon paprika

4 tablespoons chopped parsley

salt and pepper

Dumplings:

125 g (4 oz) self-raising flour

50 g (2 oz) butter

2 tablespoons finely chopped parsley

I teaspoon chopped thyme or marjoram

I tablespoon dry English mustard

I small egg, beaten

1 Heat the oil in a large saucepan and fry the onion until soft but not coloured. Add the carrots, celery, turnip and potatoes and stir well to combine. Cover closely with greaseproof paper or foil and cook very gently over a low heat for about 5 minutes to draw out the flavour of the vegetables.

2 Add the tomatoes, stock, tomato purée, paprika and half of the parsley and season with salt and pepper. Bring to the boil, then reduce the heat, cover and simmer gently for 15–20 minutes.

3 Meanwhile, prepare the dumplings. Put the flour into a large bowl, cut the butter into small pieces and rub into the flour using your fingertips until the mixture resembles fine breadcrumbs. Stir in the herbs, mustard and season with salt and pepper. Make a well in the centre, add the beaten egg and enough water to form a sticky dough.

4 Using a wet spoon, drop 8 tablespoons of the dough on to the simmering stew. Cover and cook for 20–30 minutes until the vegetables are tender and the dumplings light and fluffy. Sprinkle the remaining parsley over the stew and serve immediately.

Serves 4

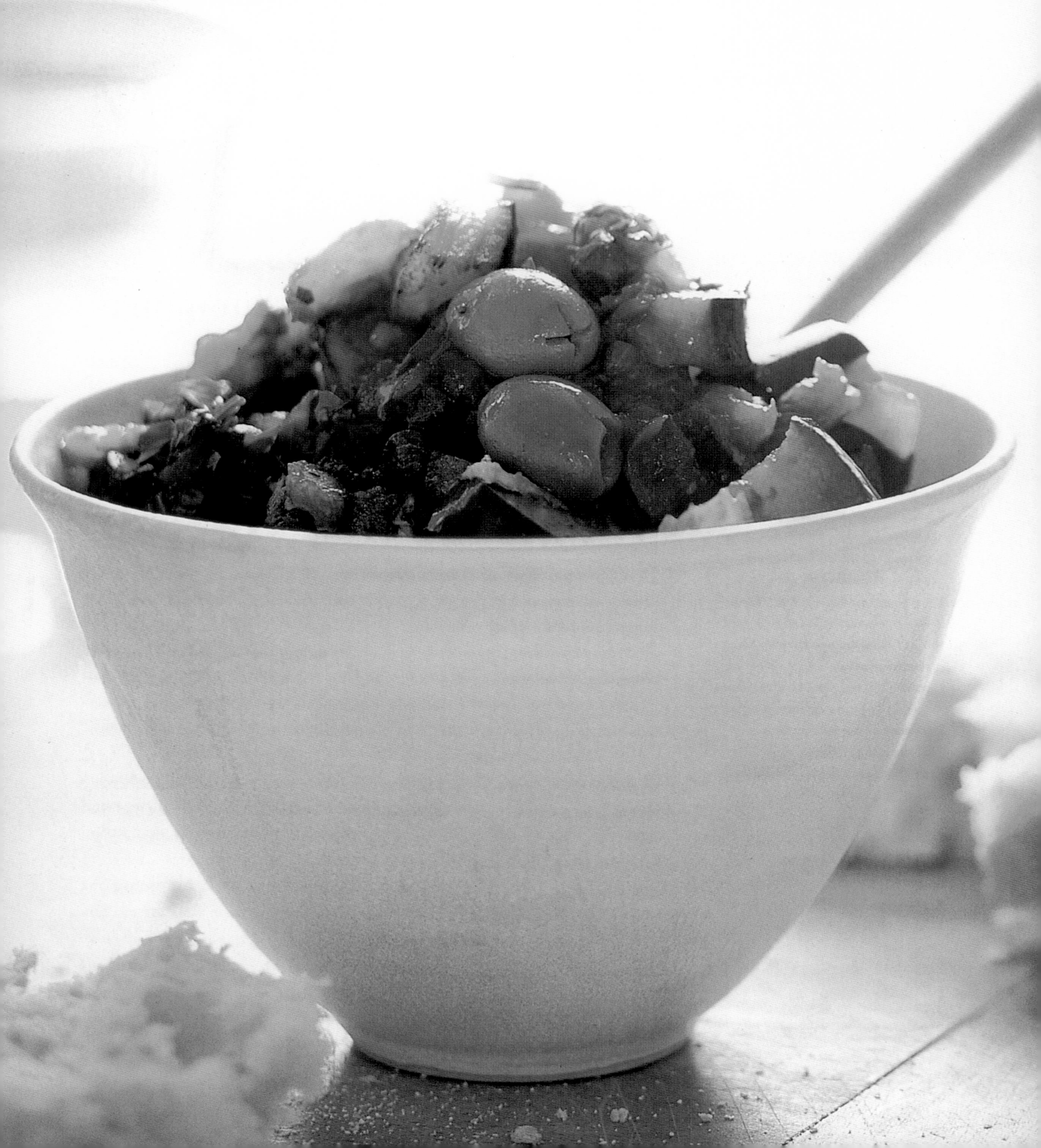

caponata

300 ml (½ pint) sunflower oil

3 large aubergines, cut into 2 cm
  (¾ inch) cubes

6 celery sticks, thinly sliced

2–3 tablespoons finely chopped flat
  leaf parsley

Tomato Sauce:

2 tablespoons extra virgin olive oil

I large onion, finely chopped

I x 400 g (13 oz) can chopped plum
  tomatoes

125 ml (4 fl oz) red wine vinegar

2 tablespoons brown sugar

50 g (2 oz) pitted green olives

3 tablespoons salted or pickled
  capers, drained and rinsed

salt and pepper

This sweet and sour vegetable stew comes from Sicily. Serve it at room temperature with plenty of good country bread and a selection of cold meats, such as salami and ham, or fish. It is also good as a relish with grilled and barbecued meats, and makes a tasty topping for bruschetta and crostini.

1 First make the sauce. Heat the oil in a large saucepan and fry the onion over a gentle heat until soft and rich golden brown. Add the tomatoes and vinegar and bubble for a few minutes to drive off the excess liquid. Stir in the sugar, olives and capers, then simmer gently for about 20 minutes to form a thick, pulpy mixture.

2 Meanwhile, heat half of the sunflower oil in a large frying pan and fry the aubergines in batches over a high heat until golden brown on all sides, adding more oil when necessary. Remove with a slotted spoon and drain on kitchen paper. Fry the celery in the remaining oil until golden brown and drain on kitchen paper.

3 Season the sauce with salt and pepper, adding extra sugar if necessary to give a distinctive sweet and sour taste, then add the aubergines and celery and cook gently for 5–10 minutes. Transfer to a bowl, leave to cool, then cover and refrigerate until required.

4 To serve, bring the caponata to room temperature and sprinkle with chopped parsley. If you plan to store the caponata for several days, float a thin film of olive oil over the top and cover the bowl with clingfilm or a lid.

Serves 6–8

ratatouille

This is my version of the pungent vegetable stew of Provence, one of the great dishes of the Mediterranean. In the recipe I have roasted the vegetables in the oven before combining them with a stew of tomatoes and herbs. This ensures they keep their texture while at the same time creating a mixture which is rich and thick. Ratatouille can be served hot or cold with crusty bread; as an accompaniment to grilled or roast meats; as a light first course or snack with eggs; in omelettes and as part of a scrambled egg mixture. It can also be used as a filling for other vegetables like courgettes and aubergines or pastry tarts. When cold, it makes a delicious salad.

1 Heat half of the oil in a roasting tin in a preheated oven, 220°C (425°F), Gas Mark 7. Add the aubergines, courgettes and peppers, toss in the hot oil, return to the oven and roast until tender, about 30 minutes.

2 While the vegetables are cooking, heat the rest of the oil in a deep saucepan and fry the onions and garlic until soft but not coloured. Add the tomato purée, plum tomatoes, basil, marjoram or oregano, thyme and paprika and season with salt and pepper. Stir to combine and cook for 10–15 minutes until the mixture is thick and syrupy.

3 Using a slotted spoon, transfer the vegetables from the roasting tin to the tomato mixture. Gently stir to combine, then add the parsley and taste for seasoning. Serve hot or cold.

Serves 8–9

125 ml (4 fl oz) olive oil

2 large aubergines, quartered
lengthways and cut into 1 cm
(½ inch) slices

2 courgettes, cut into 1 cm (½ inch)
slices

2 large red peppers, cored, deseeded
and cut into squares

1 large yellow pepper, cored,
deseeded and cut into squares

2 large onions, thinly sliced

3 large garlic cloves, crushed

1 tablespoon double concentrate
tomato purée

1 x 400 g (13 oz) can plum tomatoes

12 basil leaves, chopped

1 tablespoon finely chopped
marjoram or oregano

1 teaspoon finely chopped thyme

1 tablespoon paprika

2–4 tablespoons finely chopped
parsley

salt and pepper

beef & carrot tzimmes
with thimble dumplings

This robust and hearty stew was inspired by the wonderful rich melting sweetness that fresh new carrots have when they are combined with syrup, a Jewish cookery technique. The syrup accentuates the flavour of the carrots and creates a partnership which, although sweet, is neither sickly nor cloying. In this recipe I have used equal quantities of beef and carrots; for a vegetarian alternative, substitute the meat with 750 g (1½ lb) sturdy vegetables such as parsnips, turnip, celeriac, celery or potatoes.

1 Heat the oil in a large frying pan. Add the meat a little at a time and fry to seal in the meat juices and brown the meat well on all sides. Do not add all the meat to the pan at once or the temperature of the oil will be reduced and the meat will not brown. Using a draining spoon, transfer the meat to a large saucepan or flameproof casserole.

2 Fry the onion until beginning to colour, drain and add to the meat. Stir in the flour. Blend the syrup with a little of the warmed stock, then add to the pan with the rest of the stock, the carrots, bay leaf and seasoning. Stir to combine and bring to the boil. Cover, reduce the heat and simmer gently for 1–1½ hours until the meat is almost tender.

3 Meanwhile, make the thimble dumplings. Rub the butter into the flour until the mixture resembles fine breadcrumbs. Stir in the parsley and thyme and season with salt and pepper. Make a well in the centre, beat the egg and 2 tablespoons water together and pour into the well. Mix to a sticky dough, adding a little extra water if necessary.

4 About 20–30 minutes before the end of the cooking time for the stew, drop small teaspoonfuls of the dough on to the simmering stew. Cover and cook until the dumplings are risen, light and fluffy and the meat and vegetables are tender. Sprinkle with parsley and serve.

Serves 4

2–3 tablespoons sunflower oil
750 g (1½ lb) braising or stewing beef, such as chuck steak, topside or thick plate, cut into 2.5 cm (1 inch) slices
1 large onion, chopped
2 tablespoons plain flour
1–2 tablespoons golden syrup
750 ml (1¼ pints) beef stock
750 g (1½ lb) carrots, cut into 2.5 cm (1 inch) chunks
1 bay leaf
salt and pepper
2 tablespoons finely chopped parsley, to garnish

Thimble Dumplings:
50 g (2 oz) butter
125 g (4 oz) self-raising flour
2 tablespoons finely chopped parsley
pinch of fresh thyme
1 small egg
2–3 tablespoons cold water

pumpkin & root vegetable stew

This rich stew is substantial and filling. Serve it with some Cheesy Leek & Herb Scones (page 240), or with crusty bread or garlic mashed potatoes for a main course or supper dish. It will keep for 2–3 days in the refrigerator and actually improves with time, like most stews. Any leftovers can be turned into a gratin with the addition of thick cream and a topping of browned breadcrumbs and grated cheese.

1 Cut the pumpkin or squash in half across its widest part and remove and discard the seeds and stringy flesh. Cut into sections like a melon, then into cubes, removing the skin. You should have about 1 kg (2 lb) flesh. Take care when cutting the skin because it is very tough and the knife can easily slip.

2 Heat the oil in a large saucepan or flameproof casserole and fry the onion, garlic and chilli until soft but not coloured. Add the pumpkin and celery and fry gently for 10 minutes. Stir in the carrots, parsnip, tomatoes, tomato purée, paprika, stock and bouquet garni. Bring to the boil, then reduce the heat, cover and simmer for 1–1½ hours until the vegetables are almost tender.

3 Add the beans and cook for 10 minutes. Season with salt and pepper and sprinkle with the chopped parsley before serving.

Serves 8–10

1.5 kg (3 lb) pumpkin or squash

3 tablespoons sunflower or olive oil

1 large onion, finely chopped

3–4 garlic cloves, crushed

1 small red chilli, deseeded and chopped

4 celery sticks, cut into 2.5 cm (1 inch) lengths

300 g (10 oz) carrots, cut into 2.5 cm (1 inch) chunks

150 g (5 oz) parsnip, cut into 2.5 cm (1 inch) chunks

2 x 400 g (13 oz) cans plum tomatoes

2 tablespoons tomato purée

1 tablespoon hot paprika

150–300 ml (¼–½ pint) light vegetable stock

1 bouquet garni

2 x 400 g (13 oz) cans red kidney beans, drained

salt and pepper

3–4 tablespoons finely chopped parsley, to garnish

stir-fries,
pan-fries
& grills

peppered tuna steaks
with fennel, red onions & sugar snaps

4 tablespoons black peppercorns

1 teaspoon salt

4 trimmed tuna steaks, each
  weighing 125–150 g (4–5 oz), cut
  from the middle section of the fish

1 tablespoon olive oil

50 ml (2 fl oz) cognac

150 ml (¼ pint) concentrated fish or
  chicken stock

juice of 1 small lemon

50 g (2 oz) unsalted butter, cut into
  small dice

150 ml (¼ pint) double cream

2 tablespoons finely chopped parsley

4 flat leaf parsley sprigs, to garnish

Vegetables:

2 fennel bulbs

2 red onions

125 g (4 oz) sugar snap peas or
  mangetouts

4 potatoes

2 tablespoons olive oil

25 g (1 oz) unsalted butter

1 First prepare the vegetables. Remove the feathery fronds from the fennel bulbs, chop finely and reserve. Trim the root ends off the fennel and discard. Cut the fennel in half lengthways and cut into 5 mm (¼ inch) thick slices. Cut the onions into rings. Top and tail the sugar snaps or mangetouts and cut in half lengthways on the diagonal. Peel the potatoes.

2 Heat the oil and butter in a large pan, fry the fennel gently for 5 minutes, then add the onions. Cook over a moderate heat until the fennel and onions are tender, then increase the heat to colour slightly. Remove from the heat and keep warm. Boil the potatoes until just tender.

3 Meanwhile, coarsely crush the peppercorns with a pestle or the end of a rolling pin. Mix with the salt. Brush the tuna with the olive oil and press in the pepper mixture to coat them. Heat a large frying pan over a moderate heat. Set the steaks in the dry pan and fry for 2 minutes on one side, then turn and fry for 1 minute on the second side.

4 Add the sugar snaps or mangetouts to the fennel and onion mixture along with the fennel fronds and toss over a high heat until hot. Drain the potatoes, cut each one into 4–5 slices and keep warm. Transfer the tuna to a warmed dish and keep warm.

5 Turn the heat up under the frying pan. Add any remaining cracked pepper, pour on the cognac and a little of the stock and stir to scrape up the sediment and any fish juices. Let the mixture bubble fiercely for a few seconds, then add the rest of the stock and the lemon juice and boil rapidly until syrupy.

6 Remove the frying pan from the heat and gradually add the butter pieces, stirring to combine them with the sauce and thicken it. Add the cream, still stirring to mix well. Bring to the boil for a few seconds, add the chopped parsley and reduce the heat. Keep warm while serving the fish.

7 Divide the vegetables between 4 warm plates, arranging them in a mound in the centre. Set a tuna steak on top of this and pour a little of the peppered sauce on top of each steak and around the edge of the vegetables. Garnish each with a sprig of flat leaf parsley and serve immediately.

Serves 4

Peppered Tuna Steaks are shown on the preceding page

sweetcorn & tofu
burgers with spiked yogurt sauce

Tofu, or bean curd as it is also known, is one of the mainstays of oriental vegetarian cuisine because of its high nutritional value. It is an important source of protein, contains very little saturated fat and no cholesterol. It also provides a supply of calcium which compares well to dairy milk and contains B vitamins, niacin, phosphorus, sodium and iron. These tofu burgers can be made with finely chopped roasted red pepper added to the mixture along with 1 teaspoon sweet chilli sauce. They are also good served with a rich tomato or tomato and pepper sauce instead of the yogurt sauce. Formed into tiny rounds, they make an excellent hot or cold cocktail savoury.

1 Heat 2 tablespoons oil and fry the onion and garlic until soft but not coloured. Put the tofu in a bowl and mash with a fork. Stir in the onion and garlic. Add the sweetcorn, 300 g (10 oz) of the breadcrumbs, the parsley and basil. Mix the yeast extract with the soy sauce and beaten egg and add to the other ingredients. Stir to combine and season to taste.

2 Divide the mixture into 8 equal pieces. Shape into patties, toss in the remaining breadcrumbs and fry gently in a little hot oil until golden brown. They will take about 5–8 minutes on each side.

3 Meanwhile, make the sauce. Heat the oil and fry the garlic, mustard seeds and ginger for 3–4 minutes until colouring. Set aside to cool. Put the yogurt into a bowl, add the garlic mixture and season with salt and pepper. Stir to combine. Dust with the cayenne pepper, cover and chill.

4 Drain the cooked burgers on kitchen paper. Serve hot, with the yogurt sauce and a mixed leaf salad.

Serves 4–6

sunflower oil, for frying
175 g (6 oz) onion, finely chopped
1 garlic clove, crushed
1 x 310 g (10½ oz) carton firm tofu, drained
1 x 200 g (7 oz) can sweetcorn, drained
375 g (12 oz) wholemeal breadcrumbs
3 tablespoons finely chopped parsley
1 teaspoon finely chopped basil
1 tablespoon yeast extract
1 tablespoon soy sauce
1 small egg, beaten
salt and pepper

Spiked Yogurt Sauce:
1 tablespoon sunflower oil
1 garlic clove, finely chopped
1 tablespoon black mustard seeds
1 teaspoon grated fresh root ginger
250 ml (8 fl oz) thick plain yogurt
pinch of cayenne pepper

sweetcorn & red pepper frittata

Frittata is Italy's version of the omelette: flat, round, completely set through although still moist, and generally about two fingers thick. It is perfect served warm as a light lunch or supper dish with salad, or as part of a composed salad plate or a cocktail savoury. It is also good served cold, and is ideal for picnics because it travels so well.

1 Heat the oil and fry the onion, garlic and celery until soft but not coloured. Stir in the red pepper and continue to cook until soft and beginning to colour. Set aside to cool.

2 Break the eggs into a bowl and mix with the milk until just blended, using a fork. Transfer the cooked vegetables to the eggs with a slotted spoon, leaving behind any excess oil. Stir in the sweetcorn, parsley, breadcrumbs and half of the Parmesan. Season well.

3 Put the butter into a 15 cm (6 inch) omelette pan and heat until foaming but not brown. Pour the frittata mixture into the pan, stirring with a fork while pouring to disperse the vegetables. The pan will be almost full. Stop stirring, turn the heat down to very low and cook for about 5–10 minutes. The eggs should be set with only the top surface runny.

4 Sprinkle the remaining Parmesan on top of the frittata and slide the pan under a preheated grill for about 1 minute, just long enough to set the top and colour the cheese slightly. Leave to rest for a few minutes before sliding out on to a board or plate and cutting into wedges, fingers or cubes. Serve garnished with rocket leaves.

Serves 4 as a main course, 8 as a light snack

Makes 80 x 2 cm (¾ inch) cubes as a cocktail savoury

2–3 tablespoons light olive oil

1 onion, finely chopped

2 garlic cloves, crushed

1 celery stick, finely chopped

1 red pepper, cored, deseeded and finely diced

5 large eggs

2 tablespoons milk

1 x 200 g (7 oz) can sweetcorn, drained

3 tablespoons finely chopped parsley

2–3 tablespoons fine white fresh breadcrumbs

4 tablespoons grated Parmesan cheese

25 g (1 oz) unsalted butter

salt and pepper

rocket leaves, to garnish

wild mushroom omelette

This recipe uses one of my favourite autumn mushrooms, chanterelles. You can of course use any variety of mushrooms. If using dried mushrooms, soak them for about 30 minutes before draining, chopping and frying.

1 First prepare the filling. In a small pan (not the omelette pan), melt two-thirds of the butter and fry the mushrooms until soft and slightly coloured but still holding their shape. Stir in the herbs, flour and cream, season with salt and pepper and cook for a few minutes. Remove from the heat and keep warm.

2 Break the eggs into a shallow dish (a soup plate is ideal). Add salt, pepper and half of the remaining butter. Beat the eggs lightly with a fork, just enough to combine. Warm a 20 cm (8 inch) omelette pan, then put in the remaining butter. When it begins to foam and just before it starts to brown, pour in the eggs. Quickly stir the contents of the pan 2–3 times with the flat of the fork so that as much of the mixture as possible is exposed to the heat.

3 When the underside of the omelette has begun to set, pull the edge of the omelette into the centre with the fork and tilt the pan at the same time so that the liquid egg can flow towards the hot surface and set. The omelette is cooked when the underside is set but the top is still soft and slightly runny.

4 Spread the filling over the omelette, folding the nearest edge of the omelette into the centre using a fork or palette knife. Tilt the pan away from you, slip the fork under the fold and tip the omelette over again, rolling it towards the edge of the pan. Pull the last remaining bit of omelette from the far edge of the pan over the folded section and press down gently to seal. Keep the tilted pan over the heat for a few seconds to brown the bottom of the omelette slightly.

5 Tip the pan against the plate, holding it in such a way that it rolls golden-side uppermost on to the plate. Draw a small piece of butter over the surface of the omelette to give it a sheen, then serve immediately.

Serves 1

40 g (1½ oz) unsalted butter, cut into small cubes
50 g (2 oz) mushrooms, brushed or wiped, trimmed and finely sliced
1 teaspoon finely chopped herbs (parsley, chives, chervil)
pinch of plain flour
1–2 tablespoons double cream
3 large eggs
salt and pepper

alternative omelette fillings

Aubergine or Courgette Cut into matchstick pieces about 4 cm (1½ inches) long and fry in hot oil for 3–4 minutes. Drain and scatter over the omelette in the pan.

Avocado Finely dice avocado flesh and scatter over the omelette in the pan.

Grilled Sweet Red Pepper Finely shred grilled red pepper and add to the omelette in the pan.

Mixed Herbs Add 1 tablespoon finely chopped mixed herbs (equal quantities of flat leaf parsley, chervil and chives with a pinch of tarragon) to the beaten eggs. Or add shredded basil leaves and a little marjoram to the beaten eggs.

Ratatouille Heat 4–6 tablespoons of prepared Ratatouille (page 162) and spread over the omelette in the pan.

Shallots or Garlic Cook finely sliced shallots or garlic in oil and scatter over the omelette in the pan.

Sorrel or Watercress Finely shred a handful of tender young sorrel leaves and add to the omelette in the pan to give a wonderful sharp, sour taste. Watercress leaves used in the same way give a peppery bite.

Tomato Toss peeled, deseeded and diced tomato in a little butter, season and strew across the omelette in the pan.

stir-fried duck
with ginger & vegetables

Because duck breast, like chicken breast, is so tender, it requires very little cooking and lends itself particularly well to stir-frying. I devised this recipe for my friends Lilla and Ronnie Steel of Silver Hill Duckling in Monaghan, Ireland. It goes well with boiled rice, egg fried rice or noodles.

1 Cut the duck into finger-thick strips. Halve the peppers lengthways and remove the seeds and pith. Cut into strips about 4 cm (1½ inches) long and 3 mm (⅛ inch) thick. Peel and cut the carrot to a similar size and shape. Peel the ginger and cut into very thin pieces. Trim the spring onions and cut into 4 cm (1½ inch) lengths.

2 Combine all the ingredients for the sauce in a large measuring jug.

3 Heat the oil in a wok or large frying pan and stir-fry the duck quickly until just beginning to colour. This should take about 3 minutes. Add all of the vegetables and continue to stir-fry for a further few minutes, tossing everything together in the pan.

4 Stir the sauce to make sure it is well blended, then pour into the pan. Bring to the boil and cook for a few minutes, stirring all the time to combine the flavours while the sauce is cooking and thickening. Serve immediately.

Serves 4

2 boneless, skinless duck breasts, total weight about 500 g (1 lb)
2 peppers (1 red, 1 green)
1 large carrot
1 cm (½ inch) piece of fresh root ginger
8 spring onions
2 tablespoons sunflower oil
125 g (4 oz) bean sprouts

Sauce:
2 garlic cloves, crushed
2 tablespoons cornflour
1 tablespoon Szechuan seasoning
2 tablespoons dark soft brown sugar
1 teaspoon ground ginger
4 tablespoons soy sauce
2 tablespoons sherry
600 ml (1 pint) chicken, duck or vegetable stock

red lentil burgers
spiked with chillies and garlic

Among the vegetable cook's great resources are pulses, lentils in particular. They are inexpensive, versatile and nutritious, rich in protein, carbohydrates, vitamins and iron. Unlike beans, they don't require long soaking and cooking, and bright orange, red or yellow lentils, either whole or split, can be quickly cooked to a thick purée which forms the basis of many dishes. Because they are without a strong taste of their own, they combine perfectly with rich powerful flavours. Serve these burgers with thick natural yogurt or Cucumber & Mint Raita (page 216) and a mixed leaf salad.

1 Wash the lentils and put them into a large saucepan of boiling water. Return to the boil, then reduce the heat to a simmer. Cook gently for 20–40 minutes until the lentils are pulpy, the liquid has evaporated and the mixture is dry in texture. Stir frequently during cooking to ensure that the lentils do not burn. Spread the cooked lentils on a baking sheet and set aside to cool.

2 Meanwhile, heat the sunflower oil and fry the onion, garlic, red pepper and chilli until soft but not coloured. Set aside to cool.

3 In a large bowl, combine the lentils, onion mixture, 150 g (5 oz) of the breadcrumbs, the Cheddar cheese, tomato purée, parsley and yeast extract. Stir well, season and add the beaten egg, then mix to combine.

4 Divide the mixture into 12 pieces. Dip them in the remaining breadcrumbs and make into burgers about 7 cm (3 inches) in diameter. Heat a little oil in a large frying pan and fry the burgers for about 5–6 minutes until very hot all the way through and brown on both sides. Drain on kitchen paper and serve hot.

Makes 12 burgers, enough to serve 6

275 g (9 oz) split red lentils
750 ml (1¼ pints) boiling water
3 tablespoons sunflower oil
1 large onion, finely chopped
2–3 garlic cloves, finely chopped
65 g (2½ oz) red pepper, deseeded
  and finely chopped
1–2 small red chillies, deseeded and
  finely chopped
250 g (8 oz) fresh white breadcrumbs
150 g (5 oz) mature Cheddar cheese,
  grated
1 tablespoon tomato purée
3 tablespoons finely chopped parsley
½ teaspoon yeast extract
1 small egg, beaten
vegetable oil, for frying
salt and pepper

Spanish potato omelette

This thick, juicy, fragrant omelette, known as tortilla *in Spain, is made from eggs, onions and potatoes. It is served hot (though more generally warm) or cold, as a first course, main course, light supper or snack, and is both delicious and satisfying. Cut into wedges, it is served on its own or accompanied by fried eggs, sausages, bacon or peppers.*

1 Heat the oil in a 20–23 cm (8–9 inch) heavy non-stick frying pan. Add the slices of potato one at a time, then alternate layers of potato with layers of onion slices. Cover the pan and cook the onion and potatoes over a low heat without colouring until the potatoes are tender, lifting and turning them occasionally. This will take about 30–45 minutes. At this stage the potatoes will remain separate; they will not have formed a 'cake'.

2 Beat the eggs with a fork in a large bowl until they are slightly foamy. Season with salt and pepper. Once the vegetables are soft and well cooked, lift them out of the pan with a slotted spoon and drain them in a colander. Reserve the oil for frying the tortilla. Add the potatoes and onions to the beaten eggs, pressing them well down so that they are completely immersed. If possible, leave to stand for about 15 minutes.

3 Wipe the pan clean, then heat about 2–3 tablespoons of the reserved oil. Add the egg mixture and quickly spread it out with a palette knife. Reduce the heat and cook very gently, shaking the pan occasionally to prevent it from sticking. When the potatoes begin to brown underneath and shrink slightly from the edge of the pan after about 15 minutes, remove the pan from the heat.

4 Turn the tortilla over by placing a flat plate, slightly larger than the pan, on top of it and quickly turn the tortilla upside down on to the plate. Don't worry if the omelette sticks slightly to the pan when you turn it over, just remove the pieces and press them back into the omelette.

5 Heat another tablespoon of oil in the pan, then slide the tortilla back to brown the other side. This will take another 3–4 minutes. Alternatively, instead of turning the tortilla, just slip the pan under a preheated moderate grill and cook until the surface is golden brown. The tortilla should be golden brown on the outside and moist and juicy inside. Transfer to a plate or board and serve hot or cold.

Serves 4–6 as a main course

150 ml (¼ pint) olive oil
4 large potatoes, cut into 3 mm
 (⅛ inch) slices
1 large onion, thinly sliced
4–5 large eggs
salt and pepper

salmon & courgette brochettes

These kebabs are shown on a bed of rocket with Lime & Sesame Dressing (page 231).
They are equally delicious served on mashed potatoes flavoured with olive oil, with the
salad served separately. They can also be made with fresh tuna or swordfish.

1 You will need 8 barbecue skewers. If they are wooden, put them to soak in cold water. Prepare the marinade by combining all the ingredients in a large bowl. Add the salmon and courgette pieces and toss to combine and coat. Cover and leave to marinate for about 30 minutes.

2 Thread the salmon and courgette pieces alternately on to the barbecue skewers and cook the kebabs under a preheated very hot grill or over a very hot barbecue for about 5 minutes, turning them frequently and brushing with the marinade to keep the fish and courgettes from drying out. The fish is cooked when it is just beginning to look milky. Take care not to overcook it or it will become dry and tough. Serve immediately on a bed of rocket, garnished with whole chives and lime wedges.

Serves 4

750 g–1 kg (1½–2 lb) salmon fillet, skinned and cut into 2.5 cm (1 inch) cubes
375 g (12 oz) courgettes, cut into 1 cm (½ inch) pieces

Marinade:
8 tablespoons sunflower oil
2 tablespoons light sesame seed oil
2 tablespoons sesame seeds
1 garlic clove, crushed
1–2 tablespoons lime juice
pepper

To Serve:
rocket
whole chives
lime wedges

vegetable brochettes
with mustard & herb glaze

These brochettes, a collection of seasonal mixed vegetables grilled over a wood or charcoal fire or under an electric or gas grill, are colourful and delicious at any time of the year. Choose vegetables with firm moist flesh that will cook quickly without disintegrating; and partially pre-cook resilient vegetables like potatoes, yams and onions. This will ensure that delicate items aren't cooked to a frazzled mush while others remain inedible. I generally allow 250 g (8 oz) mixed vegetables per person.

1 Plunge the pickling onions into boiling water and blanch for 2–3 minutes. Refresh under cold water, drain and peel. Cut the pepper in half lengthways, remove the seeds and cut the flesh into 2.5 cm (1 inch) squares or wedges. Slice aubergines into 5 mm (¼ inch) rounds or cut baby ones in half lengthways. Cut courgettes into 2 cm (¾ inch) rounds and blanch for 1 minute. Cut corn-on-the-cob into 1 cm (½ inch) rounds and cook in boiling water for 2–3 minutes. Refresh and drain. Trim fennel at the root to free the leaves and cut each bulb into 2.5 cm (1 inch) pieces.

2 Arrange the vegetables in bowls on a tray. If using wooden skewers, soak them in cold water. Place a mushroom or onion at the ends of each skewer to anchor the other vegetables, then thread an assortment on each one to make a colourful and attractive display. Put the prepared brochettes on the tray.

3 Combine all the ingredients for the glaze in a bowl. Brush this generously over the brochettes, turning them so they are well coated. Cover with clingfilm and refrigerate until required, along with the remaining glaze. These can be prepared several hours in advance.

4 Grill the brochettes under a preheated grill or over a barbecue, turning them every few minutes to expose all surfaces to the heat and brushing with extra marinade as required. When the vegetables are cooked, sizzling hot and nicely browned, serve immediately with skewers of grilled chilli-flavoured new potatoes, a choice of salads and grilled bread.

Serves 4

12 pickling onions
1 large red, green or yellow pepper
2 or 3 vegetables, such as aubergines, courgettes, corn-on-the-cob or fennel bulbs
24 button mushrooms, wiped

Mustard & Herb Glaze:
2 tablespoons Dijon mustard
2 tablespoons finely chopped mixed herbs (parsley, thyme, marjoram, basil)
2 garlic cloves, crushed
4 tablespoons red wine vinegar
½–1 teaspoon sweet chilli sauce
2 teaspoons clear honey
salt and pepper

mushroom
& tofu kebabs

This recipe was inspired by one of my favourite sauces, satay sauce, the rich and spicy nutty concoction from Indonesia that is traditionally served with strips of marinated chicken. If you want a more 'meaty' kebab, add cubes of chicken breast to the marinade along with the tofu and mushrooms. For a main course, serve with white basmati rice.

250 g (8 oz) firm tofu
36 even-sized, firm button
mushrooms

Marinade:
3 tablespoons sunflower oil
3 garlic cloves, crushed
3 teaspoons ground coriander
3 teaspoons ground cumin
4–6 tablespoons clear honey
3 tablespoons sweet chilli sauce
4 tablespoons tamari or soy sauce
8 tablespoons cold water
4 tablespoons lime juice

To Garnish:
coriander sprigs
Indonesian Peanut Dipping Sauce
(page 224)

1 First make the marinade. Heat the oil in a small saucepan and fry the garlic over a low heat until soft but not coloured. Stir in the dry spices and fry for a few minutes to develop the flavours. Remove from the heat and stir in the honey, chilli and tamari or soy sauces, water and lime juice. Bring to the boil and cook for a few minutes to blend the flavours, then remove from the heat and leave to cool.

2 Drain the tofu and cut it into 2 cm (¾ inch) cubes. Wipe the mushrooms and trim the stalks level with the caps if long. Set the tofu and mushrooms in a single layer in a large, shallow non-metallic dish. Soak twelve 20 cm (8 inch) fine bamboo skewers in cold water.

3 Pour the cool marinade over the tofu and mushrooms, cover and leave for about 1 hour to marinate.

4 Thread the tofu and mushrooms alternately on the soaked skewers. Place under a preheated grill or on a barbecue and brush all over with the marinade. Cook for 8–10 minutes, turning and basting frequently until browned.

5 Serve the kebabs hot, garnished with coriander sprigs. Hand the Indonesian Peanut Dipping Sauce separately.

Serves 4 as a main course, 6 as a first course

wilted greens
with water chestnuts & black bean sauce

Oriental cooking, with its quick stir-fry technique and imaginative flavour combinations, offers the perfect example of how leafy greens can be used to create interestingly textured dishes. In this recipe I have combined the delicate leaves of pak-choi with crisp broccoli, but any leafy green cabbage can be used. They are quickly stir-fried before being enriched with a black bean sauce, a hint of chilli and toasted sesame seeds – a delicious main course served with rice or noodles.

1 First prepare the sauce. Put the cornflour into a bowl, gradually add about 2 tablespoons of the stock and mix to a smooth paste. Stir in the rest of the ingredients and season to taste. Set aside until required.

2 Shred the pak-choi, but not too finely. Trim any woody stems from the broccoli and divide the head into florets each with a little stem.

3 Heat the sunflower and sesame oils in a large wok or pan, add the onion and garlic and stir-fry until soft but not coloured. Increase the heat, add the pak-choi, broccoli and water chestnuts and stir-fry over a high heat for about 3–5 minutes until the vegetables are almost tender. Add the bean sprouts. Stir the sauce and add to the pan, tossing the vegetables in it to coat thoroughly. Bring to the boil and cook for about 1 minute to thicken the sauce. Taste for seasoning, sprinkle with the toasted sesame seeds and serve immediately.

Serves 4

Black Bean Sauce:
1 tablespoon cornflour
300 ml (½ pint) vegetable stock
2–4 tablespoons soy sauce
2 tablespoons black bean sauce
2 teaspoons sweet chilli sauce
1 tablespoon clear honey
salt and pepper

Wilted Greens:
500 g (1 lb) pak-choi
250 g (8 oz) broccoli florets
3 tablespoons sunflower oil
1 tablespoon light sesame oil
1 onion, quartered and thinly sliced
3 garlic cloves, thinly sliced
1 x 250 g (8 oz) can water chestnuts, drained and sliced
50–75 g (2–3 oz) bean sprouts
2 tablespoons sesame seeds, toasted

stir-fried noodles with
broccoli, sweetcorn, bean sprouts & smoked tofu

In this recipe I have combined dried thread egg noodles and smoked tofu with crisp broccoli, sweetcorn and bean sprouts to create an interesting variety of flavour, texture and colour. Any crunchy vegetables, such as mangetouts, sugar snaps, water chestnuts or asparagus, could be used. All the preparation can be done in advance and the ingredients stored in the refrigerator for up to 8 hours until required. The cooking, like all stir-frying, only takes a few minutes. Serve with Pickled Cucumber (page 249).

1 Cook the noodles in a large pan of boiling water according to packet instructions until just tender. Drain and refresh under cold running water until very cold. Leave to drain.

2 Heat about 5 cm (2 inches) sunflower oil in a wok or heavy-based pan and fry the tofu cubes for 3–4 minutes until crisp and lightly golden. Drain on kitchen paper and keep warm.

3 Remove all but a few tablespoons of the oil from the wok and fry the onion, ginger, garlic and chilli until soft but not browned. Remove from the heat.

4 Blanch the broccoli in a large saucepan of boiling water for about 1 minute, drain and refresh under cold water until absolutely cold. Drain again and pat dry with kitchen paper.

5 Combine all the ingredients for the sauce in a bowl and mix well.

6 Return the wok or pan with the onion mixture to the heat. When reheated, add the broccoli and stir-fry for 2–3 minutes. Add the sweetcorn and bean sprouts and stir-fry for about 3 minutes, keeping the ingredients moving. Add the sauce, toss to combine, then add the noodles and the fried tofu. Cook for another 1 minute until everything is heated through.

Serves 4

175 g (6 oz) dried thread egg noodles
sunflower oil, for frying
250 g (8 oz) firm smoked tofu, cubed
1 onion, finely chopped
1 teaspoon grated fresh root ginger
2 garlic cloves, crushed
1 small red chilli, deseeded and finely
  sliced
250 g (8 oz) broccoli florets
175 g (6 oz) baby sweetcorn, cut in
  half lengthways
175 g (6 oz) fresh bean sprouts

Sauce:
250 ml (8 fl oz) teriyaki sauce
2 tablespoons sake (Japanese rice
  wine)
2 tablespoons lemon juice
2–3 teaspoons sweet chilli sauce
2 teaspoons brown sugar

crisp green vegetables
stir-fried with mushrooms in sweet & sour sauce

2 tablespoons sunflower oil

2 garlic cloves, crushed

I onion, thinly sliced

5 cm (2 inch) piece of fresh root
   ginger, peeled and thinly sliced

125 g (4 oz) mushrooms, sliced

I green pepper, cored, deseeded and
   cut into strips

125 g (4 oz) green beans, cut in half

125 g (4 oz) mangetouts or sugar
   snap peas, left whole, cut in half or
   into three diagonally

175 g (6 oz) broccoli, trimmed, cut
   into bite-sized florets and stalks
   peeled

125 g (4 oz) celery, cut into thin 4 cm
   (1½ inch) lengths

6 spring onions, cut into thin 4 cm
   (1½ inch) lengths

salt and pepper

Sweet & Sour Sauce:

I tablespoon cornflour

3 tablespoons soy sauce

2 tablespoons sweet chilli sauce

I teaspoon oyster sauce

2 tablespoons rice wine or sherry

4 tablespoons water

2 tablespoons sunflower oil

2 tablespoons dark soft brown sugar

Stir-frying is one of the best ways of cooking vegetables to retain their colour, crispness and much of their food value. This recipe is particularly versatile because any crisp vegetables can be used. Good vegetables to choose are firm ones such as celery, peppers, fennel, broccoli and cauliflower florets, leeks, mangetouts, sugar snaps, courgettes, green beans and spring onions. Serve with rice or noodles.

1 First combine all the ingredients for the sauce in a measuring jug or bowl. Set aside.

2 Heat a wok, then add the oil. When it is hot, add the garlic, onion and ginger and stir-fry until soft but not coloured. Add the mushrooms, tossing quickly. Add the remaining vegetables and stir-fry for a further few minutes until tender but still bright in colour and crisp.

3 Pour on the sauce, tossing and turning the ingredients in the wok. Season to taste and serve immediately.

Serves 4–6

grilled vegetables
with dipping sauce

The simple technique of grilling vegetables intensifies their succulence and flavour. As the flesh softens and the juices run, they caramelize, causing the skin to wrinkle and char and produce that incomparable depth of flavour. Grilled vegetables can also be served with salad leaves, drizzled with olive oil, seasoned with pepper and scattered with Parmesan shavings – this makes an excellent light lunch or first course.

1 Put the garlic and olive oil in a bowl and leave to infuse while preparing the vegetables.

2 Slice the onion across into rings, discarding the ends. Try to keep the rings together. Place on a large plastic or metal tray. Slice the small fennel bulb through its length into about 3 flat slices or leave mini fennel whole.

3 Cut the peppers in half lengthways and remove the seeds, white membranes and stalks. Cut in half again. Place the pepper wedges on the tray. Slice the aubergines in half lengthways through the stalk if mini or small; if large, slice thinly from stalk to tip. With the point of a sharp knife, lightly score the flesh of the aubergines in a criss-cross fashion. Set beside the peppers. Top and tail the courgettes and cut in half lengthways. Set on the tray.

4 Cut the chicory in half lengthways. Peel and remove the stalks from the mushrooms. Set on the tray. Brush each vegetable with the garlic-flavoured oil.

5 Cook the vegetables on a very hot barbecue or ridged grill pan, or on a preheated very hot heavy baking sheet under a preheated grill. Start with the vegetables which take longest, gradually adding the rest until they are all done – onions and fennel take 10–20 minutes, peppers, aubergines and courgettes 15 minutes, chicory and mushrooms 5 minutes. Turn the vegetables during cooking and raise or lower the grill pan as required. If using a ridged pan, press the vegetables against the hot surface with a palette knife. When ready, the vegetables should be *al dente*, coloured and blistering.

6 Arrange the vegetables on a large platter or individual plates and garnish with lemon and parsley. Offer extra virgin olive oil separately, or any other sauce of your choice such as Pesto (page 234) or Salsa Verde (page 211). Serve warm, with crusty bread.

Serves 4

4 garlic cloves, finely chopped

10–12 tablespoons extra virgin olive oil

1 large red onion, peeled

4 mini fennel bulbs, or 1 small fennel bulb

2 large peppers (1 red, 1 yellow)

4 mini aubergines, or 2 small aubergines

4 baby courgettes, or 2 small courgettes

1 head chicory

4 large field mushrooms

To Garnish:

1 large lemon, cut into wedges

flat leaf parsley sprigs

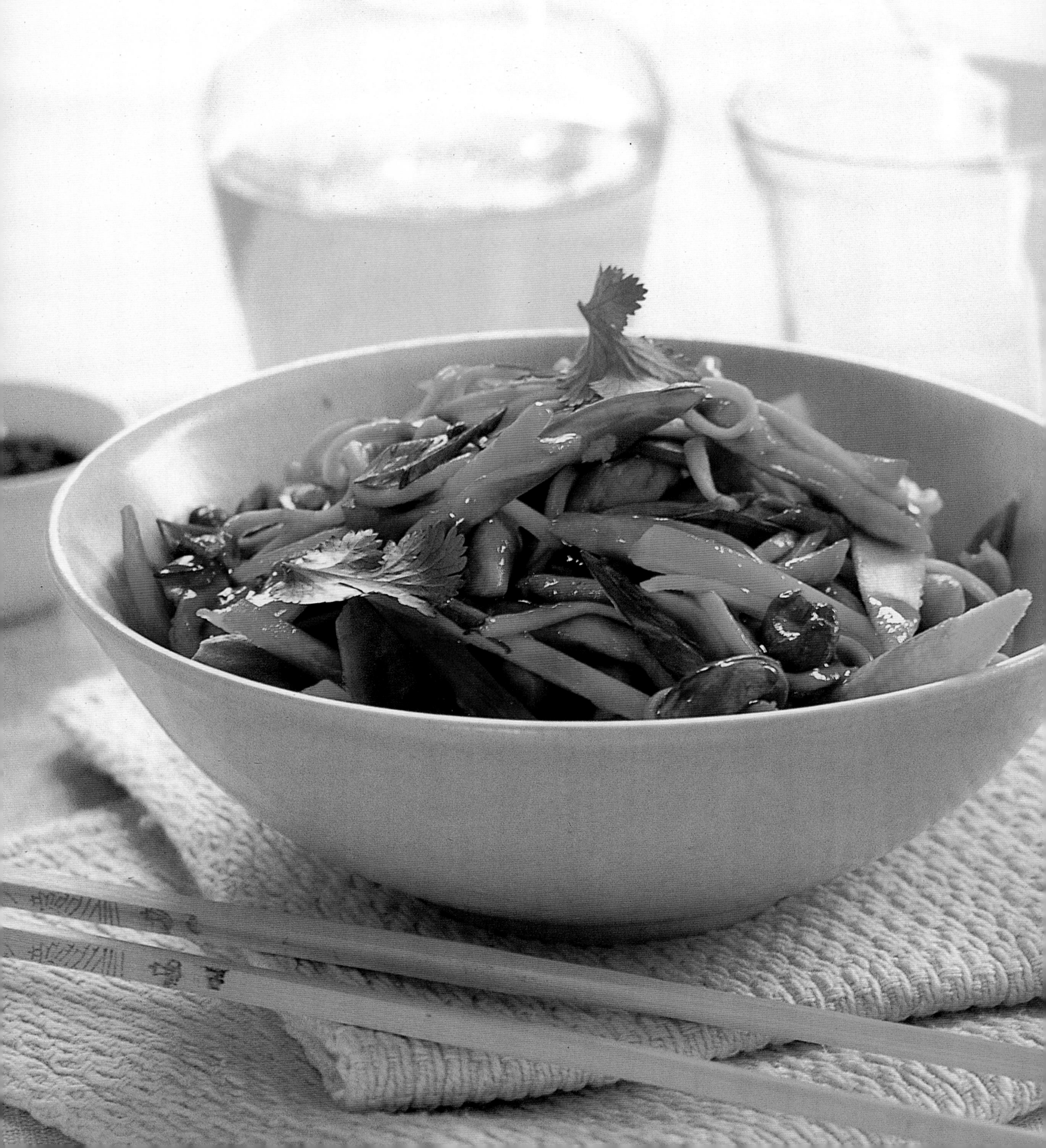

chicken with vegetables,
noodles & cashew nuts

Because the cooking time is so short, you need to have everything ready before you start cooking this dish. Pork or beef fillet or sirloin steak can be used instead of chicken.

1 First combine all the ingredients for the sauce in a jug, gradually adding the stock to make a smooth liquid.

2 Combine the sunflower and sesame oils, heat half in a wok or large frying pan and stir-fry the chicken strips until cooked. This will only take about 3 minutes. Remove from the pan. Add the remaining oil mixture and stir-fry the carrot for 1 minute, then add the peppers, mangetouts and sweetcorn, constantly tossing and frying over a high heat.

3 Stir the sauce to make sure it is well blended, then pour it into the pan. Bring to the boil and cook for a few minutes, stirring all the time. Add the noodles and chicken and cook for a further few minutes to heat thoroughly.

4 Pile a generous helping in the centre of 4 warmed plates and sprinkle over the cashew nuts, spring onions and a little of the sauce. Garnish with coriander and serve immediately.

Serves 4

50 ml (2 fl oz) sunflower oil

1 tablespoon light sesame seed oil

750 g (1½ lb) skinless, boneless chicken breasts, cut into thin strips

1 large carrot, cut into thin strips

2 large peppers (1 red, 1 yellow), cored, deseeded and cut into thin strips

175 g (6 oz) mangetouts

175 g (6 oz) baby sweetcorn

375 g (12 oz) medium egg noodles, cooked and drained

50–125 g (2–4 oz) cashew nuts, toasted

2 spring onions, thinly sliced

coriander leaves, to garnish

Sauce:

1½ tablespoons cornflour

3 garlic cloves, finely chopped

2 teaspoons finely grated fresh root ginger

3 tablespoons dark soft brown sugar

6 tablespoons tamari sauce

1 teaspoon Tabasco sauce

450 ml (¾ pint) chicken stock

roasts
& bakes

roast root vegetable tarte Tatin

This savoury version of the classic sweet tarte Tatin was inspired by the natural caramelization of roasted root vegetables and the simplicity of the crisp pastry lid – or rather base – on to which the meltingly tender vegetables cling. Try serving it with a mixed leaf salad and a piquant yogurt sauce.

1 Heat the oil in a large heavy roasting tin and add the carrots, turnips, parsnips, shallots and spices. Toss over a high heat until lightly coloured. Place in a preheated oven, 220°C (425°F), Gas Mark 7, for 20 minutes, then add the garlic cloves and roast for 10 minutes. Add the leeks and continue roasting for a further 10 minutes or until the vegetables are tender and a rich brown colour.

2 Meanwhile, cut the pastry into six 11 cm (4½ inch) circles. Cover and refrigerate until required.

3 Make the caramel. Melt the butter with the sugar, vinegar and water in a heavy frying pan. Bring to the boil, shaking the pan and stirring until the sugar dissolves, then let the mixture bubble until it turns a deep golden caramel. It will turn pink and frothy before it turns a rich gold. By this stage the liquid will have evaporated. Keep shaking the pan and drawing the spoon across the centre to disperse the heat. Quickly pour into the centre of six shallow 7 cm (3 inch) heavy pie tins, spreading it over their bases if you can. It may set immediately, but it will liquefy again in the oven.

4 Arrange the vegetables over the caramel, then place the pastry discs over them, tucking in the pastry edges so they lie on top of the vegetables inside the tins. Set on a heavy baking sheet and bake for 10–15 minutes until the pastry is crisp, risen and golden. Cool for a few minutes, then invert on to warmed plates, handling the tarts carefully as the hot juices may run out. Serve the tarts hot, pastry side down.

Serves 6

3 tablespoons olive oil

175 g (6 oz) carrots, cut into 2.5 cm (1 inch) chunks

175 g (6 oz) turnips, cut into 2.5 cm (1 inch) chunks

175 g (6 oz) parsnips, cut into 2.5 cm (1 inch) chunks

175 g (6 oz) shallots, halved if large

1 teaspoon coriander seeds, finely ground

1 teaspoon fennel seeds, finely ground

4 garlic cloves, peeled

175 g (6 oz) leeks, cut into 2.5 cm (1 inch) chunks

1 x 375 g (12 oz) packet ready rolled puff pastry

Caramel:

20 g (¼ oz) butter

40 g (1½ oz) sugar

1 tablespoon red wine vinegar

25 ml (1 fl oz) water

Roast Root Vegetable Tarte Tatin is shown on the preceding page

courgette & red pepper tian

This vegetable gratin takes its name from the dish in which it is cooked, a shallow Provençal earthenware dish which is wider across the top than the bottom. This ensures that there is much more of the crispy gratin topping than filling. You can use any lightly cooked vegetable or combination of vegetables, such as steamed, boiled or fried broccoli, cauliflower, aubergines or leeks. Macaroni or other small pasta shapes are an excellent alternative to the rice. Strips of lightly fried or poached chicken breast meat can also be added for another variation. Serve with a mixed leaf salad and crusty garlic bread.

4–5 tablespoons olive or sunflower oil

1 large onion, finely chopped

2 garlic cloves, crushed

750 g (1½ lb) courgettes, cut into 5 mm–1 cm (¼–½ inch) cubes

1 red pepper, cored, deseeded and diced

2 tablespoons finely chopped coriander

1–2 tablespoons ground coriander

75 g (3 oz) long-grain rice

2 large eggs

50 g (2 oz) mature Cheddar cheese, grated

50 g (2 oz) Parmesan cheese, freshly grated

4 tablespoons fine white breadcrumbs

salt and pepper

1 Heat 3 tablespoons of the oil in a large, heavy wide-based saucepan and fry the onion and garlic until soft but not coloured. Add the rest of the oil, increase the heat, then add the courgettes, red pepper and chopped coriander. Fry for 5–10 minutes, then stir in the ground coriander and fry for a few minutes to develop the flavour.

2 Meanwhile, cook the long-grain rice in a large pan of boiling salted water for 11 minutes, or according to the packet instructions, until just tender. Drain the rice well. Beat the eggs in a large bowl, season with salt and pepper and then stir into the courgette mixture. Add the rice and two-thirds of the Cheddar and Parmesan cheeses.

3 Lightly oil a 1 litre (1¾ pint) gratin dish about 5 cm (2 inches) deep and fill with the vegetable mixture. Mix the remaining cheese with the breadcrumbs and scatter on top. Bake in a preheated oven, 180°C (350°F), Gas Mark 4, for 20–30 minutes until the mixture is set and the top is beginning to turn crisp and golden brown. I generally flash the tian under a very hot grill to speed up the process. Serve hot or cold.

Serves 4

roast fillet of salmon

with tomato & avocado compote

This is a wonderfully simple recipe for an elegant summer meal. It can be prepared in advance and takes just a few minutes to cook and assemble. I use the chef's method of frying and roasting for cooking the salmon, but it can of course be completely cooked in the pan or under the grill, turning the fish once during cooking. I generally use a cast iron pan with an ovenproof handle, which can be transferred directly to the oven.

1 First prepare the compote. Put the tomatoes, avocado, olive oil and lime juice into a bowl and add a dash each of Worcestershire and Tabasco sauces. Add salt and pepper to taste, cover and refrigerate until required.

2 Brush a heavy frying pan lightly with oil and warm over a high heat. Season the salmon fillets with salt and pepper, place flesh-side down in the pan and cook over a high heat for 2 minutes to brown the flesh. The fish should have a seared appearance.

3 Carefully transfer the fish, skin-side down, to a lightly oiled baking sheet. Transfer the baking sheet to a preheated oven, 240°C (475°F) Gas Mark 9, and cook for 7–9 minutes depending on thickness. To tell if the fish is cooked, take a peek inside the salmon by slightly opening the flesh with a palette knife: if it is still a little pink, cook for a little longer. Don't forget, it will continue to cook after it has been removed from the oven.

4 Divide the compote between 4 large plates, arranging it in the centre of each one. Shake the dressing, then drizzle it over and around the compote. Set a piece of salmon on each mound of compote, garnish with basil leaves and serve immediately.

Serves 4

½ tablespoon sunflower oil
4 x 150–175 g (5–6 oz) pieces of
    salmon fillet, skin on but scaled
Fresh Basil Dressing (page 230)
4 basil leaves, to garnish
salt and pepper

Compote:
4 ripe tomatoes, peeled, deseeded
    and cut into 5 mm (¼ inch) dice
1 large firm, ripe avocado, stoned,
    peeled and cut into 5 mm (¼ inch)
    dice
1–2 tablespoons extra virgin olive oil
4–5 tablespoons lime juice
dash of Worcestershire sauce
dash of Tabasco sauce

carrot, mushroom
& mixed nut roast

This rich vegetable and mixed nut roast spiked with herbs and flavourings is moist and succulent. I make it in a large ring mould because this way it cuts into perfect slices. It also looks good on a festive or buffet table, the centre filled with fresh watercress, tender young salad leaves, or a vegetable like Brussels sprouts, mixed green beans, broccoli florets or roasted baby beetroots. It can of course also be made in a large loaf tin or individual tins or rings. Any combination of nuts and vegetables can be used with carrot as the principal character. It is excellent hot or cold and is perfect with Spicy Tomato Sauce (page 232).

1 Lightly oil a 24 cm (9½ inch) ring mould or eight 10 cm (4 inch) individual ring moulds. Line carefully with clingfilm, taking care to smooth out any folds or wrinkles. Oil lightly.

2 Heat the oil and fry the onion, celery and garlic until soft. Add the mushrooms and fry until colouring. Stir in the carrots and cook for 5 minutes.

3 Meanwhile, combine all the nuts in a food processor and process until finely chopped but still with a texture, or chop by hand. Put them into a large bowl with the breadcrumbs, lemon rind, marjoram, parsley, mace and thyme and season with salt and pepper. Add the onion mixture and the eggs and stock or water. Mix well to blend and check the seasoning.

4 Pack the mixture into the mould or moulds, smooth the top and make sure there are no air spaces. Cover with oiled foil. Set on a heavy baking sheet and bake in a preheated oven, 190°C (375°F), Gas Mark 5, until firm to the touch. This will take 1½ hours for the large mould or 45 minutes for the small ones.

5 When cooked, remove the foil and carefully invert the nut roast on to a warm serving dish or warmed individual plates. Remove the clingfilm and serve hot or cold.

Gives about 30 slices, enough to serve 8

2 tablespoons olive or sunflower oil

1 onion, about 175 g (6 oz), finely chopped

1 celery stick, finely chopped

1 garlic clove, finely chopped

250 g (8 oz) mushrooms, finely chopped

175 g (6 oz) carrots, grated

250 g (8 oz) can chestnuts, whole and peeled (or vacuum packed)

250 g (8 oz) hazelnuts, walnuts, peanuts, Brazil nuts or pecan nuts

250 g (8 oz) fine wholemeal breadcrumbs

1 teaspoon grated lemon rind

1 teaspoon finely chopped marjoram

2 tablespoons finely chopped parsley

1 teaspoon ground mace

pinch of dried thyme

3 large eggs, beaten

150 ml (¼ pint) vegetable stock or water

salt and pepper

courgette, tomato & basil tart

A crisp melting pastry case filled with a single vegetable or a mixture of vegetables and set in a light custard is one of the classic dishes of any culinary repertoire. Here I have combined three of the summer garden's best – baby courgettes, flavoursome tomatoes and sweet basil. For mixed vegetable tarts, use whatever vegetables you fancy. Each tart needs 300 g (10 oz) vegetables – or 65 g (2½ oz) for individual tartlets. One of my favourite combinations is onion, red and green pepper, courgette and tomato, all finely chopped and cooked in a little hot oil until soft. The custard mixture and pastry quantity remain the same. One of the secrets of success is that the pastry should be rolled out thinly – no more than 3 mm (⅛ inch) thick. Serve warm or cold.

1 First make the pastry. Sift the flour and salt into a bowl. Cut the fats into small pieces and coat with the flour. Rub the fat into the flour until it resembles fine breadcrumbs. Mix together the egg yolk and water. Make a well in the centre of the flour and add the liquid. Mix with a broad-bladed knife to form a stiff dough, adding a little extra water if necessary. Place in a plastic bag and chill for about 30 minutes.

2 For the large tart, roll the pastry into 1 large circle to line a 20 x 4 cm (8 x 1½ inch) tart tin. For tartlets, divide the pastry into quarters and roll out into circles just larger than four 11 x 2 cm (4½ x ¾ inch) tartlet tins, allowing just enough to cover the base and sides. Press the pastry against the sides of the tin or tins, keeping it an even thickness all the way round. Cut off any excess pastry with a knife. Prick the pastry base gently with a fork, line with foil and fill with baking beans. Set on a baking sheet and bake blind in a preheated oven, 200°C (400°F), Gas Mark 6, for 8–10 minutes. Remove the baking beans and foil and bake for a further 8–10 minutes.

3 While the pastry is baking, make the filling. Heat the oil and fry the onion until soft but not coloured, then stir in the chopped tomato and basil.

4 Spoon the filling into the cooked tart ot tartlet shells and arrange the courgette slices decoratively on top. Reduce the oven temperature to 180°C (350°F), Gas Mark 4. Beat the eggs and cream together, add salt and pepper and pour over the filling. Sprinkle with grated Cheddar cheese and bake for 25–30 minutes for the large tart, 20–25 minutes for the tartlets, until just set and light golden.

Serves 4

1–2 tablespoons olive oil
1 onion, finely chopped
1 large tomato, peeled, deseeded and chopped
4 basil leaves, finely chopped
8 tiny courgettes, cut into wafer-thin slices
2 large eggs
150 ml (¼ pint) double cream
50 g (2 oz) mature Cheddar cheese, grated
salt and pepper

Rich Shortcrust Pastry:
125 g (4 oz) plain flour
pinch of salt
50 g (2 oz) solid block vegetable margarine or butter
25 g (1 oz) solid block white fat
1 egg yolk
1 tablespoon cold water

couscous-filled
aubergines

4 large aubergines

2 tablespoons lemon juice

1 tablespoon olive oil

125 g (4 oz) mature Cheddar cheese, grated

50 g (2 oz) Parmesan cheese, freshly grated

chopped coriander and coriander sprigs, to garnish

Filling:

40 g (1½ oz) couscous

150 ml (¼ pint) boiling water

2 tablespoons olive oil

1 large onion, finely chopped

3 garlic cloves, finely chopped

1 small green pepper, cored, deseeded and diced

1 small red chilli, deseeded and finely chopped

1 x 400 g (13 oz) can chopped plum tomatoes

75 g (3 oz) black olives, pitted and sliced

2 tablespoons double concentrate tomato purée

1 teaspoon demerara sugar

3 tablespoons finely chopped coriander

salt and pepper

This recipe was a popular dish in my delicatessen and restaurant, and has been a family favourite over the years. I allow 1 large aubergine per person for a main course, half a small to medium aubergine for a first course. Serve them either hot or cold, with thick natural yogurt flavoured with chopped coriander and lime juice, or with Spicy Tomato Sauce (page 232).

1 Cut the aubergines in half lengthways. With a sharp, pointed knife, draw a shallow line around the flesh about 5 mm (⅛ inch) in from the skin. Make criss-cross cuts in the flesh and rub the cut surface with lemon juice. Brush the skin with a little oil. Arrange the aubergines skin-side down on an oiled baking sheet and place in a preheated oven, 240°C (475°F), Gas Mark 9, for about 30 minutes until the flesh is tender.

2 Meanwhile, make the filling. Soak the couscous in the boiling water. Heat the oil and fry the onion and garlic until soft but not coloured, then add the pepper and chilli and continue to fry until beginning to colour. Stir in the tomatoes, olives, tomato purée, sugar and coriander. Cover and cook over a gentle heat for about 20 minutes.

3 Remove the aubergines from the oven. Using a dessertspoon, carefully scoop out the flesh inside the line, taking care not to damage or break the skin. Chop the flesh finely and add to the filling mixture. Fork through the couscous and add to the filling. Season to taste.

4 Pile the filling in the aubergine shells. Mix together the Cheddar and Parmesan cheeses, scatter over the filling and return to the oven for 15–30 minutes until crisp and golden brown. Garnish with chopped coriander and coriander sprigs before serving.

Serves 4

CHEF'S TIP If the filling is very hot when the shells are filled, you can melt the cheese topping under a very hot grill. The couscous filling is excellent for other vegetables, such as courgettes and peppers, and it can also be used in a moussaka instead of meat.

spinach & cheese filo pie

I kg (2 lb) fresh spinach or 500 g
(1 lb) frozen spinach
2 tablespoons olive oil
I large onion, finely chopped
3 garlic cloves, crushed
75 g (3 oz) feta cheese, crumbled
75 g (3 oz) ricotta or cottage cheese
50 g (2 oz) Parmesan cheese, freshly
grated
2 tablespoons finely chopped parsley
3 eggs, beaten
freshly grated nutmeg
75 g (3 oz) unsalted butter
12–14 sheets fresh or defrosted filo
pastry, each sheet measuring
32 x 17.5 cm (12½ x 7½ inches)
pepper

This recipe, with its filling of spinach, cheese and eggs, is based on the Greek filo pie known as spanakopitta. *Although feta is the traditional cheese to use, I have used a combination of feta for sharpness and saltiness, ricotta or cottage cheese for a cool mellow taste, and Parmesan, which melts during cooking and holds the filling together.*

1 Remove any large tough spines from the spinach and wash in cold salted water. Shake to remove excess water, then put the spinach into a large saucepan with only the water that clings to the leaves. Cover with greaseproof paper and a lid and cook over a moderate heat until the spinach is tender, shaking the pan occasionally. This will take 5–8 minutes. Drain well and press out as much water as possible, then chop roughly and put into a large bowl.

2 Heat the oil in a frying pan and fry the onion and garlic until soft but not coloured. Add to the spinach. Cool, then add the feta, ricotta or cottage cheese, Parmesan and parsley. Mash together with a fork. Stir in the beaten eggs and season with nutmeg and pepper. Mix well.

3 Melt the butter and generously butter a shallow 20 cm (8 inch) circular or square cake tin with a removable base or an ovenproof dish 2.5–4 cm (1–1½ inches) deep. Use the rest to brush each sheet of filo pastry before peeling the sheet off the pile. Work carefully with the pastry, using only one sheet at a time as required. Keep the rest of the filo pastry covered with clingfilm and a damp tea towel to prevent it from drying out and becoming brittle.

4 Line the tin with 2–3 sheets of filo pastry, pushing it into the sides and letting the surplus overhang the edges. Butter another 6 sheets, fold each one in half lengthways and place over the tin, angling them all slightly differently so that the points of the overhanging edges radiate like the petals of a flower. Spoon in the spinach mixture. Lay 2 more sheets of buttered filo pastry on top, tucking them in to fit the pie. Bring the overhanging lining sheets over the top layer of pastry, then place the last 3 sheets on top, scrunching them to fit into the tin. Brush the pastry well with butter, then bake in a preheated oven, 190°C (375°F), Gas Mark 5, for 45–60 minutes until crisp and golden brown.

5 Cool slightly, then remove from the tin by inverting a serving plate over the pie and turning it out. Put another plate over the bottom of the pie and turn it the right way up. Serve hot or cold.

Serves 6–8

broccoli
& coriander chicken

This was one of my mother's favourites, often served for Monday supper – made from the leftovers of Sunday's roast chicken. In this recipe I use raw chicken and gently poach it in chicken stock before combining it with the broccoli. The sauce is lighter and sharper than the original, using crème fraîche rather than a classic béchamel. I have also added curry paste for a touch of spice, but it is equally good without it. Serve with a crisp green salad and garlic bread.

1 Cut the chicken into finger strips, about 8 x 2 cm (3½ x ¾ inch) long. Heat the stock, then poach the chicken gently for 4–6 minutes until just cooked. Remove the chicken from the stock with a slotted spoon and set aside.

2 Trim the broccoli into florets and peel the stalks. Plunge the florets into a large pan of boiling water, cook for 2 minutes, then drain. Refresh under cold running water until very cold. Drain again and dry with kitchen paper.

3 Prepare the topping by melting the butter in a large frying pan and gently frying the breadcrumbs until golden brown.

4 Make the sauce. Melt the butter in a large saucepan and fry the onion and garlic until soft but not coloured. Stir in the curry paste and fry for a few minutes to develop the flavour. Add the crème fraîche, lemon juice and coriander, season to taste with salt and pepper and mix well. Bring to the boil.

5 Arrange the cooked chicken in a 30 x 23 x 5 cm (12 x 9 x 2 inch) baking dish. Pour the hot sauce over the chicken. Scatter the cheese on top followed by the breadcrumbs. Bake in a preheated oven, 200°C (400°F), Gas Mark 6, for 30–40 minutes until bubbling hot and golden brown. To crisp the top, flash under a preheated grill, if necessary.

Serves 6

**4 boneless, skinless chicken breast
fillets, total weight 600–750 g
(1¼–1½ lb)**
600 ml (1 pint) chicken stock
750 g (1½ lb) broccoli

Gratin Topping:
50 g (2 oz) butter
125 g (4 oz) fresh white breadcrumbs
**50–75 g (2–3 oz) mature Cheddar
cheese, grated**

Sauce:
50 g (2 oz) butter
1 large onion, finely chopped
3 garlic cloves, crushed
**2–3 tablespoons rogan josh curry
paste**
750 ml (1¼ pints) crème fraîche
1½ tablespoons lemon juice
**3 tablespoons finely chopped
coriander**
salt and pepper

chicory & smoked bacon gratin

Witloof chicory has a slightly bitter taste and delicately wilted texture when cooked. It combines beautifully with rich creamy sauces and sharp, piquant flavours like lemon and orange juice, olives, capers and anchovies. In this recipe I have fried the heads in butter and lemon juice before sprinkling them with crisp bacon. They are then baked in cream flavoured with Dijon mustard and cheese. Wicked, but delicious.

8 chicory heads

25 g (1 oz) butter

juice of 1 large lemon

8 large thin rashers of lightly smoked bacon, rinded, chopped and fried until crisp

2 tablespoons Dijon mustard

300 ml (½ pint) single cream

150 g (5 oz) Gruyère or mature Cheddar cheese, grated

salt and pepper

chervil sprigs, to garnish

1 Trim a thin slice from the root end of the chicory, if discoloured, and remove any damaged or brown leaves. If it is just the tips of the leaves that have developed a brown edge, trim them with scissors. Cut each chicory head in half lengthways and remove the central core, leaving the head intact.

2 Melt the butter in a large frying pan, add the chicory cut-side down and sprinkle with the lemon juice. Fry until browning, turning several times and taking care to keep the heads together.

3 Transfer the chicory to a 2–2.5 litre (3½–4 pint) gratin dish and scatter with the fried bacon. Mix together the mustard, cream, and two-thirds of the cheese, season with salt and pepper and pour over the chicory. Scatter over the remaining cheese and place in a preheated oven, 200–225°C (400–425°F), Gas Mark 6–7, for about 20 minutes until bubbling and golden. Finish the browning under a hot grill, if necessary. Garnish with chervil sprigs and serve.

Serves 4

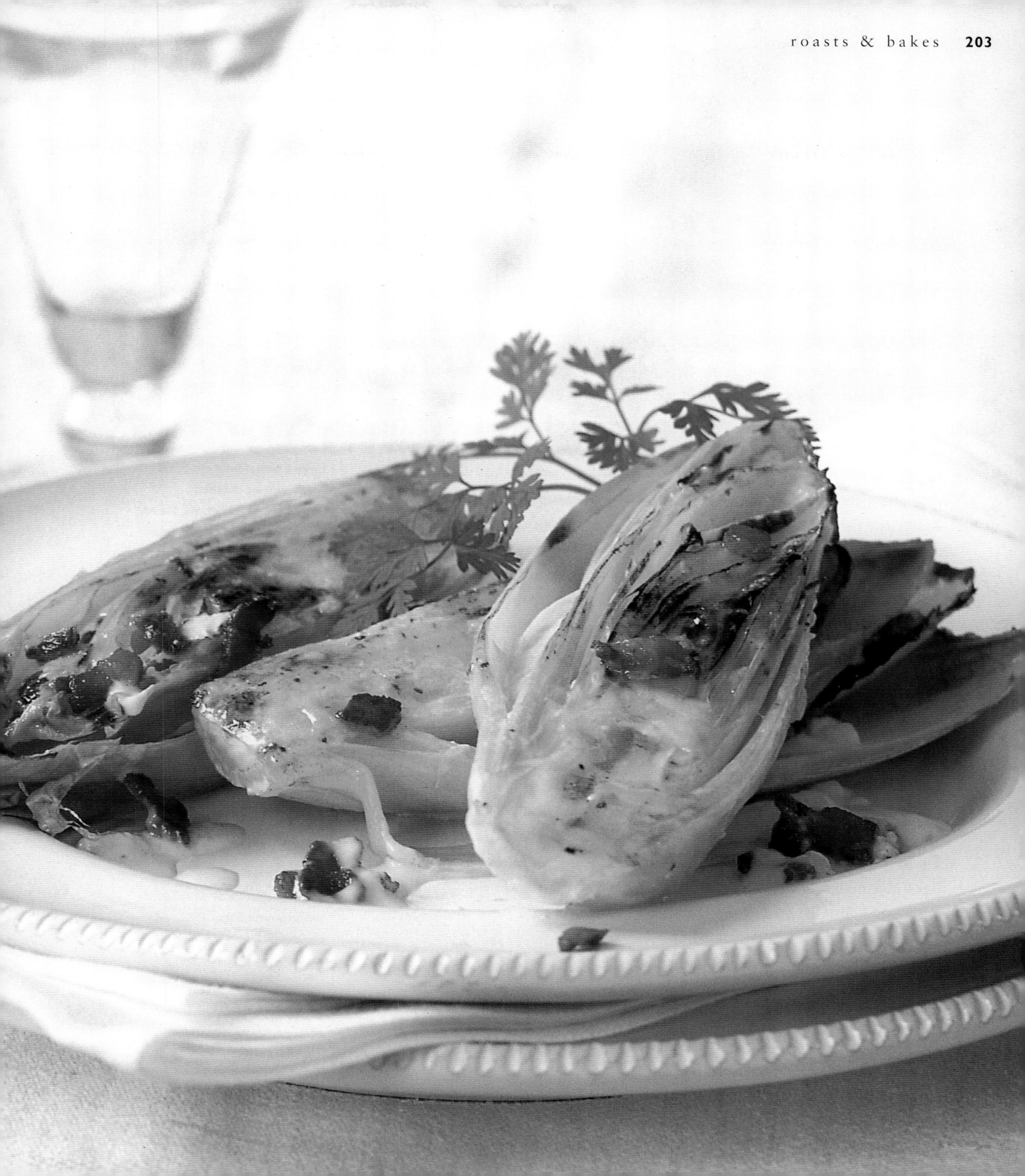

melange of vegetables
with coconut & cheese topping

In this tasty gratin the vegetables are fried first, then allowed to cook in their own juices before being moistened with a rich cheesy white sauce and baked in the oven. Serve with wholegrain brown rice, a crisp salad and Cucumber & Mint Raita (page 216).

1 Heat the oil in a large frying pan and fry the onion and garlic until soft but not coloured. Add the mushrooms and fry until browning. Add the peppers, courgettes and cauliflower and fry for a few minutes. Add the chilli powder, cumin and turmeric and season with salt and pepper, stir well to combine and fry for a few minutes to develop the flavours. Press a piece of greaseproof paper or foil on top of the vegetables and sweat them gently for 20 minutes to draw out the juices, stirring from time to time. The vegetables will produce their own liquid, but if they show signs of drying out and sticking, add a few tablespoons of water to the pan.

2 While the vegetables are cooking, prepare the cheese sauce. Melt the butter in a saucepan and stir in the flour. Remove from the heat and gradually blend in the warm milk, making sure no lumps form. Return the pan to the heat and stir constantly until the sauce has thickened. Add the mustard and half of the Cheddar cheese and season to taste with salt and pepper. Stir in the coconut and coriander.

3 Pour the sauce over the vegetables and carefully fold in with a large spoon. Tip into a 1.8 litre (3 pint) gratin dish and scatter the rest of the cheese on top. Bake in a preheated oven at 220°C (425°F), Gas Mark 7, for 30–40 minutes until bubbling. Alternatively, brown under a preheated grill. Serve immediately.

Serves 4

3 tablespoons sunflower oil
I large onion, finely chopped
2 garlic cloves, crushed
150 g (5 oz) mushrooms, sliced
2 small peppers (I red, I green), cored, deseeded and cut into I cm (½ inch) pieces
2 courgettes, sliced into rings
¼ large cauliflower, broken into florets
I teaspoon chilli powder
I teaspoon ground cumin
I teaspoon ground turmeric
salt and pepper

Cheese Sauce:
25 g (I oz) butter
25 g (I oz) plain flour
300 ml (½ pint) milk, warmed
½ teaspoon English mustard powder
150–175 g (5–6 oz) mature Cheddar cheese, grated
4 tablespoons coconut flakes
3 tablespoons finely chopped coriander
salt and pepper

potato, mushroom & bacon gratin

25 g (1 oz) butter

2 tablespoons olive oil

8 rashers of back bacon, rinded and
  cut into strips

1 large onion, finely chopped

2 garlic cloves, crushed

150 g (5 oz) mushrooms, sliced

750 g–1 kg (1½–2 lb) cooked potatoes
  (boiled or steamed with their
  skins on)

150–200 ml (5–7 fl oz) double cream

1 tablespoon finely chopped parsley

75 g (3 oz) mature farmhouse
  Cheddar cheese, grated

50 g (2 oz) Parmesan cheese, freshly
  grated

salt and pepper

Use a floury potato such as Maris Piper, King Edward or Pentland Square, which will absorb the cooking juices and make the sauce thick and rich.

1 Melt half of the butter with half of the oil and fry the bacon until browning. Remove from the pan with a slotted spoon and put into a large bowl. Add the remaining butter and oil if necessary and fry the onion and garlic until soft. Add the mushrooms and continue to fry until all the vegetables are beginning to colour. With the slotted spoon, transfer all the vegetables to the bowl with the bacon and mix together.

2 Cut the potatoes into wedges and arrange them with the other vegetables in an ovenproof gratin dish. Mix the cream with the parsley, season with salt and pepper and pour it over the vegetables. Mix the Cheddar and Parmesan cheeses together and scatter on top. Set the dish on a baking sheet and bake in a preheated oven, 180°C (350°F) Gas Mark 4, for 20–30 minutes until crisp and golden. Serve immediately.

Serves 4

red lentil, pepper & mushroom bake

This has been a family favourite for many years. It is rich and substantial, with a deep earthy flavour. As the lentils need to be cooked to a purée, it is best to use the split red variety. They don't need to be presoaked. Other suitable vegetables instead of the pepper and mushrooms are diced courgettes and aubergines, tomatoes and celery, in any combination. Serve with a salad of mixed leaves or crunchy green vegetables.

1 Put the lentils into a saucepan and cover with the boiling water. Return to the boil, then reduce the heat and simmer gently for about 20 minutes, stirring occasionally, until the lentils are tender and all the water has been absorbed.

2 Lightly oil a 900 ml–1.2 litre (1½–2 pint) ovenproof dish about 5 cm (2 inches) deep. Heat the remaining oil in a large pan and fry the onion until soft but not coloured. Add the green pepper and mushrooms and fry for about 10 minutes on a higher heat to colour the vegetables slightly.

3 Add the lentils, chilli powder, Tabasco, paprika, tomato purée, tamari, yeast extract and salt and pepper. Stir well to combine, then turn into the dish.

4 Mix the topping ingredients together and sprinkle over the lentil mixture. Bake in a preheated oven, 190°C (375°F), Gas Mark 5, for about 30 minutes until bubbling hot and toasted golden. Serve hot.

Serves 4

175 g (6 oz) split red lentils
600 ml (1 pint) boiling water
3 tablespoons sunflower or olive oil
1 large onion, finely chopped
1 large green pepper, cored, deseeded
  and diced
175 g (6 oz) mushrooms, sliced
1 teaspoon chilli powder
½ teaspoon Tabasco sauce
1 teaspoon paprika
1 tablespoon tomato purée
2 tablespoons tamari sauce
1 teaspoon yeast extract
salt and pepper

Topping:
25 g (1 oz) wholewheat breadcrumbs
25 g (1 oz) pine nuts, chopped
25 g (1 oz) pumpkin seeds
50 g (2 oz) Cheddar cheese, grated

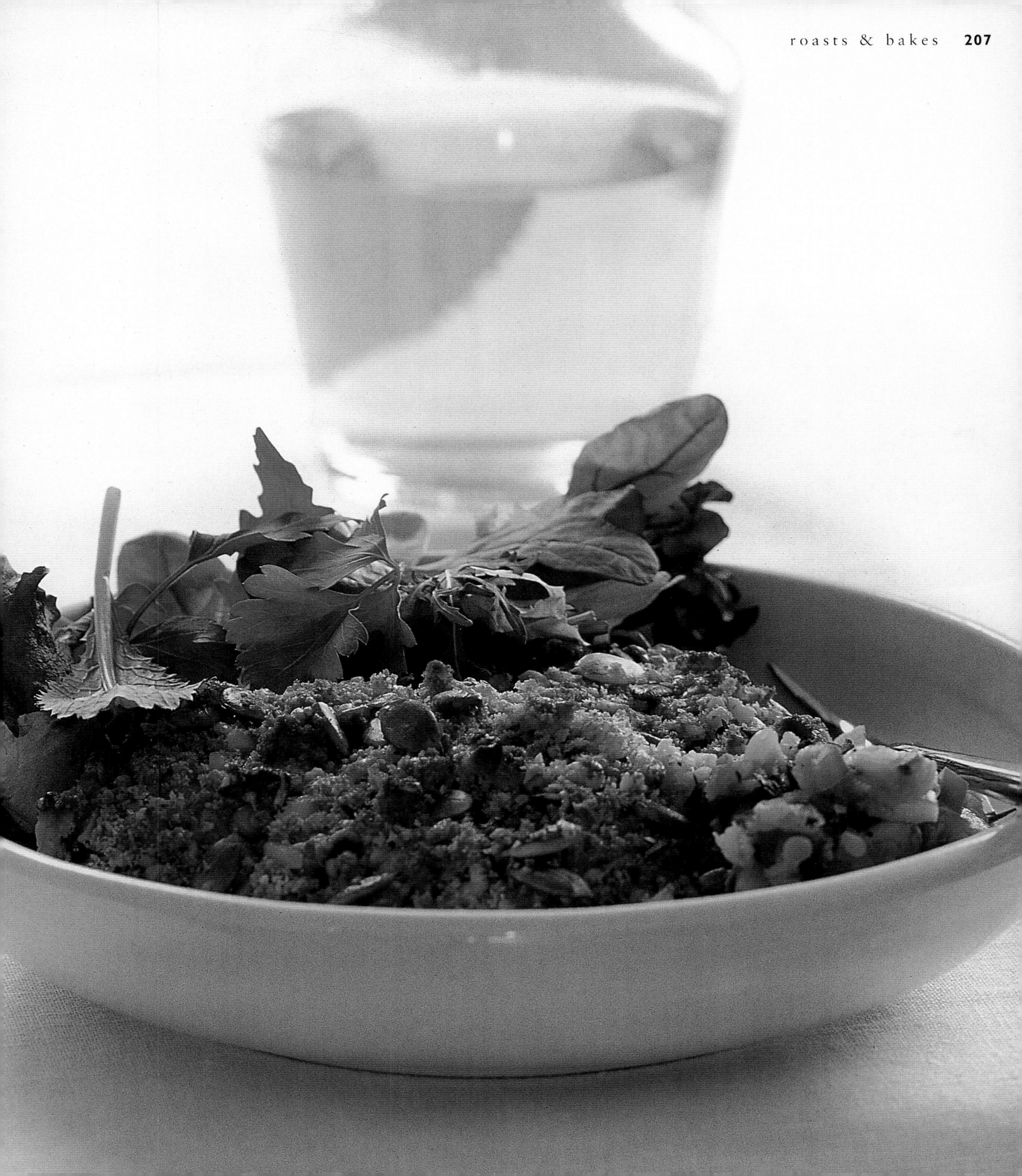

dips &
salsas

sweet & sour
aubergine relish

This is a tangy relish that is excellent with samosas, Vegetable Beignets (page 130) or Vegetable Pakoras (page 132). It will keep for about 1 week in the refrigerator.

1 Heat 2 tablespoons of the oil and fry the onion and garlic until soft and beginning to colour. Using a slotted spoon, transfer to a large saucepan.

2 Heat one-third of the remaining oil until very hot and fry one-third of the aubergines very quickly until browned on all sides. Using the slotted spoon, transfer them to the pan with the onion. Repeat with the remaining oil and aubergines.

3 Stir the lemon juice, sugar, cumin and cayenne into the fried aubergine and onion mixture and season with salt to taste. Return to the heat and cover closely with a circle of greaseproof paper and the saucepan lid. Cook gently, stirring occasionally, for about 20 minutes until the mixture is thick and pulpy but still with texture.

4 Transfer to a bowl and leave to cool. Cover and refrigerate until required. Serve at room temperature.

Makes 1 litre (1¾ pints), enough to serve 8–10

150 ml (¼ pint) sunflower oil
1 large onion, halved and thinly sliced
3 garlic cloves, crushed
1 kg (2 lb) firm aubergines, cut into
    1 cm (½ inch) dice
6 tablespoons lemon juice
3–4 tablespoons demerara sugar
1 teaspoon ground cumin
¼ teaspoon cayenne pepper
salt

Sweet and Sour Aubergine Relish is shown on page 208

salsa verde

6 tablespoons finely chopped flat leaf parsley
3 tablespoons finely chopped basil
2 garlic cloves, crushed
2 tablespoons capers, drained, rinsed and finely chopped
2 canned anchovy fillets, rinsed and finely chopped
I teaspoon Dijon mustard
150 ml (¼ pint) olive oil
I–3 tablespoons lemon juice or white wine vinegar
pepper

This rich, unctuous sauce is perfect with boiled artichokes, grilled vegetables or steak. It is also delicious tossed with warm pasta, baby new potatoes, cooked white beans or hard-boiled eggs.

1 Combine the parsley, basil, garlic, capers, anchovies and mustard in a bowl, whisk in the oil and add lemon juice or wine vinegar to sharpen. Transfer to a screw-top jar and store in the refrigerator for up to 1 week.

Makes 250 ml (8 fl oz), enough to serve 8.

CHEF'S TIP Don't over chop the ingredients – they should have a little texture rather than being pounded to a pulp. You can ring the changes by using other fresh herbs, such as lovage, fennel fronds, chervil or rocket, with the parsley, or you can include the finely grated rind from the lemon with the juice. Alternatively, add 1 tablespoon finely chopped gherkin instead of the capers and lime or orange juice instead of the lemon.

hot tomato salsa

1 Put the red onion into a small bowl and cover with boiling water. Leave for a few minutes, then drain and refresh under cold water. Drain again and pat dry with kitchen paper.
2 Combine all the ingredients together, mixing lightly. Cover and chill for 30–60 minutes, to let the flavours develop before serving.

Makes 375 ml (13 fl oz), enough to serve 4

VARIATIONS Any of the following can be added to the basic tomato salsa: avocado, peeled, diced and tossed in lime juice to prevent discoloration; papaya, peeled, deseeded and diced; pineapple, peeled and diced; mango, peeled, stoned and diced; chopped fresh herbs, such as mint, fennel, lovage, oregano, marjoram, dill, tarragon. For a more gentle salsa, leave out the chilli.

I small red onion, finely diced
I garlic clove, finely chopped
500 g (I lb) sweet ripe tomatoes, peeled, deseeded and diced
I–2 sweet, moderately hot red chillies, deseeded and finely chopped
3 tablespoons finely chopped coriander
I tablespoon finely chopped parsley
juice of ½ lime
3 tablespoons olive oil
pinch of salt
pinch of sugar
pepper

Salsa Verde is shown on page 208 and Hot Tomato Salsa is shown on page 209

avocado & tomato salsa

2–3 tablespoons lime juice

I tablespoon olive oil

a few drops of Tabasco sauce

I small garlic clove, finely chopped

½ small red onion, finely diced

2 large firm, ripe tomatoes, peeled, deseeded and finely diced

2 large firm, ripe avocados, stoned, peeled and diced

2 tablespoons finely chopped coriander

salt and pepper

1 Put the lime juice, olive oil, Tabasco and garlic in a bowl and whisk well to combine. Stir in the onion, add the diced tomato and avocado and toss gently in the dressing along with the chopped coriander. Season to taste.

Serves 4

hot papaya & roasted pepper salsa

A sweet, tangy salsa, the colour of a flaming sunset, this is warm and inviting to look at and refreshing to eat. Delicious with grilled and fried meat, chicken, fish and vegetables.

1 Combine the lime juice, olive oil and balsamic vinegar in a bowl. Add the papayas, chilli, spring onions and roasted red peppers and toss gently until combined. Season with salt and pepper and stir in the coriander. Cover and chill for about 30 minutes before serving to allow the flavours to blend and develop. Best eaten on the same day.

Makes 500 g (1 lb)

juice of 1–2 limes

4 tablespoons light olive oil

¼ teaspoon balsamic vinegar

2 ripe papayas, halved, deseeded and cut into 1 cm (½ inch) dice

½ small red chilli, finely chopped

2 spring onions, finely sliced

2 roasted red peppers, cored, deseeded and cut into 5 mm (¼ inch) dice

I tablespoon finely chopped coriander

salt and pepper

chargrilled sweetcorn & avocado salsa

This is delicious with grilled or roasted meats and fish, Red Lentil Burgers (page 176), Vegetable Brochettes (page 180) and Grilled Vegetables (page 186). If it is kept longer than a few hours the avocado will discolour and lose its vibrancy, so make it only far enough ahead to allow the flavours to mingle and develop. Alternatively, prepare the salsa in advance without the avocado, adding it about 30 minutes before serving. An excellent variation is to omit the avocado altogether and replace it with another corn-on-the-cob and a small diced red pepper.

1 Plunge the corn cobs into a pan of boiling water, return to the boil and blanch for 3–4 minutes. Drain, rub with a little of the olive oil, and place under a preheated very hot grill for 10–15 minutes until tender and well toasted. Leave to cool slightly, then scrape the kernels from the cobs with a knife; you need about 150 g (5 oz). Put the kernels into a bowl and set aside to cool.

2 Put the onion in a small bowl and cover with boiling water. Leave for a few minutes, then drain and refresh under cold water. Drain again and pat dry with kitchen paper. Add the onion to the corn with the lime juice, jalapeño sauce, chilli, red pepper, tomato, ground and chopped coriander, the remaining oil and salt and pepper. Toss gently to combine, then fold in the avocado. Taste and adjust the seasoning as necessary. Cover and refrigerate until required.

Serves 4

2 corn-on-the-cob, stripped of husks and threads
3 tablespoons olive oil
1 tablespoon red onion, finely diced
3–4 tablespoons lime juice
2 dashes of jalapeño sauce
1 small red chilli, deseeded and finely diced
¼ small red pepper, cored, deseeded and finely diced
1 large firm, red plum tomato, peeled, deseeded and finely diced
¼ teaspoon ground coriander
2 tablespoons finely chopped coriander
1 firm, ripe avocado, stoned, peeled and diced
salt and pepper

black olive salsa
with capers, onion & anchovies

This salsa is wonderful to look at and delicious to eat. Serve it on bruschetta, with pasta or seared salmon steaks, or as part of a mixed leaf salad with fresh Parmesan shavings.

1 Drain the anchovy fillets, rinse well under cold running water and soak in a little milk while preparing the rest of the ingredients.

2 Put the red onion into a small bowl and cover with boiling water. Leave for a few minutes, then drain and refresh under cold water. Drain again and pat dry with kitchen paper.

3 Remove the anchovies from the milk and rinse well under cold running water. Pat dry with kitchen paper and chop roughly. Put into a bowl and add the rest of the ingredients. Stir to combine, cover and leave to marinate for at least 30 minutes. The salsa will keep for several days in the refrigerator.

Makes 500 ml (16 fl oz), enough to serve 5–6

1 x 50 g (2 oz) can anchovy fillets in oil

milk, for soaking

50 g (2 oz) red onion, finely diced

50 g (2 oz) red pepper, cored, deseeded and finely diced

50 g (2 oz) capers in salt or vinegar, drained and rinsed

150 g (5 oz) black olives, pitted and diced

2 large garlic cloves, finely chopped

1 small red chilli, deseeded and finely chopped

150 ml (¼ pint) extra virgin olive oil

1 tablespoon lemon juice

1 tablespoon balsamic vinegar

2 tablespoons finely chopped coriander

3 tablespoons finely chopped flat leaf parsley

pepper

avocado salsa

The word salsa *means sauce, in both Italian and Mexican cooking. In Mexico and the United States it is generally used to describe a slightly chunky relish based on chillies, tomatoes, onion, garlic, coriander and salt. There are many variations on this theme, but in general salsas are characterized by their vibrant colours and hand-chopped ingredients. They make a refreshing addition to grilled food, such as chicken, fish, beef steaks, lamb cutlets, vegetable burgers and patties, sausages and kebabs, and are equally good piled on top of bruschetta or crostini to be served as a snack or light lunch.*

1 Run a cut line lengthways through the centre of the avocado as far as the stone, then gently twist the two halves apart. The stone will remain in one half. Remove the stone carefully without damaging the delicate flesh. Peel off the skin and cut the avocado into 1 cm (½ inch) dice.

2 Put the avocado flesh into a bowl with the lime juice, coriander and spring onions. Season to taste with salt and pepper and toss lightly to combine without breaking up the avocado. Cover and refrigerate until required.

Serves 4

1 firm, ripe avocado
2 tablespoons lime juice
1 tablespoon finely chopped coriander
2 spring onions, finely sliced
salt and pepper

cucumber & mint raita

A mild-flavoured and refreshing Indian yogurt dish, this is the perfect accompaniment to any spicy, highly seasoned meat, fish or vegetable, and traditionally served with Vegetable Pakoras (page 132). Occasionally I add a little chopped fresh chilli or mint sauce, or some freshly chopped coriander.

1 Put the yogurt in a bowl and beat lightly with a fork or whisk until smooth. Add the remaining ingredients and stir to combine. Cover and refrigerate until required. Serve chilled, garnished with mint sprigs.

Makes 300 ml (½ pint), enough to serve 4–6

200 ml (7 fl oz) natural yogurt
7 cm (3 inch) piece of cucumber,
** peeled and coarsely grated or**
** chopped**
2 tablespoons chopped mint
pinch of ground cumin
pepper
squeeze of lemon or lime juice
mint sprigs, to garnish

mango & cucumber
salsa with chilli

This salsa is quick and easy to make, and can be as fiery or cooling as you wish — just adjust the amount of chillies or leave them out altogether. It is excellent with grilled, roasted or fried foods, particularly herrings and salmon, but is also perfect with cold meats, such as salami, bresàola or Parma ham. It will keep for several days in the refrigerator.

½ cucumber, peeled

1 large mango, ripe but still firm

3 tablespoons finely chopped red
  onion

1 small green chilli, deseeded and
  finely chopped

1 tablespoon finely chopped flat leaf
  parsley

juice of 1½ limes

salt and pepper

chopped flat leaf parsley, to garnish

1 Cut the cucumber into 2.5–5 mm (⅛–¼ inch) cubes and leave in a sieve to drain. Cut down each side of the flat central stone of the mango. Discard the stone and cut each piece of mango flesh into long strips 2.5–5 mm (⅛–¼ inch) thick. Remove the skin by slipping the knife between the flesh and skin and running it along its length. Cut into dice. Combine the cucumber and mango in a bowl.

2 Put the onion in a small bowl, cover with boiling water and soak for a few minutes. Drain and refresh under cold water, then pat dry with kitchen paper (this helps to soften the flavour of the onion).

3 Add the onion to the cucumber and mango with the rest of the ingredients. Stir gently to combine. Cover and chill for a few hours to allow the flavours to mingle and develop. Serve chilled, garnished with chopped flat leaf parsley.

Makes 600 ml (1 pint), enough to serve 6

guacamole

This thick creamy purée from Mexico can be used as a dip for Crudités (page 129), fresh tortilla chips or hot pitta bread, or eaten Mexican-style with tortillas. It can also be used as a sauce for fish and chicken. Don't purée the avocado flesh in a food processor or blender as this produces too smooth a texture.

2 large ripe avocados, halved, stoned and peeled
juice of 1 lime or lemon
1 garlic clove, crushed
1 tablespoon finely chopped onion
1 large tomato, skinned, deseeded and finely diced
1–2 fresh green chillies, deseeded and finely chopped
1 tablespoon finely chopped coriander
pinch of sugar
salt and pepper
coriander sprigs, to garnish

1 Put the avocado flesh in a bowl along with the lime or lemon juice and mash with a fork to make a textured paste. Stir in the garlic, onion, tomato, chillies, coriander and sugar. Season with salt and pepper and add some extra lime or lemon juice, if required. Spoon the mixture into a serving bowl and garnish with coriander sprigs. Cover with clingfilm to prevent discoloration and chill in the refrigerator until required.

Makes about 500 ml (17 fl oz)

lentil, green peppercorn
& mustard dip

Serve with crisp robust vegetables or fried or grilled fish. It also goes well with Crudités (page 129), Vegetable Brochettes (page 180) or Grilled Vegetables (page 186).

25 g (1 oz) green le Puy lentils
1–2 tablespoons green peppercorns in brine, drained
2 tablespoons Dijon mustard
4 tablespoons sunflower oil
1 tablespoon lemon juice
1 tablespoon warm water

1 Bring a large saucepan of water to the boil, add the lentils and return to the boil. Cook for 10–15 minutes until just tender and beginning to turn mushy. Drain and refresh under cold water until completely cold.
2 Crush the peppercorns until roughly broken using a pestle and mortar. Stir in the mustard and gradually beat in the oil, adding a little at a time. Stir in the lemon juice, warm water and cooked lentils. Pile into a serving bowl, cover with clingfilm and store in the refrigerator. The dip will keep for several days.

Makes 150 ml (¼ pint)

harissa

This is a traditional North African accompaniment to soups, stews and couscous. It is fiery hot and not for the faint hearted. Some more aromatic versions include herbs like mint and coriander, but they are no less fiery. Harissa can be bought in tubes and cans from Middle Eastern shops, good delicatessens and supermarkets. Its only substitute is a spice paste from Indonesia called sambal oelek*. A simple version of harissa can be made quickly by adding as much Tabasco sauce, paprika, cayenne pepper and crushed garlic as you like to tomato purée along with a little oil and lemon juice.*

1 If using dried chillies, soak them with or without their seeds in hot water for 1 hour. The seeds add to the fieriness of the harissa.

2 Wearing rubber gloves, drain the chillies and cut them into small pieces. If using fresh chillies, deseed them if desired, then chop finely. Pound in a mortar with the garlic and salt until puréed, or whizz in a food processor or blender. I find pounding more successful as it gives a finer purée.

3 Put the coriander, cumin and caraway seeds in a dry frying pan and shake over a low heat for a few minutes to roast and develop their flavour. Grind in a spice mill and add to the chilli mixture with enough oil to make a thick paste. Whizz again. Put into a screw-top jar and drizzle on enough oil to cover and seal. Cover with a lid and store in the refrigerator until required. It will keep for several months.

Makes 75 ml (3 fl oz)

50 g (2 oz) dried or fresh red chillies
4 garlic cloves, crushed
½ tablespoon salt
½–1 teaspoon coriander seeds
½–1 teaspoon cumin seeds
½–1 teaspoon caraway seeds
1–2 tablespoons sunflower oil

chilli bean dip

This spicy dip is excellent with raw vegetables, corn chips or fingers of warm or toasted pitta bread. It is also good spread on bruschetta and crostini, like a pâté.

1 Halve the peppers lengthways and deseed. Lightly brush the pepper inside and out with a little oil. Place on a lightly oiled baking sheet and roast in a pre-heated oven, 240°C (475°F), Gas Mark 9, for 15 minutes. Turn the peppers over and continue to roast until the edges begin to blacken and the flesh and skin begin to crumple. This will probably take another 15 minutes. Remove the peppers from the oven and leave until cool enough, then peel off the skins.

2 Work the red pepper flesh, garlic and chilli in a food processor or blender until well chopped. Add the beans and paprika and continue to process until a coarse purée forms. This won't take long. Season with Tabasco (if using) and salt and pepper. With the machine running, add the rest of the oil to make a thick paste.

3 Pile the bean purée into a bowl and sprinkle with the chives. Cover and refrigerate until required.

Makes about 400 ml (14 fl oz), enough to serve 4

2 large red peppers

2 tablespoons olive oil

2 garlic cloves, crushed

I small red chilli, deseeded and finely chopped

I x 400 g (13 oz) can red kidney beans, drained

½ teaspoon paprika

few drops of Tabasco sauce (if required)

salt and pepper

2 tablespoons snipped chives, to garnish

aubergine & sesame dip

750 g (1½ lb) aubergines

3 tablespoons lemon juice

2 tablespoons olive oil

2 garlic cloves, crushed

5 tablespoons finely chopped
  coriander or flat leaf parsley

3 tablespoons tahini paste

dash of Tabasco sauce

½ tablespoon white sugar

¼ teaspoon chilli powder

2 tablespoons thick Greek yogurt

salt and pepper

To Serve:

coriander or flat leaf parsley sprigs

paprika or black pepper

1 tablespoon toasted sesame seeds

This smooth and smoky tasting paste makes an excellent dip for crudités or warm pitta bread. It can also be used as a spread for crostini, bruschetta or crackers. In a covered bowl, it keeps for about 1 week in the refrigerator.

1 Cut the aubergines in half lengthways and brush the cut sides with lemon juice. Brush a heavy baking sheet with a little olive oil, place the aubergines cut-side down on the sheet and bake in a preheated oven, 240°C (475°F), Gas Mark 9, for 20–30 minutes until the flesh is tender and the shells collapsed. Turn them cut-side up and leave to cool.

2 With a metal spoon, scoop the aubergine flesh into a food processor or blender. Add the garlic, coriander or parsley and the remaining lemon juice and whizz to form a smooth purée. Add the tahini, Tabasco, sugar, chilli powder, yogurt and salt and pepper to taste, and whizz again. Taste for seasoning.

3 Pile the dip into a bowl and float the remaining oil on top. Cover and chill until required. Before serving, stir in the oil and garnish with coriander or parsley sprigs, a little paprika or black pepper and the toasted sesame seeds.

Makes about 600 ml (1 pint), enough to serve 5

hummus

1 x 400 g (13 oz) can chickpeas or
   75 g (3 oz) dried chickpeas, soaked
   and cooked
2 garlic cloves, crushed
2–3 tablespoons lemon juice
150 ml (¼ pint) tahini paste
about 150 ml (¼ pint) olive or
   sunflower oil
2–4 tablespoons natural set yogurt,
   chickpea cooking liquor or hot
   water
salt and pepper
cayenne or paprika pepper, to serve

*It takes seconds to make hummus using canned chickpeas and a food processor or
blender and it is much less expensive than buying it ready made.*

1 Drain and rinse the chickpeas (reserving the cooking liquor if you are using
dried chickpeas) and put them into a food processor or blender with the garlic,
lemon juice, tahini paste, 1 teaspoon salt and pepper to taste. Process to a
smooth paste.

2 Very gradually add the oil as if you were making mayonnaise. Stir in the
yogurt, cooking liquor or hot water to give the required consistency. Taste and
adjust the seasoning, if necessary.

3 Spoon the hummus into a serving dish and smooth with the back of a
spoon. Pour over a little oil and dust with a sprinkling of cayenne or paprika.

Makes 300–350 ml (10–12 fl oz), enough to serve 4

skordalia

*This garlicky purée is the Greek equivalent of Aïoli (opposite page). It was traditionally
served with fried vegetables during Lent, as it was made without egg. Breadcrumbs,
mashed potatoes, ground almonds or walnuts were used instead.*

1 Crush the garlic and pound with the salt in a pestle and mortar (or use a
heavy bowl and the end of a wooden rolling pin). Soak the bread in the hot
water until it forms a thick paste. Add to the garlic and pound well to blend.
Continue to pound while gradually adding the almonds.

2 When the mixture is a homogenous mass, start adding the oil very gradually,
drop by drop at first, just like making mayonnaise. Pound well between each
addition until the sauce is thick, rich and emulsified. Add lemon juice to taste,
pepper and extra salt if required. If the sauce is too thick, add more oil and a
little hot water to give the desired consistency.

Makes 350 ml (12 fl oz), enough to serve 8–12

1 large head garlic, about 8–10 fat
   cloves, peeled
1 teaspoon salt
50 g (2 oz) stale white bread
5 tablespoons hot water
50 g (2 oz) ground almonds
150–300 ml (5–10 fl oz) olive oil
25–50 ml (1–2 fl oz) lemon juice
freshly ground white pepper

aïoli

This Provençal sauce is a strongly flavoured mayonnaise in which garlic is pounded to a very smooth paste before the egg yolks and oil are added. It is not just a case of adding crushed garlic to mayonnaise. The quantity of garlic can range from 4 cloves to 2 heads, depending on taste. It is generally left raw, but whole heads may be roasted first, for a less harsh flavour. Lemon juice may be added to cut through the oil and sharpen the taste, and finely chopped herbs, such as oregano and flat leaf parsley, can be stirred into the finished sauce for variety. For additional flavour and colour, a pinch of saffron can be soaked in 1 tablespoon warm water and added in place of the boiled water. For a less rich sauce, replace half of the olive oil with sunflower oil. Aïoli is traditionally served with salt cod, squid, octopus, lobster, snails and boiled potatoes.

6 large garlic cloves

2 egg yolks

300 ml (½ pint) extra virgin olive oil

2 tablespoons lemon juice

1 teaspoon cooled boiled water

salt and white pepper

1 Crush the garlic to a smooth paste using a pestle and mortar (or use a heavy bowl and the end of a wooden rolling pin). I generally crush the cloves in a garlic press first.

2 Unless the mortar is very large, transfer the garlic to a large bowl, add the egg yolks and continue to pound with the pestle, or use an electric hand-mixer. Although the mixer would be frowned on by the purists, it is much quicker and easier. The traditional method is time-consuming, and food processors or blenders are unsuitable because they make the garlic bitter.

3 When the garlic and yolks are well blended, begin adding the oil, just as when making mayonnaise, drop by drop to begin with until the sauce begins to thicken and about half of the oil has been added. Continue to add the oil in a thin stream, beating all the time. If the mayonnaise becomes too thick, add a few drops of the lemon juice. Continue like this until all the oil and lemon juice have been incorporated. The consistency should be very thick, almost solid, and rich and glistening. Season with salt and pepper and stabilize with the cooled boiled water. If the sauce should curdle or separate (because the oil has been added too quickly and the mixture not beaten well enough), put a third egg yolk into a fresh bowl and very gradually beat the curdled aïoli into it until it holds again.

4 Pile the sauce into a bowl, cover and store in the refrigerator until required. The garlic flavour will continue to develop for several hours after the sauce has been made.

Makes about 300 ml (½ pint), enough to serve 4

Indonesian peanut dipping sauce

This recipe was inspired by one of my favourite sauces, satay, the rich, spicy, nutty Indonesian concoction made from peanuts, peanut butter, ginger and chilli. In this recipe I have made the sauce thicker and richer than normal so that it can be used as a dip. It is delicious with any type of vegetable brochette or kebab, with chunky pieces of grilled vegetables and grilled skewered meats, particularly chicken.

1 Heat the oil in a saucepan and fry the onion, garlic, ginger and ground peanuts for 10 minutes to develop the flavours. Add the rest of the ingredients, stirring well to combine. Bring to the boil, reduce the heat and cook gently for a further 10 minutes. The sauce will be thick and rich.

Makes 250 ml (8 fl oz)

2 tablespoons sunflower oil

1 small onion, finely grated

2 garlic cloves, crushed

2.5 cm (1 inch) piece of fresh root ginger, peeled and grated

50 g (2 oz) dry roasted peanuts, ground in a blender or nut mill

a large pinch of hot chilli powder

½ teaspoon soy sauce

2 tablespoons crunchy peanut butter

1–2 tablespoons muscovado sugar

2 tablespoons lime juice

1 x 200 ml (7 fl oz) carton coconut cream

hoisin sauce

A strongly flavoured, distinctive and versatile Chinese sauce, which can be used as a dressing or dip for raw or cooked vegetables. It makes an excellent addition to a stir-fry of leafy greens or robust vegetables, and is a good marinade for meat or fish.

1 Heat the oil and fry the onion, garlic and ginger until soft but not coloured. Add the lemon grass and gradually stir in the rest of the ingredients. Transfer to a bowl or jar, leave to cool, then cover and store in the refrigerator until required. The sauce will keep for several days.

Makes 300 ml (½ pint)

3 tablespoons light sesame oil

¼ small onion, finely chopped

2 garlic cloves, finely chopped

2.5 cm (1 inch) piece of fresh root ginger, peeled and finely sliced

1 lemon grass stalk, finely chopped

150 ml (¼ pint) concentrated vegetable stock

5 tablespoons hoisin sauce

2 tablespoons soy sauce

3 tablespoons red wine vinegar

2 tablespoons clear honey

Szechuan dipping sauce

3 tablespoons soy sauce

2 tablespoons light sesame oil

2 tablespoons lime juice

I tablespoon rice wine vinegar

I tablespoon sweet chilli sauce

I tablespoon clear honey

2 garlic cloves, finely chopped

I teaspoon toasted sesame seeds

2.5 cm (I inch) piece of fresh root
   ginger, peeled and finely grated

2 large spring onions, finely chopped

I tablespoon finely chopped
   coriander

A hot peppery dipping sauce, which takes its name from the fiery cooking of the Szechuan province of China. Although hot, it is also slightly sweet and spicy. Serve with Crudités (page 129) and robust grilled vegetables.

1 Combine all the ingredients except the spring onions and coriander in a screw-top jar. Shake well to combine. Leave for a few hours so that the flavours can mingle and develop.

2 Just before serving, stir in the spring onions and coriander. This sauce will keep for several weeks, as long as the onions and herbs have not been added.

Makes 65 ml (2½ fl oz)

tapenade

A rich robust purée of olives from Provence. There is no absolute recipe – although most have capers, they are not obligatory; others also include anchovies. The olives can vary too, and the tapenade made with any variety, black or green. Serve as a dip for Crudités (page 129), a stuffing for hard-boiled eggs, or a spread on savoury biscuits, crackers or crostini. Tapenade can also be tossed with pasta and sturdy vegetables like broccoli, or combined with vinaigrette to be used as a dressing for salads and cold meats.

200 g (7 oz) black olives, pitted

I x 50 g (2 oz) can anchovy fillets,
   drained and rinsed

2–3 tablespoons capers, drained

juice of I small lemon

1–2 garlic cloves, crushed

½ teaspoon Dijon mustard

50 ml (2 fl oz) extra virgin olive oil

pepper

1 Put the olives, anchovies, capers, lemon juice, garlic and mustard into a food processor or blender. With the machine at full speed, pour in the olive oil to produce a coarse or smooth paste as required. Taste and season with pepper, if necessary. Transfer to a screw-top jar and pour a little oil on top to cover and seal. Cover with the lid and refrigerate. It will keep almost indefinitely.

Makes 250 ml (8 fl oz)

sauces
& dressings

sweet & sour sauce

A hot, spicy sauce to serve with lightly steamed or grilled vegetables, or Vegetable Beignets (page 130), sturdy salad leaves and grilled meat, poultry or fish. If stored in an airtight container without the coriander and spring onions, it will keep in the refrigerator for several weeks.

175 ml (6 fl oz) rice wine vinegar
75 ml (3 fl oz) water
2 tablespoons teriyaki sauce
2 tablespoons lime juice
2 tablespoons muscovado sugar
2–3 garlic cloves, crushed
1–3 tablespoons sweet chilli sauce
1 tablespoon finely chopped
   coriander
3 spring onions, finely chopped
salt

1 Combine all the ingredients, except the coriander and spring onions, in a saucepan. The amount of sweet chilli sauce you add will depend on how hot you want the sauce to be and the strength of the sauce itself. Gently bring to the boil, stirring to blend and dissolve the sugar. Reduce the heat and simmer for about 5 minutes. Set aside to cool, then stir in the chopped coriander and spring onions.

Makes 300 ml (½ pint), enough to serve 10–20

Sweet & Sour Sauce is shown on page 226

ginger & lime pickle mayonnaise

This recipe was inspired by the wonderful range of pickles and chutneys made by Mrs Bassa's Indian Kitchen. They're superb just as they are, but mixed with a rich mayonnaise or thick natural yogurt, they make an excellent saucy dip.

1 Using a vegetable peeler, remove the rind from the lime in very thin strips, leaving the white pith attached to the flesh. Cut the rind into julienne. Remove the pith from the lime with a serrated knife and cut the flesh into segments.

2 Make the mayonnaise. Put the egg yolk and mustard in a bowl, then add the oil, drop by drop, beating continually with a hand or electric whisk. After about 25 ml (1 fl oz) oil has been incorporated, add the rest in a fine, thread-like stream, still beating continually.

3 Squeeze the juice from half of the lime segments into the mayonnaise, then stir in the remaining lime segments and half of the lime julienne, the pickle or chutney, ginger and coriander. Season as necessary, garnish with the remaining lime julienne, then cover and refrigerate until required.

Makes 300 ml (½ pint)

I lime
I large egg yolk
¼ teaspoon English mustard powder
150 ml (¼ pint) sunflower oil
4 tablespoons lime pickle, brinjal pickle or mango chutney
I piece stem ginger preserved in syrup, cut into slivers
I tablespoon finely chopped coriander
salt and pepper

Ginger & Lime Pickle Mayonnaise is shown on page 227

fresh basil dressing

1 Put all the ingredients in a screw-top jar and shake vigorously to emulsify.

Makes about 200 ml (7 fl oz)

150 ml (¼ pint) extra virgin olive oil
juice of 1 large lemon
50 g (2 oz) basil leaves, finely chopped
pinch of salt
pinch of cracked black peppercorns

vinaigrette

1 Put all the ingredients in a screw-top jar and shake vigorously to emulsify. Taste and adjust the seasoning if necessary.

Makes 75 ml (3 fl oz)

½ teaspoon Dijon mustard
1 small garlic clove, crushed
25 ml (1 fl oz) pine nut or hazelnut oil
25 ml (1 fl oz) sunflower oil
1 teaspoon cider or white wine
  vinegar
salt and pepper

lime & sesame dressing

1 Put all the ingredients in a screw-top jar and shake vigorously to emulsify.

Makes 100 ml (3½ fl oz)

50 ml (2 fl oz) light sesame oil
25 ml (1 fl oz) sunflower oil
2 tablespoons lime juice
pinch of sugar
salt and pepper

spicy tomato sauce

A rich, pulpy homemade tomato sauce is one of the essentials in any kitchen. It can be made in large or small quantities, and freezes well, ready for use when needed. In the absence of large, sweet, flavoursome, sun-ripened tomatoes in this country, a more satisfactory result is obtained by using canned tomatoes. Shop around, try a few different brands, then stick to the one that gives you the best results. All sorts of flavours can be added to the basic sauce: diced red or green hot chillies (seeds removed), Tabasco sauce, olives, anchovy fillets or fresh herbs like basil and oregano.

1 Heat the oil in a heavy saucepan and fry the onion and garlic until soft but not coloured. This will take about 10 minutes. Add the rest of the ingredients. Bring to the boil, then lower the heat, cover and simmer for 20 minutes to reduce the liquid and concentrate the flavours. Taste and adjust the seasoning and serve the sauce just as it is, thick and pulpy, or liquidize to give a smooth finish. It may be necessary to adjust the consistency slightly, depending on how the sauce is to be used.

Makes 600 ml (1 pint), enough to serve 4

I tablespoon olive oil
I large onion, finely chopped
2 garlic cloves, finely crushed
I x 400 g (13 oz) can chopped plum tomatoes
65 ml (2½ fl oz) vegetable stock
2 tablespoons tomato purée
I teaspoon sugar
I bay leaf
I teaspoon finely chopped basil
pinch of ground cinnamon
salt and pepper

Hollandaise sauce

It is a long time since I made Hollandaise sauce the classic way. This food processor method is quick, easy and more or less foolproof.

1 Put the shallot, cracked peppercorns, lemon juice and vinegar into a small saucepan. Bring to the boil and cook quickly to reduce the liquid to about 2 tablespoons. Strain into a food processor. Add the egg yolks and process for a few seconds to mix.

2 Melt the butter in a small saucepan over a low heat. With the processor motor running, very gradually pour the butter through the funnel in a thin steady stream, leaving the residue from the butter still in the pan. The mixture will thicken very slightly.

3 Pour the sauce into a bowl and set over a pan of simmering water. The water should not touch the bottom of the bowl. Whisk continually with a balloon whisk until the sauce warms and thickens, taking care that it does not overheat or it may separate and curdle. If it begins to show signs of curdling, quickly remove the bowl from the hot water and beat in 1 tablespoon cold water. Season with salt and extra lemon juice or vinegar, if necessary. If you are not serving the sauce immediately, turn the heat down very low and keep the sauce warm, whisking from time to time.

Makes about 350 ml (12 fl oz), enough to serve 4

I shallot, finely chopped
I teaspoon cracked white
  peppercorns
4 tablespoons lemon juice
I tablespoon white wine vinegar
3 egg yolks
250 g (8 oz) unsalted butter
sea salt

pesto

The word pesto comes from the Italian word pestare, *meaning 'to pound' or 'to bruise'. The sauce originated in Liguria in northern Italy, and in Provence in the south of France, they make a similar sauce called* pistou. *The ingredients for pesto are traditionally pounded together in a mortar to form a brilliant green paste, slightly speckled in appearance, with a heady perfume and a rich flavour. Today purists still use a pestle and mortar, but most of us are satisfied with using a food processor or blender. The secret is not to over-process. Pesto can also be made with herbs like parsley, coriander, sage, sorrel or rocket, but with different results. Although traditionally served with pasta, it has many other uses. It can be stirred into risotto or mashed potatoes, or soups such as minestrone, mixed vegetable and tomato. It can liven up baked tomatoes, sandwiches and crostini, and it combines beautifully with slices of sweet fragrant tomato and buffalo mozzarella cheese.*

1 Put the pine nuts and garlic into a food processor and process briefly. The pesto should not be totally smooth, but have a slight texture. Add the Parmesan and basil and process briefly.

2 With the motor running, gradually add the oil through the funnel in a thin stream until it is all incorporated and a thick, slightly runny paste has formed. Check the seasoning, adding salt and pepper as necessary.

3 Serve as required or store in the refrigerator in an airtight container, covered with a little oil to retain the colour. It will keep well for at least 1 month. Once the container is opened, the sauce needs to be used within 2–3 days.

Makes about 250 ml (8 fl oz)

40 g (1½ oz) pine nuts
1–2 garlic cloves, crushed
40 g (1½ oz) Parmesan cheese, freshly grated
50 g (2 oz) basil leaves
150 ml (¼ pint) light extra virgin olive oil
salt and pepper

mushroom sauce

This richly flavoured sauce can be made with cultivated or wild mushrooms, or even a combination of both. It can also be made without the cream. The liquid can be half stock and half red wine, or all milk, depending on the result required and what it is to be served with. It is particularly good with savoury roulades or pasta.

25 g (1 oz) butter

1 onion, finely chopped

1 garlic clove, crushed

175 g (6 oz) mushrooms, thinly sliced

40 g (1½ oz) butter

40 g (1½ oz) plain flour

500 ml (17 fl oz) mushroom or
  vegetable stock

75 ml (3 fl oz) cream

1 tablespoon mushroom ketchup
  (optional)

salt and pepper

1 Melt the butter in a large saucepan and gently fry the onion over a low heat until soft but not coloured. Add the garlic and mushrooms to the saucepan and fry until beginning to colour.

2 Melt the butter in another saucepan, stir in the flour and cook for a few minutes. Gradually add the stock, stirring to form a smooth consistency. Bring to the boil, stirring frequently, then cook over a gentle heat for 5 minutes to develop the flavour.

3 Add the cream, mushroom ketchup (if using) and season to taste. Return to the boil and use as required.

Makes 750 ml (1¼ pints), enough to serve 8

acco

mpaniments

seeded cheese sablés

Serve these crisp savoury biscuits with soup, raw vegetable salads, such as Vegetable Carpaccio (page 128) or Crudités (page 129), and roasted or grilled vegetables. They are perfect with cheese and chutney too, and also good as a cocktail biscuit. They can be cut into any shape, served hot or cold, and they freeze well.

1 Work the flour, butter, mustard, cayenne and salt in a food processor until the mixture resembles fine breadcrumbs. Add the Cheddar and continue to process for a few seconds until the mixture begins to come together to make a soft dough. Turn on to a lightly floured surface and knead gently. Wrap in clingfilm and refrigerate for about 30 minutes.

2 Roll out the pastry on a lightly floured surface to about 2.5 mm (⅛ inch) thick. Cut into circles with a 6 cm (2½ inch) fluted pastry cutter. Knead the trimmings together, roll out and cut more circles.

3 Line 2 heavy baking sheets with nonstick baking paper and place the sablés on them. Sprinkle with Parmesan and dust with mustard and poppy seeds. Bake in a preheated oven, 200°C (400°F), Gas Mark 6, for 9–12 minutes until crisp and light golden. Transfer to a wire rack with a palette knife. Serve hot, or set aside to cool and store in an airtight container to serve later.

Makes about 30

125 g (4 oz) plain flour

75 g (3 oz) unsalted butter, cut into
  small pieces

1 tablespoon English mustard powder

pinch of cayenne pepper

pinch of salt

125 g (4 oz) mature Cheddar cheese,
  finely grated

40–50 g (1½–2 oz) Parmesan cheese,
  finely grated

2 tablespoons black mustard seeds

1 tablespoon poppy seeds

Seeded Cheese Sablés are shown on the preceding page

tomato & olive bruschetta

Bruschetta are pieces of coarse-textured crusty country bread, more than two days old, cut into 1 cm (½ inch) slices and toasted on both sides on a ridged cast iron grill pan or barbecue grill. Traditionally they were cooked over a wood fire, but nowadays they are more often grilled or baked in a very hot oven, 220°C (425°F), Gas Mark 7, for about 10 minutes until crisp and golden. While still warm, the toasted bread is rubbed with cut garlic, seasoned with sea salt and drizzled with fragrant extra virgin olive oil. Sometimes the bread is brushed with oil before grilling or baking, but this is not strictly authentic. Bruschetta are an excellent way of using up bread which is past its best but not yet stale. It can be served plain, or as a base for an infinite variety of toppings, such as salsa, tapenade, pesto, roasted Mediterranean vegetables, pâté, grilled goat's cheese, sautéed mushrooms and scrambled eggs.

2 large garlic cloves, peeled

8–10 baby tomatoes, cut into thin slices

8 black olives, pitted and roughly chopped

8 green olives, pitted and roughly chopped

2 sun-dried tomatoes in oil, drained and roughly chopped

40 ml (1½ fl oz) extra virgin olive oil

1 teaspoon balsamic vinegar

2 tablespoons finely chopped flat leaf parsley

4 slices of bread

4–8 basil leaves, torn into pieces

salt and pepper

1 Finely chop 1 garlic clove and put it in a bowl with the tomatoes, black and green olives, sun-dried tomatoes, half of the oil and the vinegar. Season with salt and pepper to taste and add half of the parsley. Toss very gently to combine and leave to marinate for 10–15 minutes.

2 Toast the bread on both sides. Cut the remaining garlic clove in half, then lightly rub each side of the toast with the cut sides of the garlic. Brush with the remaining oil. Arrange the bread on a serving plate and spoon the tomato and olive mixture on top. Sprinkle with the remaining parsley and the basil leaves, then drizzle with a little of the remaining oil. Serve immediately.

Makes 4

cheesy leek & herb scones

These are light and puffy, excellent with savoury dishes like soups and stews, and the flavourings can be changed to complement the dish they accompany. Onion or garlic can be used instead of the leek or chives; thyme instead of the basil or marjoram; chilli powder, paprika or cayenne instead of black pepper. Finely chopped and fried bacon also gives a very tasty result. If buttermilk is not available, use thin yogurt or soured cream.

1 Sift the flour, bicarbonate of soda, cream of tartar and salt into a bowl. Cut the butter into small pieces and rub into the flour until the mixture resembles fine breadcrumbs. Stir in half of the Cheddar, the leek or chives, parsley, basil or marjoram and pepper.

2 Make a well in the centre and add almost all of the buttermilk, mixing with a wooden spoon or broad-bladed knife to form a soft dough. Take care not to overwork the dough or it will be heavy and tough. Turn on to a lightly floured surface and knead very gently to form a round shape. Pat or roll to about 2–2.5 cm (¾–1 inch) thick, then cut into scones using a 4.5 cm (1¾ inch) pastry cutter.

3 Place the scones a few inches apart on a lightly floured baking sheet and brush with a little egg or milk to glaze. Top with the remaining cheese and a light dusting of paprika. Bake the scones in a preheated oven, 220°C (425°F), Gas Mark 7, for 15–20 minutes until well risen and light golden in colour. Serve hot or cold, with butter.

Makes 15

250 g (8 oz) plain flour, plus extra
   for dusting
1 teaspoon bicarbonate of soda
1 teaspoon cream of tartar
pinch of salt
25 g (1 oz) butter, plus extra to serve
50–75 g (2–3 oz) mature farmhouse
   Cheddar cheese, grated
2 tablespoons finely chopped leek or
   snipped chives
1 tablespoon finely chopped parsley
1 teaspoon finely chopped basil or
   marjoram
pinch of black pepper
200 ml (7 fl oz) buttermilk
beaten egg or milk, to glaze
paprika, for dusting

herby grain bread

The perfect accompaniment to soups, stews and savoury dishes as well as cheese, this bread has a close, coarse texture and nutty flavour. Any flour or combination of flours can be used to create different tastes and textures, and other flavourings can be added, such as finely chopped fried bacon, nuts and seeds, even a strongly flavoured grated cheese. For a sweet bread, substitute sugar and dried fruit for the herbs.

1 Thickly spread half of the butter over the inside of a 500 g (1 lb) loaf tin.

2 Combine the flours, porridge oats, sugar and salt and pepper in a large bowl. Sift in the bicarbonate of soda and cream of tartar and stir to mix well. Cut the remaining butter into small pieces and rub into the mixture until it resembles fine breadcrumbs. Add the leek and herbs and mix well to combine.

3 Make a well in the centre of the mixture and pour in all but 25 ml (1 fl oz) of the buttermilk. The quantity of liquid required will depend on the type and absorbency of the flours used. Working quickly and lightly with your hand, mix the buttermilk into the dry ingredients. The less working the lighter the bread will be, and the mixture should resemble thick, slightly sloppy porridge.

4 Scrape the dough into the buttered tin and shape it with a spoon so that it is slightly domed in the centre and without any air spaces. The bread will rise and level out during cooking. Sprinkle with the seeds and a little extra wholegrain flour, then gently rough up the surface with the prongs of a fork.

5 Cook in a preheated oven, 200°C (400°F), Gas Mark 6, for 30 minutes, then cover loosely with foil, reduce the temperature to 180°C (350°F), Gas Mark 4 and cook for a further 30 minutes.

6 Remove the bread from the oven and leave to cool in the tin, still covered with the foil. When cold, remove from the tin and wrap in a clean tea towel or napkin. The bread will keep well for several days and can be reheated in the oven if cut into slices and wrapped in foil.

Makes one 500 g (1 lb) loaf

50 g (2 oz) butter
175 g (6 oz) extra-coarse wholegrain flour
175 g (6 oz) malted grain flour
75 g (3 oz) plain flour
75 g (3 oz) porridge oats
25 g (1 oz) demerara sugar
1 teaspoon salt
1 tablespoon pepper
2 teaspoons bicarbonate of soda
1 teaspoon cream of tartar
50 g (2 oz) leek, washed and finely chopped
4 tablespoons finely chopped parsley
2 tablespoons finely snipped chives
1 teaspoon finely chopped thyme
1 teaspoon finely chopped oregano
400–475 ml (14–16 fl oz) buttermilk
1 tablespoon pumpkin, sesame or poppy seeds

cheesy crisps

These can be served as a savoury bite with drinks, or as an accompaniment to soup, roasted vegetables or leafy salads. The cheese can be mixed with 25 g (1 oz) chopped walnuts, pecans or hazelnuts, and seasoned with fresh thyme, ground black pepper, a little paprika or cayenne. When cold, the crisps can be stored in an airtight container for about 1 week or frozen for several weeks. If they soften, return them to a hot oven to crisp up.

125 g (4 oz) mature farmhouse or vegetarian Cheddar, Gruyère or raclette cheese, coarsely grated or diced

1 Line several baking sheets with nonstick baking paper. Place 2 mounds of cheese on each sheet, no more than 8 cm (3½ inches) in diameter and at least 10 cm (4 inches) apart. The cheese will spread and form rough biscuit shapes.

2 Bake in a preheated oven, 220°C (425°F), Gas Mark 7, for 10 minutes until the cheese bubbles and begins to turn a very pale cream colour. Too golden in colour and it will taste bitter.

3 Allow the crisps to cool slightly, then transfer them with a spatula to a wire rack to cool completely. Serve or store as required.

Serves 7–8

Gruyère crisps
with pecans & thyme

140 g (4½ oz) **Gruyère cheese,
coarsely grated**

25 g (1 oz) **pecan nuts, walnuts,
hazelnuts or pine nuts, chopped**

2 teaspoons **chopped thyme
pepper**

1 teaspoon **hot paprika**

These are perfect with salads, roasted or grilled vegetables, spicy stews and stir-fries. They also make excellent cocktail biscuits. They will keep for about 1 week in an airtight container, and can be very quickly crisped up in the oven if they become soft during storage. They can also be frozen in a rigid airtight container.

1 Line a large baking sheet with nonstick baking paper. Pile small spoonfuls of the grated Gruyère on the paper, leaving about 10 cm (4 inches) between each pile to allow the cheese to spread. Sprinkle on the nuts and thyme and dust each mound with freshly ground black pepper and a shake of paprika.

2 Bake in a preheated oven, 180°C (350°F), Gas Mark 4, for 8–12 minutes until the cheese starts to bubble and turn a light golden brown. Take care not to let the cheese brown too much or the crisps will taste bitter.

3 Remove from the oven and allow to cool slightly before transferring to a wire rack with a palette knife. Leave to cool completely before serving, or store as required.

Makes 14

filo & Emmenthal wafers

These crisp savoury wafers are composed of gossamer thin sheets of filo pastry layered with butter and finely grated Emmenthal cheese. Serve with soup, roasted vegetables, salads and spicy vegetable stir-fries. They make excellent biscuits to serve with drinks, and can be stored in an airtight container for 3–4 days.

1 Lightly brush 1 sheet of filo pastry with butter and scatter with a little of the cheese. Put a second sheet on top, brush with melted butter and scatter with more cheese. Repeat with a third sheet, finishing with the cheese. Do the same with the remaining 3 sheets of filo pastry so that you have 2 stacks of pastry. Using a 7 cm (3 inch) plain round pastry cutter, cut the filo layers into circles and place them on a heavy baking sheet. Alternatively, divide the pastry into rectangular 10 x 3 cm (4 x 1¼ inch) wafers.

2 Bake in a preheated oven, 180°C (350°F), Gas Mark 4, for 15 minutes until crisp and light brown. Remove from the baking sheet and cool on a wire rack.

Makes 20 round biscuits or 36 rectangular ones

6 sheets filo pastry, 31 x 21 cm (12½ x 8½ inches), defrosted if frozen
75 g (3 oz) butter, melted
175 g (6 oz) Emmenthal cheese, finely grated

piroshki

These are small crescent-shaped pastries traditionally served as an accompaniment to borscht and other Russian soups, but also excellent as a cocktail savoury. They freeze very well in their raw state, to be defrosted and baked as required.

15 g (½ oz) butter

1 small onion, very finely chopped

2 garlic cloves, crushed

75 g (3 oz) mushrooms, very finely chopped

125 g (4 oz) cooked meat (chicken, beef, ham), very finely chopped or minced, or chopped mixed vegetables fried in a little butter until soft

1 hard-boiled egg, very finely chopped

2 tablespoons very finely chopped parsley

2 tablespoons very finely chopped dill

1 tablespoon lemon juice

beaten egg or milk, to glaze

salt and pepper

Pastry:

250 g (8 oz) plain flour

pinch of salt

125 g (4 oz) butter or hard margarine

50 g (2 oz) hard white fat

1 egg yolk

3 tablespoons soured cream

1 First prepare the pastry. Sift the flour and salt into a bowl. Cut the fats into small pieces and rub them into the flour until the mixture resembles fine breadcrumbs. This can be done in a food processor, stopping and starting the machine to ensure that the pastry does not become over-processed. Mix the egg yolk with the soured cream, then sprinkle on to the crumbled pastry and stir to make a dough. If you are using a food processor, pulse several times, just enough to meld the dough together. Turn on to a lightly floured work surface, gather together into a ball and knead lightly. Cover and chill while making the filling.

2 Melt the butter in a frying pan and gently fry the onion and garlic until soft but not coloured. Stir in the mushrooms and fry until cooked and all the moisture has been driven off. Stir in the cooked meat or fried vegetables, the egg, parsley and dill. Season to taste with salt and pepper and add the lemon juice to sharpen. Set aside to cool.

3 Roll out the pastry very thinly – no more than about 2 mm (¹⁄₁₆ inch) thick on a lightly floured surface. Cut 6 cm (2½ inch) circles from the dough and place a little of the cold filling on one half of each circle. Brush the edge of the other half with beaten egg and fold the pastry over to enclose the filling. Press the edges together and crimp with the prongs of a fork. Place the piroshki on a lightly greased baking sheet. Brush with beaten egg or milk to glaze and bake in a preheated oven, 220°C (425°F), Gas Mark 7, for 5–8 minutes until golden.

Makes about 32

Jerusalem artichoke chips

These have a crisp exterior, yet are meltingly tender inside. They have a subtle flavour and make an excellent accompaniment for grilled or roast poultry and game. When thinly sliced, they can be served like potato crisps and are good scattered over Jerusalem Artichoke Soup (page 124) or through a leafy salad.

1 Peel the artichokes and cut them into chips about 5 cm (2 inches) long and 1 cm (½ inch) wide, or cut them into thin slices as required. Rinse and dry the pieces carefully.

2 Heat the oil in a deep-fryer or large saucepan to 180–190°C (350–375°F), or until a cube of bread browns in 30 seconds. Deep-fry the artichoke pieces in small batches until tender, crisp and golden in colour. Drain on kitchen paper, season generously and serve immediately.

Serves 4–6

CHEF'S TIP The chips or slices can be prepared in advance, cooked only until they are pale in colour, then reheated in batches in hot oil at 200°C (400°F) before serving.

500–750 g (1–1½ lb) large smooth Jerusalem artichokes
vegetable oil, for deep-frying

croûtons

Small cubes of bread fried in oil are frequently added to soup, vegetables and salad dishes to add extra texture, flavour and interest. For garlic or chilli croûtons, infuse the oil with 2–3 crushed garlic cloves or 1 small chopped fresh chilli for several hours before straining the oil and frying the bread. Nut-flavoured oils can also be used.

3 slices of white bread, about 5 mm (¼ inch) thick
4–5 tablespoons sunflower or olive oil

1 Remove the crusts from the bread and cut the bread into 5 mm (¼ inch) cubes. The croûtons can be larger, depending on what they are to be served with. When used as a soup garnish, they are more elegant when small.

2 Heat the oil in a frying pan and add the cubes of bread, tossing and turning them to coat in the oil. Fry over a gentle heat until evenly coloured and a light golden brown. Drain on kitchen paper and use as required. Croûtons can be stored in an airtight container for several weeks, or they can be frozen.

Makes 75 g (3 oz) croûtons, enough to serve 6

pickled cucumber

Pickling is an easy and tasty way to use up excess cucumbers. Pickled cucumber needs to mature for several hours or overnight, so prepare in advance. It will keep well in the refrigerator for several weeks.

1 Combine all the ingredients in a non-metallic bowl, cover and leave to marinate for several hours. Pack into a sterilized jar, cover and refrigerate.

Makes 400 g (13 oz), enough to serve 4–6

250 g (8 oz) cucumber, cut into little sticks, 5 mm (¼ inch) wide
6 tablespoons rice vinegar
2 tablespoons sweet cooking sake (mirin)
50 ml (2 fl oz) cider vinegar
¼ teaspoon dried chilli flakes
2 garlic cloves, chopped
½ teaspoon salt
2 teaspoons brown sugar
pinch of ground cloves
pinch of ground cinnamon
pepper

polenta cakes

Polenta, also known as cornmeal or yellow meal, is ground maize. It is usually sunshine yellow in colour, but there is also a white variety, and a beautiful dark purple one, a strain of Indian maize known as blue cornmeal. Whatever its colour, polenta is an essential ingredient in the cooking of northern Italy, the southern states of the USA and the West Indies. It has a sweet nutty taste and comes in varying degrees of coarseness, ranging from the most commonly used Italian golden polenta, which is coarse ground, to finely ground American cornmeal and West Indian ground maize, which may be coarse or fine. In Italy, polenta is traditionally used for making a thick porridge with water, stock or milk, which is eaten 'wet' with lots of butter and Parmesan cheese. These grilled polenta cakes, made from cold polenta, are another traditional dish.

1 Melt the butter in a large saucepan and fry the onion until soft but not browned. Add the water and bring to the boil. Gradually pour in the polenta, stirring all the time, first with a wire whisk and then with a wooden spoon, so the polenta remains smooth and there are no lumps. Cook over a gentle heat for about 4–5 minutes, or follow the instructions on the packet. Stir in the Parmesan cheese and season with salt and pepper.

2 Lightly oil a 33 x 23 x 1 cm (13 x 9 x ½ inch) Swiss roll tin. Line the tin with clingfilm and oil it. Tip the prepared polenta into the tin and smooth the top. Cover with a piece of greaseproof paper and leave until cool and set. This will take about 20 minutes, but the polenta can be made the day before, ready for cutting and grilling as required.

3 When the polenta is set, turn it out on to a board. Cut it into 6 squares, then 12 triangles. Brush a heavy baking sheet with a little oil and set the polenta triangles on top. Brush each one with a little oil.

4 Cook the polenta triangles on a ridged cast iron grill pan or under a pre-heated grill for about 3 minutes on each side. Serve hot.

Makes 12

50 g (2 oz) butter
I large onion, finely chopped
I litre (1¾ pints) water
250 g (8 oz) instant polenta
50 g (2 oz) Parmesan cheese, freshly
  grated
2 tablespoons olive oil
salt and pepper

mung dhal

A rich lentil purée, quick and easy to prepare using split lentils that do not need pre-soaking. Serve with any spicy vegetable stew, or with rice or Indian bread. Mung dhal also makes an excellent spread for crostini or crisp biscuits. When mixed with finely chopped spring onion, it makes a delicious sandwich filling.

1 Wash and drain the lentils. Put them in a large saucepan with the turmeric, chilli powder, cinnamon and vegetable stock. Stir to combine and bring to the boil. Reduce the heat immediately, cover and simmer gently for 20–40 minutes until the lentils are soft and the stock almost absorbed. The mixture should have a creamy consistency, but the lentils should retain some of their texture.

2 Heat the ghee or oil in a frying pan and fry the onion and garlic until a light golden colour. Stir in the cumin seeds and fry until they begin to splutter. Pour over the lentil mixture and stir to combine. Stir in the coriander, season with salt and serve sprinkled with the garam masala.

Makes 825 g (1 lb 11 oz), enough to serve 4–6

250 g (8 oz) split red lentils
½ teaspoon turmeric
½ teaspoon chilli powder
2.5 cm (1 inch) piece of cinnamon stick
750 ml (1¼ pints) hot vegetable stock or water
2–3 tablespoons ghee or sunflower oil
1 large onion, thinly sliced
1–2 garlic cloves, crushed
½ teaspoon cumin seeds
1 tablespoon finely chopped coriander
salt
¼ teaspoon garam masala, to serve

index

bold page numbers refer to entries in the directory

A

accompaniments 236–51
acorn squash **90**
aïoli 223
Allium cepa see onions; shallots
Allium porrum see leeks
Allium sativum see garlic
almonds
  skordalia 222
anchovies
  black olive salsa with capers, onion & anchovies 214
  tapenade 225
Apium graveolens see celeriac; celery
artichokes *see* globe artichokes; Jerusalem artichokes
asparagus **36–7**
  asparagus & white wine risotto 143
  grilled asparagus 136
Asparagus officinalis see asparagus
aubergines **97**
  aubergine & sesame dip 221
  caponata 161
  couscous-filled aubergines 199
  omelette 173
  ratatouille 162
  sweet & sour aubergine relish 210
avocado **95**
  avocado & tomato salsa 212
  avocado salsa 211
  chargrilled sweetcorn & avocado salsa 213
  guacamole 218
  Mexican bean stew with avocado & tomato salsa 150
  omelette 173
  roast fillet of salmon with tomato & avocado compote 194

B

bacon
  chicory & smoked bacon gratin 202
  potato, mushroom & bacon gratin 205
bakes & roasts 190–207
basil
  courgette, tomato & basil tart 197
  fresh basil dressing 230
  pesto 234
  salsa verde 211
  tomato & orange soup with basil cream 120

bean curd *see* tofu
bean sprouts
  stir-fried duck with ginger & vegetables 174
  stir-fried noodles with broccoli, sweetcorn, bean sprouts & smoked tofu 184
beans *see individual types of bean*
beef
  beef & carrot tzimmes with thimble dumplings 163
  spicy beef koftas in pizzaiola sauce 146
beetroot **58**
  beetroot borscht with soured cream & chives 114
beignets, vegetable 130
Beta vulgaris see beetroot; Swiss chard
biscuits
  seeded cheese sablés 238
bitter melon *see* Chinese bitter melon
black bean sauce
  wilted greens with water chestnuts & black bean sauce 182
black kidney beans
  Mexican bean stew with avocado & tomato salsa 150
black truffles **104**
Boletus edulis see ceps
borscht
  beetroot borscht with soured cream & chives 114
Brassica campestrio see turnips
Brassica juncea see Chinese mustard greens
Brassica napus see swedes
Brassica oleracea
  Acephala group *see* kale
  Botrytis group *see* cauliflower
  Capitata group *see* cabbage
  Gemmifera group *see* Brussels sprouts
  Gongylodes group *see* kohlrabi
  Italica group *see* broccoli
Brassica rapa chinensis see pak-choi
Brassica rapa nipposinica see mizuna greens
Brassica rapa pekinensis see Chinese cabbage
brassicas & leafy greens **13–31**
bread
  croûtons 249
  herby grain bread 242
  tomato & olive bruschetta 239
Breton beans with cheese & herb crust 147
broad beans **78**
broccoli **23**
  broccoli & coriander chicken 201
  green vegetables with Thai-spiced coconut sauce 152

stir-fried noodles with broccoli, sweetcorn, bean sprouts & smoked tofu 184
  wilted greens with water chestnuts & black bean sauce 182
brochettes
  salmon & courgette brochettes 179
  vegetable brochettes with mustard & herb glaze 180
bruschetta, tomato & olive 239
Brussels sprouts **22**
burgers
  red lentil burgers spiked with chillies & garlic 176
  sweetcorn & tofu burgers with spiked yogurt sauce 169
butter, clarifying 137
butter beans
  Breton beans with cheese & herb crust 147
butternut squash **90**
button mushrooms **101**

C

cabbage **20–1**
cabbage, Chinese *see* Chinese cabbage
capers
  black olive salsa with capers, onion & anchovies 214
  tapenade 225
caponata 161
Capsicum annuum see peppers
Capsicum frutescens see chilli peppers
cardoon **39**
carpaccio, vegetable 128
carrots **62–3**
  beef & carrot tzimmes with thimble dumplings 163
  carrot, mushroom & mixed nut roast 196
  vegetable carpaccio with Parmesan shavings 128
cashew nuts
  chicken with vegetables, noodles & cashew nuts 189
cauliflower **18**
  hot spiced stew with potatoes & cauliflower 156
  vegetable pakoras 132
celeriac **35**
  creamed celeriac & Parmesan soup 122
celery **34**
  celery & lovage soup with herb cream & croûtons 118
  vegetable carpaccio with Parmesan shavings 128
ceps **102**
chanterelles **102**
chard, Swiss *see* Swiss chard
chargrilled sweetcorn & avocado salsa 213
chayote **96**

cheese
  Breton beans with cheese & herb crust 147
  cheesy crisps 243
  cheesy leek & herb scones 240
  chicory & smoked bacon gratin 202
  courgette & red pepper tian 193
  couscous-filled aubergines 199
  creamed celeriac & Parmesan soup 122
  eggs Florentine 140
  filo & Emmenthal wafers 246
  goat's cheese with peppers & pine nuts 135
  Gruyère crisps with pecans & thyme 245
  leek & spinach filo triangles 133
  melange of vegetables with coconut & cheese topping 204
  mushroom & green herb pâté 137
  potato, mushroom & bacon gratin 205
  pumpkin soup with crusty cheese topping 111
  red lentil burgers spiked with chillies & garlic 176
  rustic Greek salad 139
  seeded cheese sablés 238
  spinach & cheese filo pie 200
  spinach & chickpea stew 151
  spinach & ricotta gnocchi 141
  vegetable carpaccio with Parmesan shavings 128
chestnut mushrooms **101**
chestnuts
  carrot, mushroom & mixed nut roast 196
chicken
  broccoli & coriander chicken 201
  chicken with vegetables, noodles & cashew nuts 189
chickpeas
  hummus 222
  spinach & chickpea stew 151
chicory **28–9**
  chicory & smoked bacon gratin 202
chilli peppers **84**
  chilli bean & pepper soup 110
  chilli bean dip 220
  guacamole 218
  harissa 219
  hot tomato salsa 215
  mango & cucumber salsa with chilli 217
  red lentil burgers spiked with chillies & garlic 176
Chinese bitter melon **94**
Chinese cabbage **27**
Chinese mustard greens **15**
chips, Jerusalem artichoke 248
chowder, sweetcorn 116

Cichorium intybus see chicory
clarifying butter 137
coconut
  green vegetables with Thai-spiced coconut sauce 152
  melange of vegetables with coconut & cheese topping 204
collards **16**
Colocasia esculenta see taro
coriander
  broccoli & coriander chicken 201
  mushroom & green herb pâté 137
corn-on-the-cob **79**
  chargrilled sweetcorn & avocado salsa 213
courgette flowers **87**
courgettes **87**
  Breton beans with cheese & herb crust 147
  courgette & dill soup 112
  courgette & red pepper tian 193
  courgette, tomato & basil tart 197
  green vegetables with Thai-spiced coconut sauce 152
  omelette 173
  ratatouille 162
  salmon & courgette brochettes 179
couscous
  couscous-filled aubergines 199
  saffron-spiced vegetable couscous 148
cream, soured *see* soured cream
creamed celeriac & Parmesan soup 122
crème fraîche
  eggs Florentine 140
crisps
  cheesy crisps 243
  Gruyère crisps with pecans & thyme 245
crookneck squash **90**
croûtons 249
crudités 129
cucumber **85**
  cucumber & mint raita 216
  gazpacho Andaluz 115
  mango & cucumber salsa with chilli 217
  pickled cucumber 249
Cucumis sativus see cucumber
Cucurbita maxima see pumpkin
Cucurbita pepo see courgettes; marrow; squashes
cultivated mushrooms **100–1**
curly kale **16**
Cynara cardunculus see cardoon
Cynara scolymus see globe artichokes

D
Daucus carota see carrots
dill
  courgette & dill soup 112
Dioscora see yams
dipping sauce, grilled vegetables with 186
dips
  aïoli 223
  aubergine & sesame dip 221
  chilli bean dip 220
  guacamole 218
  hummus 222
  Indonesian peanut dipping sauce 224
  lentil, green peppercorn & mustard dip 218
  skordalia 222
  Szechuan dipping sauce 225
  tapenade 225
dressings
  fresh basil dressing 230
  lime & sesame dressing 231
  vinaigrette 231
dried mushrooms **103**
duck
  stir-fried duck with ginger & vegetables 174
dumplings
  beef & carrot tzimmes with thimble dumplings 163
  potato gnocchi with pesto sauce 142
  spinach & ricotta gnocchi 141
  vegetable stew with mustard & herb dumplings 159
Dutch cabbage **21**

E
eggs
  eggs Florentine 140
  sweetcorn & red pepper frittata 170
  see also omelettes

F
fennel **42**
  peppered tuna steaks with fennel, red onions & sugar snaps 168
  vegetable carpaccio with Parmesan shavings 128
field mushrooms **103**
filo pastry
  filo & Emmenthal wafers 246
  spinach & cheese filo pie 200
  leek & spinach filo triangles 133
fish *see* salmon; tuna
Foeniculum vulgare see fennel
fragrant mixed vegetable stew 154
French beans **75**
fricassée of mushrooms 155
frittata, sweetcorn & red pepper 170
fritters
  vegetable beignets 130
  vegetable pakoras 132
fruiting vegetables **80–97**

G
garlic **54–5**
  aïoli 223
  harissa 219
  omelette 173
  red lentil burgers spiked with chillies & garlic 176
  roasted pepper soup with tomatoes, garlic & fragrant herbs 123
  skordalia 222
gazpacho Andaluz 115
ginger
  ginger & lime pickle mayonnaise 227
  stir-fried duck with ginger & vegetables 174
globe artichokes **40–1**
gnocchi
  potato gnocchi with pesto sauce 142
  spinach & ricotta gnocchi 141
goat's cheese with peppers & pine nuts 135
grain bread, herby 242
gratins
  broccoli & coriander chicken 201
  chicory & smoked bacon gratin 202
  potato, mushroom & bacon gratin 205
Greek salad, rustic 139
green vegetables with Thai-spiced coconut sauce 152
grills, stir-fries & pan-fries **166–89**
Gruyère crisps with pecans & thyme 245
guacamole 218

H
harissa 219
hazelnuts
  carrot, mushroom & mixed nut roast 196
Helianthus tuberosus see Jerusalem artichokes
herb omelette 173
herby grain bread 242
Hibiscus esculentus see okra
hoisin sauce 224
hollandaise sauce 233
horn of plenty **103**
hubbard squash **90**
hummus 222

I
Indonesian peanut dipping sauce 224
Ipomoea batatas see sweet potatoes

J
Jerusalem artichokes **65**
  Jerusalem artichoke chips 248
  Jerusalem artichoke soup 124
julienne, orange 120

K
kabocha squash **90**
kale **16–17**
kantola **94**
kebabs
  mushroom & tofu kebabs 181
  salmon & courgette brochettes 179
  vegetable brochettes with mustard & herb glaze 180
kidney beans *see* red kidney beans
koftas
  spicy beef koftas in pizzaiola sauce 146
kohlrabi **38**

L
lamb
  Mediterranean lamb stew with tomatoes, olives & pasta 158
leaf beet **31**
leafy greens **12–31**
leeks **52–3**
  cheesy leek & herb scones 240
  leek & spinach filo triangles 133
lentils
  hot spiced stew with potatoes & cauliflower 156
  lentil, green peppercorn & mustard dip 218
  mung dhal 251
  red lentil burgers spiked with chillies & garlic 176
  red lentil, pepper & mushroom bake 206
lime
  ginger & lime pickle mayonnaise 229
  lime & sesame dressing 231
little gem squash **90**
lovage
  celery & lovage soup with herb cream & croûtons 118
Lycopersicon esculentum see tomatoes

M
maize *see* sweetcorn
mangetouts **77**
  green vegetables with Thai-spiced coconut sauce 152
mango & cucumber salsa with chilli 217
marrow **88**
mayonnaise
  aïoli 223
  ginger & lime pickle mayonnaise 227
meat
  piroshki 247
  see also beef; lamb *etc*
Mediterranean lamb stew with tomatoes, olives & pasta 158
melange of vegetables with coconut & cheese topping 204

melon, Chinese bitter *see*
   Chinese bitter melon
Mexican bean stew with
   avocado & tomato salsa 150
mint
   cucumber & mint raita 216
   minted green pea soup with hot
      paprika & croûtons 119
mizuna greens **26**
Momordica charantia see
   Chinese bitter melon
morels **103**
mung dhal 251
mushrooms **98–105**
   carrot, mushroom & mixed nut
      roast 196
   crisp green vegetables stir-fried
      with mushrooms in sweet &
      sour sauce 185
   fricassée of mushrooms 155
   mushroom & green herb pâté
      137
   mushroom & tofu kebabs 181
   mushroom sauce 235
   piroshki 247
   potato, mushroom & bacon
      gratin 205
   red lentil, pepper & mushroom
      bake 206
   wild mushroom omelette 172
mustard
   lentil, green peppercorn &
      mustard dip 218
   seeded cheese sablés 238
   vegetable brochettes with
      mustard & herb glaze 180
   vegetable stew with mustard &
      herb dumplings 159
mustard greens, Chinese *see*
   Chinese mustard greens

N
New Zealand spinach **31**
noodles
   chicken with vegetables,
      noodles & cashew nuts 189
   stir-fried noodles with broccoli,
      sweetcorn, bean sprouts &
      smoked tofu 184
nuts
   carrot, mushroom & mixed nut
      roast 196
   see also almonds; peanuts *etc*

O
okra **72**
olives
   black olive salsa with capers,
      onion & anchovies 214
   Mediterranean lamb stew with
      tomatoes, olives & pasta 158
   rustic Greek salad 139
   spicy beef koftas in pizzaiola
      sauce 146
   tapenade 225
   tomato & olive bruschetta 239
omelettes
   aubergine 173

avocado 173
courgette 173
garlic 173
grilled sweet red pepper 173
mixed herbs 173
ratatouille 173
shallots 173
sorrel 173
Spanish potato 177
tomatoes 173
watercress 173
wild mushroom 172
onion family **44–55**
onion squash **90**
onions **46**
   peppered tuna steaks with
      fennel, red onions & sugar
      snaps 168
   rustic Greek salad 139
   vegetable pakoras 132
oranges
   julienne 120
   tomato & orange soup with
      basil cream 120
oyster mushrooms **101**

P
pak-choi **24**
   wilted greens with water
      chestnuts & black bean sauce
      182
pakoras, vegetable 132
pan-fries, stir-fries & grills
   166–89
papaya
   hot papaya & roasted pepper
      salsa 212
parsley
   mushroom & green herb pâté
      137
   salsa verde 211
parsnips **67**
pasta
   Mediterranean lamb stew with
      tomatoes, olives & pasta 158
Pastinaca sativa see parsnips
pastries
   filo & Emmenthal wafers 246
   leek & spinach filo triangles
      133
   piroshki 247
   see also pies; tarts
pastry, rich shortcrust 197
pâté, mushroom & green herb
   137
pattypan squash **90–1**
peanuts
   Indonesian peanut dipping
      sauce 224
peas **76–7**
   green vegetables with Thai-
      spiced coconut sauce 152
   minted green pea soup with hot
      paprika & croûtons 119
pecan nuts
   Gruyère crisps with pecans &
      thyme 245
peppercorns

lentil, green peppercorn &
   mustard dip 218
peppered tuna steaks with
   fennel, red onions & sugar
   snaps 168
peppers **82–3**
   chilli bean & pepper soup 110
   courgette & red pepper tian
      193
   gazpacho Andaluz 115
   goat's cheese with peppers &
      pine nuts 135
   grilled sweet red pepper
      omelette 173
   hot papaya & roasted pepper
      salsa 212
   ratatouille 162
   red lentil, pepper & mushroom
      bake 206
   roasted pepper soup with
      tomatoes, garlic & fragrant
      herbs 123
   spicy beef koftas in pizzaiola
      sauce 146
   stir-fried duck with ginger &
      vegetables 174
   sweetcorn & red pepper frittata
      170
   vegetable carpaccio with
      Parmesan shavings 128
   vegetable pakoras 132
   see also chilli peppers
Persea americana see avocados
pesto 234
   potato gnocchi with pesto
      sauce 142
Phaseolus coccineus see runner
   beans
Phaseolus vulgaris see French
   beans
pickled cucumber 249
pickling onions **46**
pied de mouton **103**
pies
   spinach & cheese filo pie 200
pine nuts
   goat's cheese with peppers &
      pine nuts 135
   pesto 234
piroshki 247
Pisum sativum see peas
pizzaiola sauce, spicy beef koftas
   in 146
podded vegetables **70–9**
polenta cakes 250
poppy seeds
   seeded cheese sablés 238
potatoes **69**
   hot spiced stew with potatoes
      & cauliflower 156
   potato gnocchi with pesto
      sauce 142
   potato, mushroom & bacon
      gratin 205
   Spanish potato omelette 177
   vegetable pakoras 132
puffballs, giant **103**
pumpkin **86**

pumpkin & root vegetable stew
   164
pumpkin soup with crusty
   cheese topping 111
purple kale **17**

R
radishes **68**
   vegetable carpaccio with
      Parmesan shavings 128
   raita, cucumber & mint 216
Raphanus sativus see radishes
ratatouille 162
   omelette 173
red cabbage **21**
red kidney beans
   chilli bean & pepper soup
      110
   chilli bean dip 220
   Mexican bean stew with
      avocado & tomato salsa
      150
red onions **46**
relish, sweet & sour aubergine
   210
rice
   asparagus & white wine risotto
      143
   courgette & red pepper tian
      193
   risotto, asparagus & white wine
      143
roasts & bakes **190–207**
roots & tubers **56–69**
   pumpkin & root vegetable stew
      164
   roast root vegetable tarte Tatin
      192
runner beans **74**
rustic Greek salad 139

S
sablés, seeded cheese 238
saffron-spiced vegetable
   couscous 148
salad, rustic Greek 139
salmon
   roast fillet of salmon with
      tomato & avocado compôte
      194
   salmon & courgette brochettes
      179
salsas
   avocado & tomato salsa 212
   avocado salsa 211
   black olive salsa with capers,
      onion & anchovies 214
   chargrilled sweetcorn &
      avocado salsa 213
   hot papaya & roasted pepper
      salsa 212
   hot tomato salsa 215
   mango & cucumber salsa with
      chilli 217
   salsa verde 211
sauces
   aïoli 223
   hoisin sauce 224

hollandaise sauce 233
Indonesian peanut dipping
    sauce 224
mushroom sauce 235
pesto 234
skordalia 222
spicy tomato sauce 232
sweet & sour sauce 226
Szechuan dipping sauce 225
tapenade 225
Savoy cabbage **21**
scones, cheesy leek & herb 240
Sechium edule see chayote
seeded cheese sablés 238
sesame oil
    lime & sesame dressing 231
shallots **50–1**
    omelette 173
shiitake mushrooms **101**
shortcrust pastry 197
silver kale **17**
skordalia 222
Solanum melongena see
    aubergines
Solanum tuberosum see potatoes
sorrel omelette 173
soups **109–24**
    beetroot borscht with soured
        cream & chives 114
    celery & lovage soup with herb
        cream & croûtons 118
    chilli bean & pepper soup 110
    courgette & dill soup 112
    creamed celeriac & Parmesan
        soup 122
    gazpacho Andaluz 115
    Jerusalem artichoke soup 124
    minted green pea soup with hot
        paprika & croûtons 119
    pumpkin soup with crusty
        cheese topping 111
    roasted pepper soup with
        tomatoes, garlic & fragrant
        herbs 123
    sweetcorn chowder 116
    tomato & orange soup with
        basil cream 120
soured cream
    beetroot borscht with soured
        cream & chives 114
spaghetti squash **91**
Spanish onions **46**
Spanish potato omelette 177
spicy beef koftas in pizzaiola
    sauce 146
spicy tomato sauce 232
Spinacea oleracea see spinach
spinach **30–1**
    eggs Florentine 140
    leek & spinach filo triangles
        133
    spinach & cheese filo pie 200
    spinach & chickpea stew 151
    spinach & ricotta gnocchi 141
spring greens **21**
spring onions **46**
squashes **89–91**
stalks & stems **32–43**

starters **126–43**
stems & stalks **32–43**
stews **144–64**
    beef & carrot tzimmes with
        thimble dumplings 163
    Breton beans with cheese &
        herb crust 147
    caponata 161
    fragrant mixed vegetable stew
        154
    fricassée of mushrooms 155
    green vegetables with Thai-
        spiced coconut sauce 152
    hot spiced stew with potatoes
        & cauliflower 156
    Mediterranean lamb stew with
        tomatoes, olives & pasta 158
    Mexican bean stew with
        avocado & tomato salsa
        150
    pumpkin & root vegetable stew
        164
    ratatouille 162
    saffron-spiced vegetable
        couscous 148
    spicy beef koftas in pizzaiola
        sauce 146
    spinach & chickpea stew 151
    vegetable stew with mustard &
        herb dumplings 159
stir-fries, pan-fries & grills
    166–89
sugar snaps **77**
    peppered tuna steaks with
        fennel, red onions & sugar
        snaps 168
summer truffles **104**
swedes **60**
sweet & sour aubergine relish
    210
sweet & sour sauce 228
    crisp green vegetables stir-fried
        with mushrooms in sweet &
        sour sauce 185
sweet potatoes **66**
sweetcorn **79**
    chargrilled sweetcorn &
        avocado salsa 213
    stir-fried noodles with broccoli,
        sweetcorn, bean sprouts &
        smoked tofu 184
    sweetcorn & red pepper frittata
        170
    sweetcorn & tofu burgers with
        spiked yogurt sauce 169
    sweetcorn chowder 116
Swiss chard **14**
Szechuan dipping sauce 225

T
tahini paste
    aubergine & sesame dip 221
    hummus 222
tapenade 225
taro **61**
tarts
    courgette, tomato & basil tart
        197

roast root vegetable tarte Tatin
    192
thimble dumplings, beef &
    carrot tzimmes with 163
thyme
    Gruyère crisps with pecans &
        thyme 245
tian, courgette & red pepper 193
tofu
    mushroom & tofu kebabs 181
    stir-fried noodles with broccoli,
        sweetcorn, bean sprouts &
        smoked tofu 184
    sweetcorn & tofu burgers with
        spiked yogurt sauce 169
tomatoes **92–3**
    avocado & tomato salsa 212
    caponata 161
    courgette, tomato & basil tart
        197
    gazpacho Andaluz 115
    hot tomato salsa 215
    Mediterranean lamb stew with
        tomatoes, olives & pasta 158
    Mexican bean stew with
        avocado & tomato salsa 150
    omelette 173
    roast fillet of salmon with
        tomato & avocado compôte
        194
    roasted pepper soup with
        tomatoes, garlic & fragrant
        herbs 123
    rustic Greek salad 139
    spicy beef koftas in pizzaiola
        sauce 146
    spicy tomato sauce 232
    spinach & chickpea stew 151
    tomato & olive bruschetta 239
    tomato & orange soup with
        basil cream 120
tortilla 177
truffles **104**
tubers & roots **56–69**
tuna
    peppered tuna steaks with
        fennel, red onions & sugar
        snaps 168
Turk's turban squash **91**
turnips **59**
tzimmes
    beef & carrot tzimmes with
        thimble dumplings 163

V
vegetables
    chicken with vegetables,
        noodles & cashew nuts 189
    crisp green vegetables stir-fried
        with mushrooms in sweet &
        sour sauce 185
    crudités 129
    fragrant mixed vegetable stew
        154
    green vegetables with Thai-
        spiced coconut sauce 152
    grilled vegetables with dipping
        sauce 186

melange of vegetables with
        coconut & cheese topping
        204
    Mexican bean stew with
        avocado & tomato salsa 150
    pumpkin & root vegetable stew
        164
    ratatouille 162
    roast root vegetable tarte Tatin
        192
    saffron-spiced vegetable
        couscous 148
    vegetable beignets 130
    vegetable brochettes with
        mustard & herb glaze 180
    vegetable carpaccio with
        Parmesan shavings 128
    vegetable pakoras 132
    vegetable stew with mustard &
        herb dumplings 159
Vicia faba see broad beans
Vidalia onions **48**
vinaigrette 231

W
wafers, filo & Emmenthal 246
water chestnuts
    wilted greens with water
        chestnuts & black bean sauce
        182
watercress omelette 173
white cabbage **21**
white mushrooms **101**
white onions **48**
white truffles **104**
wild mushrooms **102–3**
    wild mushroom omelette 172
wilted greens with water
    chestnuts & black bean sauce
    182
wine
    asparagus & white wine risotto
        143

Y
yams **64**
yellow onions **48**
yogurt
    cucumber & mint raita 216
    sweetcorn & tofu burgers with
        spiked yogurt sauce 169

Z
Zea mays see sweetcorn

Author's Acknowledgements:

I am indebted to many people for their assistance on this book.

To the Professionals: To Laura Bamford for her confidence in the project; to Polly Manguel, for her patience and understanding; to Sasha Judelson for commissioning this book; to Jeni Wright, for her sensitive editing; to Katey Day, for always being there, particularly in the final pressured editing phase; to Sandra Lane, who has brought the text to life with her photography and to the designer, Geoff Fennell, who has fashioned a very beautiful and seductive book.

To Friends: To Owen and Ann Harry, for providing me with the most perfect writing house in which to be inspired and for supplying a variety of homegrown vegetables for my recipe tests; to Ronnie and Gwen Buchanan, for their constant support and friendship; to Maureen and Roy Haybeard, who, at short notice, included dishes from my experimenting on their meal table; to Alison Gray, for her kindness and patience in typing the finished work and deciphering my pencil jottings; and last but by no means least, to my constant companion and friend, Bruce, without whose love, support and understanding this book would not have been written.

Photographic Acknowledgements:
Patrick McLeavey/Conran Octopus page 39

Notes
Both metric and imperial measurements have been given in all recipes. Use one set of measurements only and not a mixture of both.

Standard level spoon measurements are used in all recipes.
1 tablespoon = one 15 ml spoon
1 teaspoon = one 5 ml spoon

Eggs should be medium (size 3) unless otherwise stated.

Milk should be full fat unless otherwise stated.

Pepper should be freshly ground black pepper unless otherwise stated.

Fresh herbs should be used unless otherwise stated.

Ovens should be preheated to the specific temperature – if using a fan-assisted oven, follow the manufacturer's instructions for adjusting the time and temperature.